Where do I go for answers to my travel questions?

What's the best and easiest way to plan and book my trip?

frommers.travelocity.com

Frommer's, the travel guide leader, has teamed up with **Travelocity.com,** the leader in online travel, to bring you an in-depth, easy-to-use resource designed to help you plan and book your trip online.

At **frommers.travelocity.com**, you'll find free online updates about your destination from the experts at Frommer's plus the outstanding travel planning and purchasing features of Travelocity.com. Travelocity.com provides reservations capabilities for 95 percent of all airline seats sold, more than 47,000 hotels, and over 50 car rental companies. In addition, Travelocity.com offers more than 2,000 exciting vacation and cruise packages. Travelocity.com puts you in complete control of your travel planning with these and other great features:

> **Expert travel guidance from Frommer's** - over 150 writers reporting from around the world!

> **Best Fare Finder** - an interactive calendar tells you when to travel to get the best airfare

> **Fare Watcher** - we'll track airfare changes to your favorite destinations

> **Dream Maps** - a mapping feature that suggests travel opportunities based on your budget

> **Shop Safe Guarantee** - 24 hours a day / 7 days a week live customer service, and more!

Whether traveling on a tight budget, looking for a quick weekend getaway, or planning the trip of a lifetime, Frommer's guides and Travelocity.com will make your travel dreams a reality. You've bought the book, now book the trip!

Here's what the critics say about Frommer's:

"Amazingly easy to use. Very portable, very complete."

—Booklist

♦

"The only mainstream guide to list specific prices. The Walter Cronkite of guidebooks—with all that implies."

—Travel & Leisure

♦

"The best series for travelers who want one easy-to-use guidebook."

—U.S. Air Magazine

P O R T A B L E

Vancouver
1st Edition

by Shawn Blore

HUNGRY MINDS, INC.

New York, NY • Cleveland, OH • Indianapolis, IN
Chicago, IL • Foster City, CA • San Francisco, CA

ABOUT THE AUTHOR

A native of California and resident by turns in Ottawa, Amsterdam, Moscow, and (for the past half-decade) Vancouver, **Shawn Blore** is a newspaper journalist, award-winning magazine writer, and best-selling author of *Vancouver: Secrets of the City*.

Published by:

HUNGRY MINDS, INC.

909 Third Ave.
New York, NY 10022
www.frommers.com

ISBN 0-7645-6347-5
ISSN 1531-7501

Editor: Myka Carroll
Production Editor: Heather Gregory
Photo Editor: Richard Fox
Design by Michele Laseau
Cartographer: Roberta Stockwell
Production by Hungry Minds Indianapolis Production Services
Cover photo: Totem poles in Stanley Park

SPECIAL SALES

For general information on Hungry Minds' products and services, please contact our Customer Care department within the U.S. at 800-762-2974, outside the U.S. at 317-572-3993, or fax 317-572-4002. For sales inquiries and reseller information, including discounts, bulk sales, customized editions, and premium sales, please contact our Customer Care department at 800-434-3422.

Manufactured in the United States of America

5 4 3 2 1

Contents

List of Maps

AN INVITATION TO THE READER

In researching this book we have discovered many wonderful places—hotels, restaurants, shops, and more. We're sure you'll find others. Please tell us about them, so we can share the information with your fellow travelers in upcoming editions. If you were disappointed with a recommendation, we'd love to know that, too. Please write to:

Frommer's Portable Vancouver, 1st Edition
Hungry Minds, Inc.
909 Third Avenue
New York, NY 10022

AN ADDITIONAL NOTE

Please be advised that travel information is subject to change at any time, and this is especially true of prices. We therefore suggest that you write or call ahead for confirmation when making your travel plans. The authors, editors, and publishers cannot be held responsible for the experiences of readers while traveling. Your safety is important to us, however, so we encourage you to stay alert and be aware of your surroundings. Keep a close eye on cameras, purses, and wallets, all favorite targets of thieves and pickpockets.

WHAT THE SYMBOLS MEAN
✪ Frommer's Favorites

Our favorite places and experiences—outstanding for quality, value, or both.

The following abbreviations are used for credit cards:

AE	American Express	EC	Eurocard
CB	Carte Blanche	JCB	Japan Credit Bank
DC	Diners Club	MC	MasterCard
DISC	Discover	V	Visa
ER	EnRoute		

FIND FROMMER'S ONLINE

www.frommers.com offers up-to-the-minute listings on almost 200 cities around the globe—including the latest bargains and candid, personal articles updated daily by Arthur Frommer himself. No other Web site offers such comprehensive and timely coverage of the world of travel.

Planning Your Trip to Vancouver

*W*hether you're coming to Vancouver for business or shopping, dining or dancing, beach walking or backwoods trekking, or all of the above at once, here are some tips to help you plan your trip.

1 Visitor Information & Entry Requirements

VISITOR INFORMATION

You can get Canadian tourism information at consulate offices in most major American cities. The provincial and municipal Canadian tourism boards are also great sources of travel information. Contact **Super Natural British Columbia–Tourism B.C.,** Box 9830 Stn. Prov. Government, Victoria, B.C. V8W 9W5 (☎ **800/HELLO-BC [435-5622]** or 604/435-5622; www.hellobc.com; www.snbc-res.com for reservations), for information about travel and accommodations throughout the province.

Tourism Vancouver's **Vancouver Tourist Info Centre,** 200 Burrard St., Vancouver, B.C. V6C 3L6 (☎ **604/683-2000;** www.tourismvancouver.com), can help you with everything from booking accommodations to making suggestions for what to see and do.

For cultural information, check out the Web site for *Vancouver Magazine* at **www.vanmag.com**. Other helpful Web sites include Discover Vancouver (**www.discovervancouver. com**), In Vancouver! (**www.vancouver-bc.com**), and VancouverToday.Com (**www.vancouvertoday.com**).

ENTRY REQUIREMENTS

If you're driving from Seattle, you'll clear Customs at the Peace Arch crossing (open 24 hours) in Blaine, Washington. You'll pass through **Canadian Customs** (☎ **800/461-9999** or

204/983-3500) to enter Canada, and **U.S. Customs (☎ 360/ 332-5771**) on your departure. Duty-free shops are located in Blaine at the last exit before the border going into Canada. On the Canadian side, the shops are a little more difficult to find. They're on the right, just after the speed limit drops to 35 kilometers per hour (22 m.p.h.).

If you fly directly into Vancouver International Airport from another country, you'll clear Customs in the new International Terminal. Once you get through passport control, you and your luggage will go through Customs before you leave the terminal. (Even if you don't have anything to declare, Customs officials randomly select a few passengers and search their luggage.)

DOCUMENTS FOR U.S. CITIZENS

Citizens or permanent U.S. residents don't require visas to enter Canada. American citizens need to show proof of citizenship and residence; a passport or birth certificate plus a driver's license is sufficient. Naturalized citizens should carry their naturalization certificates.

Permanent U.S. residents who are not U.S. citizens should carry their passports and Resident Alien Card (U.S. form I-151 or I-551). Foreign students and other noncitizen U.S. residents should carry their passports or a Temporary Resident Card (form 1688) or Employment Authorization Card (1688A or 1688B); a visitor's visa; I-94 Arrival-Departure Record; a current I-20 copy of IAP-66 indicating student status; proof of sufficient funds for a temporary stay; and evidence of return transportation. In either case, citizens of other countries traveling to Canada from the United States should check with the Canadian Consulate before departure to see if a visitor's visa is required.

If you're bringing children into Canada, you must have proof of legal guardianship. Lack of it can cause long delays at the border, because there have been cases of parents involved in custody cases abducting their children and attempting to flee to Canada (despite the fact that the Canadian and U.S. governments cooperate closely to resolve matters of this sort). If you're under 18 and not accompanied by a parent or guardian, you should bring a permission letter signed by your parent or legal guardian allowing you to travel to Canada.

DOCUMENTS FOR COMMONWEALTH CITIZENS

Citizens of Great Britain, Australia, and New Zealand don't require visas to enter Canada, but they do need to show proof of commonwealth citizenship (such as a passport), as well as evidence of funds sufficient for a temporary stay (credit cards work well here). Naturalized citizens should carry their naturalization certificates. Permanent residents of commonwealth nations should carry their passports and resident status cards. Foreign students and other residents should carry their passports or temporary resident cards or employment authorization cards; a visitor's visa; arrival-departure record; a current copy of student status; proof of sufficient funds for a temporary stay; and evidence of return transportation. Check with the Canadian Consulate before departure to see if you will also need a visitor's visa.

CUSTOMS REGULATIONS

Your personal baggage can include the following: boats, motors, snowmobiles, camping and sports equipment, appliances, TV sets, musical instruments, personal computers, cameras, and other items of a personal or household nature. If you are bringing excess luggage, be sure to carry a detailed inventory list that includes the acquisition date, serial number, and cost or replacement value of each item. It sounds tedious, but it can speed things up at the border. Customs will help you fill in the forms that allow you to temporarily bring in your effects. This list will also be used by U.S. Customs to check off what you bring out. You will be charged Customs duties for anything left in Canada.

If you're over 18, you're allowed to bring in 40 ounces of liquor and wine or 24 12-ounce cans or bottles of beer and ale, and 50 cigars, 400 cigarettes, or 14 ounces of manufactured tobacco per person. Any excess is subject to duty. Gifts not exceeding C$60 (US$40) and not containing tobacco products, alcoholic beverages, or advertising material can be brought in duty-free. Meats, plants, and vegetables are subject to inspection on entry. There are restrictions, so contact the Canadian Consulate for more details if you want to bring produce.

For more information concerning items you wish to bring in and out of the country, contact the **Canadian Customs Office** (☎ **800/461-9999** or 204/983-3500).

2   Money

CURRENCY   The Canadian currency system is decimal and resembles both British and U.S. denominations. Canadian monetary units are dollars and cents, with dollars coming in different colors, just like British currency. The standard denominations are C$5 (US$3.35), C$10 (US$7), C$20 (US$13), C$50 (US$34), and C$100 (US$67). The "loonie" (so named because of the loon on one side) is the C$1 (US65¢) coin that replaced the C$1 bill. A C$2 (US$1.35) coin, called the "toonie" because it's worth two loonies, has replaced the Canadian C$2 bill.

Banks and other financial institutions offer a standard rate of exchange based on the daily world monetary rate. The best exchange rates can be had by withdrawing funds from bank ATMs. Hotels will also gladly exchange your notes, but they usually give a slightly lower exchange rate. Almost all stores and restaurants accept American currency, and most will exchange amounts in excess of your dinner check or purchase. However, these establishments are allowed to set their own exchange percentages, and generally offer the worst rates of all.

The exchange rate between Canadian and U.S. dollars should always be kept in mind. The *figures* charged in hotels and restaurants in Vancouver are often incrementally higher than in comparable U.S. cities; the *cost* is typically about one-third less. Canada, at the moment, is a bargain. The prices cited in this guide are given in both Canadian and U.S. dollars, with all dollar amounts over $5 rounded to the nearest dollar. Note that the Canadian dollar is worth 30% less than the U.S. dollar but buys nearly as much. As we go to press, C$1 is worth US67¢, which means that your C$100-a-night hotel room will cost only US$67 and your C$6 breakfast only US$4.

TRAVELER'S CHECKS   Traveler's checks in Canadian funds are the safest way to carry money and are universally accepted by banks (which may charge a small fee to cash them), larger stores, and hotels. If you are carrying American Express or Thomas Cook traveler's checks, you can cash them at the local offices of those companies free of charge.

ATM NETWORKS   The 24-hour PLUS and Cirrus ATM systems are available in Vancouver. The systems convert

Canadian withdrawals to your account's currency within 24 hours, so don't panic if you call your bank and hear a one-to-one balance immediately after conducting a transaction. Cirrus network cards work at ATMs at the **Bank of Montreal** (☎ 604/665-2703), **CIBC** (☎ 800/465-2422), **Hong Kong Bank of Canada** (☎ 604/685-1000), **Royal Bank** (☎ 800/769-2511), and **Toronto Dominion** (☎ 800/983-2265), and at all other ATMs that display the Cirrus logo. None of these ATM systems provides your current balance. You must have a four-digit PIN to access Canadian ATMs.

CREDIT & DEBIT CARDS   Major U.S. credit cards are widely accepted in British Columbia, especially American Express, MasterCard, and Visa. British debit cards like Barclay's Visa debit card are also accepted. Diners Club, Carte Blanche, Discover, JCB, and EnRoute are taken by some establishments, but not as many. The amount spent in Canadian dollars will automatically be converted by your issuing company to your currency when you're billed—generally at rates that are better than you'd receive for cash at a currency exchange.

3 When to Go

CLIMATE   Tree experts say that a rain forest species like the Western Red Cedar needs at least 30 inches of precipitation a year. Vancouver gets about 47 inches a year, a cause for no small celebration amongst the local cedar population. Homo sapiens simply learn to adjust.

For example, most of that precipitation arrives in the wintertime, when with a 30-minute drive to the mountains you can trade the rain for snow. Skiing and snowboarding are popular and are practiced from mid-December until the mountain snowpack melts away in June. Except in Whistler, hotels in the winter are quiet. Restaurants are uncluttered. This is also when Vancouver's cultural scene is at its most active.

Around mid-February, the winds begin to slacken—the sun shines a bit more, and the blossoms on the cherry trees begin to poke their heads out, timid at first, but gaining more confidence with each day until, by the beginning of March, there's a riot of pink on every street. The sun comes out, and stays out; there are 16 hours of daylight in mid-June, which means more hours at the beach, shopping, or in the mountains than in other parts of North America. From then until the rains close in again in mid-October is prime visiting time for sun junkies. Of course, that's also when most other visitors arrive.

HOLIDAYS   The official British Columbian public holidays are as follows: New Year's Day (January 1); Good Friday, Easter, Easter Monday (April 13 to 16, 2001); Victoria Day (May 21, 2001); Canada Day (July 1); B.C. Day (August 6, 2001); Labour Day (September 3, 2001); Thanksgiving (October 8, 2001); Remembrance Day (November 11); Christmas (December 25); and Boxing Day (December 26).

VANCOUVER CALENDAR OF EVENTS

Festivals held in Vancouver draw millions of visitors each year. Things may seem a little quiet in the winter and early spring, but that's because most residents simply head for the ski slopes. If no contact number or location is given for any of the events listed below, Tourism Vancouver (☎ **604/683-2000**) should be able to provide further details.

January

• **Polar Bear Swim,** English Bay Beach. Thousands of hardy citizens show up in elaborate costumes to take a dip in the icy waters of English Bay. January 1.

February

• **Chinese New Year,** Chinatown. This is when the Chinese traditionally pay their debts and forgive old grievances to start the new lunar year with a clean slate. These Chinese communities launch a 2-week celebration, ringing in the new year with firecrackers, dancing dragon parades, and other festivities. Late January or early February.

March

✪ **International Wine Festival.** This is a major wine-tasting event featuring the latest international vintages. Each winery sets up a booth where you may try as many varieties as you like. Cheese and pâté are laid out on strategically placed tables. Late March or early April.

April

- **Baisakhi Day Parade.** The Sikh Indian New Year is celebrated with a colorful parade around Ross Street near Marine Drive and ends with a vegetarian feast at the temple. Contact **Khalsa Diwan Gurudwara Temple** (☎ **604/324-2010**) for more information. Mid-April.
- **Vancouver Sun Run.** This is Canada's biggest 10K race, featuring over 40,000 runners, joggers, and walkers who race through 10 scenic kilometers (6.2 miles). The run starts and finishes at B.C. Place Stadium. Late April.

May

- **Vancouver International Marathon.** Runners from all over the world gather to compete in a run through the streets. For information, call ☎ **604/872-2928.** First Sunday in May (May 6, 2001).
- **New Play Festival.** Emerging playwrights show off their latest works at Granville Island. Call ☎ **604/685-6228** for more information. Mid-May.

June

- **International Children's Festival.** Activities, plays, music, and crafts for children are featured at this annual event held in Vanier Park on False Creek. For information, call ☎ **604/708-5655.** Late May or early June (May 28 to June 3, 2001).
- **SlugFest,** Richmond Nature Park, 1185 Westminster Hwy. (☎ **604/273-7015**). Kids compete to find the biggest slug in the park. There are slug races as well as awards for the fastest, slowest, and ugliest slugs. Usually first weekend in June.
- **VanDusen Flower and Garden Show.** Presented at the **VanDusen Botanical Garden,** 5251 Oak St., at 37th Street (☎ **604/878-9274**), this is Vancouver's premier flora gala. Early June.
- **National Aboriginal Day Community Celebration.** This event offers the public an opportunity to learn about Canada's First Nations cultures. Many events take place at the **Vancouver Aboriginal Friendship Centre,** 1607 E. Hastings at Commercial Street (☎ **604/251-4844**). June 24.
- ✪ **Alcan Dragon Boat Festival.** Traditional dragon-boat racing is a part of the city's cultural scene. Watch the races from False Creek's north shore, where more than 150 local and international teams compete. Four stages of music, dance, and Chinese

acrobatics are presented at the **Plaza of Nations** (☎ 604/
688-2382). Third week in June.

❂ **DuMaurier International Jazz Festival.** More than 800 international jazz and blues players perform at 25 venues ranging
from the Orpheum Theatre to the Roundhouse. Includes a
large number of free performances. Call the **Jazz Hotline**
(☎ **604/872-5200**) or visit www.jazzvancouver.com for more
information. Late June or early July.

❂ **Bard on the Beach Shakespeare Festival,** Vanier Park. The
best backdrop for Shakespeare you will ever see! The Bard's
plays are performed in a tent overlooking English Bay. Plays are
different every summer. Call the box office (☎ **604/739-0559**)
during the performance season, check www.bardonthebeach.
org, or phone 604/737-0625 October through April. Mid-June
to late September, Tuesday through Sunday.

• **Festival d'ete francophone de Vancouver,** various venues,
includes street festival. A 4-day festival celebrating francophone
music from around the world. Performers often include well-
known Québec artists. Call ☎ **604/736-9806** for information. Mid-June.

July

❂ **Canada Day.** Canada Place Pier (☎ **604/775-8687;** www.
canadaplace.ca) hosts an all-day celebration that begins with the
induction of new Canadian citizens. Music and dance are performed outdoors throughout the day. There's a 21-gun salute at
noon, precision aerobatics teams perform overhead during the
afternoon, and a nighttime fireworks display on the harbor tops
off the festivities. Other locations that host Canada Day events
include Granville Island and Grouse Mountain. July 1.

• **Steveston Salmon Festival,** Steveston. A parade, salmon barbecue, special crafts exhibits, and other forms of entertainment
take place in this heritage fishing village at the Gulf of Georgia
Cannery National Historic Site (☎ **604/664-9009**). July 1.

• **Ecomarine Kayak Marathon.** Competitors race sea kayaks in
the Georgia Strait's open waters. The **Ecomarine Kayak Centre** (☎ **604/689-7575**), at Jericho Beach, hosts the race and
can provide details. Early July.

• **Dancing on the Edge.** Canadian and international dance
groups perform modern and classic works at the **Firehall Arts
Centre** and other venues. Call (☎ **604/689-0691**) for more
information. Early to mid-July.

- **Vancouver Folk Music Festival.** International folk music is played outdoors at Jericho Beach Park. Contact the **Vancouver Folk Music Society** (☎ **604/602-9798;** www.thefestival. bc.ca). Second or third weekend in July.

✪ **Illuminares,** Trout Lake Park. Evening lantern procession circling Trout Lake is a phantasmagoric experience. Drums, costumes, fire-breathing apparitions, and lots of elaborate handcrafted lanterns—floating lanterns, kids' lanterns, 10-foot-high four-person lanterns. Various performances start at dusk. For info call ☎ **604/879-8611.** End of July, always on Saturday.

- **Powell Street Festival.** An annual festival of Japanese culture that includes music, dance, food, and more. Contact the Powell Street Festival Society at ☎ **604/739-9388** for more information. Last weekend of July or first weekend of August.

August

- **Vancouver Pride Parade.** Sponsored by the Vancouver Pride Society, this colorful gay- and lesbian-pride parade covers a route along Denman and Davie streets, beginning at noon. Celebrations at many local gay and lesbian nightclubs take place the same weekend. For more information, visit the Pride Society's Web site (www.vanpride.bc.ca) or call the Pride Society (☎ **604/687-0955**). First Sunday in August (B.C. Daylong weekend).

✪ **Benson & Hedges Symphony of Fire.** Three international fireworks companies compete for a coveted title by launching their best displays accompanied by music over English Bay Beach. Don't miss the big finale on the fourth evening, which attracts as many as 500,000 spectators to the West End. (*Note:* Because of the crowds, the West End's streets and Kits Point are closed to vehicles each night.) Other prime viewing locations include Kitsilano Beach and Jericho Beach. End of July through first week in August.

- **International Comedy Festival.** Comedians from all over Canada and the United States perform at a variety of venues around town. Contact the Festival office at ☎ **604/683-0883** or www.comedyfest.com for more information. Last week of July, first week in August.

- **Greater Vancouver Open** (**Air Canada Championship**), Surrey. This PGA tour event attracts professional golfers and golf fans from around the world to the Northview Golf

Country Club, 6857–168 St., Surrey. Call ☎ **604/575-0324** for details. Late August.

- **Pacific National Exhibition.** The years 2001 or 2002 may be the final ones for the tenth-largest North American country-style fair, as the city council has voted to convert the grounds to green space. Offerings include one of North America's best all-wooden roller coasters, many other rides, big-name entertainment, and a demolition derby. Special events include livestock demonstrations, logger sports competitions, fashion shows, and a midway. Contact the Pacific National Exhibition (☎ **604/253-2311;** www.pne.bc.ca) for more details. Mid-August to Labour Day.

September

- **Molson Indy.** The CART Indy Series holds its biggest annual event in the streets of Yaletown and False Creek, attracting more than 500,000 spectators. Contact **Molson Indy** (☎ **604/684-4639;** www.molsonindy.com) for information or tickets. Labour Day.

- ✪ **The Fringe—Vancouver's Theatre Festival.** The best place to catch new theater. Centered around Granville Island and with venues around the Commercial Drive area (the Havana and the Cultch) and Yaletown's Roundhouse, the Fringe Festival features more than 500 innovative and original shows performed by over 100 groups from across Canada and around the world. All plays cost under C$12 (US$8). Call ☎ **604/257-0350,** or visit www.vancouverfringe.com for more info. September 6 to 16, 2001.

- **Mid-Autumn Moon Festival,** Dr. Sun Yat-sen Garden. This outdoor Chinese celebration includes a lantern festival, storytelling, music, and, of course, moon cakes. For more info call the Garden at ☎ **604/662-3207.** Early to mid-September, according to the lunar cycle (15th day of the 8th month of the Chinese calendar).

October

- ✪ **Vancouver International Film Festival.** This highly respected film festival features 250 new works, revivals, and retrospectives, representing filmmakers from 40 countries. Asian films are particularly well represented. Attendance reaches more than 110,000 viewers, not including the stars and celebrities who appear annually. Contact the Vancouver International Film

Festival (☎ **604/685-0260;** www.viff.org) for details. Late September and first 2 weeks of October.

- **Cranberry Harvest Festival,** Richmond Nature Park, 1185 Westminster Hwy. (☎ **604/273-7015**). Cranberries are indigenous to British Columbia's bogs, and the Richmond Nature Park has one of the few remaining wild patches. The Saturday of Thanksgiving weekend, early October.

- **Vancouver International Writers Festival.** Public readings conducted by Canadian and international authors as well as writers' workshops take place on Granville Island and at other locations in the lower mainland. Call ☎ **604/681-6330** for details. Mid-October.

- **Vancouver Snow Show,** B.C. Place Stadium (☎ **604/ 878-0754;** www.skiandboardshow.com). If you ski, Canada's largest annual ski show, sale, and swap is a must. Sporting-goods stores unload the previous year's inventory, and people consign their own skis to raise money for the Vancouver Ski Foundation's youth programs. Late October.

- **Parade of Lost Souls,** Grandview Park. A bizarre and intriguing procession takes place around Commercial Drive to honor the dead and chase away bad luck. For more information, call ☎ **604/879-8611.** Last Saturday of October.

November

- **Remembrance Day.** Celebrated throughout Canada, this day commemorates Canadian soldiers who gave their lives in war. Vintage military aircraft fly over Stanley Park and Canada Place, and at noon a 21-gun salute is fired from Deadman's Island. November 11.

- **Christmas Craft and Gift Market,** Van Dusen Botanical Garden. Popular craft and gift market in a beautiful garden setting. For info, call ☎ **604/878-9274.** November and December.

December

- **Christmas Carol Ship Parade,** Vancouver Harbour. Harbour cruise ships decorated with colorful Christmas lights sail around English Bay, while onboard guests sip cider and sing their way through the canon of Christmas carols. Throughout December.

- **Festival of Lights,** Van Dusen Botanical Garden. Throughout December, the garden is transformed into a magical holiday land with seasonal displays and over 20,000 lights illuminating the garden. Call ☎ **604/878-9274** for info. December.

• **First Night.** The city's New Year's Eve performing arts festival and alcohol-free party. Vancouver closes the downtown streets for revelers. Events and venues change from year to year. Contact **Tourism Vancouver** at ☎ **604/683-2000** for more information. December 31.

4 Tips for Travelers with Special Needs

FOR TRAVELERS WITH DISABILITIES

According to *We're Accessible,* a newsletter for travelers with disabilities, Vancouver is "the most accessible city in the world." There are more than 14,000 sidewalk wheelchair ramps, and motorized wheelchairs are a common sight in the downtown area. The stairs along Robson Square have built-in ramps. Most major attractions and venues have ramps or level walkways for easy access. Many Vancouver hotels have at least partial wheelchair accessibility, if not rooms built completely to suit. Most SkyTrain stations and the SeaBus are wheelchair accessible, and most bus routes are lift equipped. For more information about accessible public transportation, contact **Translink** (☎ **604/521-0400;** www.translink.bc.ca; or phone the department of accessible transit at 604/540-3400) and ask for its brochure, *Rider's Guide to Accessible Transit.*

Many downtown hotels are equipping rooms with visual smoke alarms and other facilities for hearing-impaired guests. You'll also notice that downtown crosswalks have beeping alert signs to guide visually impaired pedestrians.

FOR GAY & LESBIAN TRAVELERS

What San Francisco is to the United States, Vancouver is to Canada—the laid-back town on the coast with a large, thriving gay community. Much of the social activity centers in the West End—particularly Denman and Davie streets—where many gay singles and couples live. The best way to find out what's going on is to pick up a copy of the biweekly gay and lesbian tabloid, *Xtra! West,* which is available throughout the West End. To obtain a copy ahead of time, contact *Xtra! West,* 501–1033 Davie St., Vancouver, B.C. V6E 1M7 (☎ **604/ 684-9696**). Also check out the **Vancouver Pride Society** Web site (**www.vanpride.bc.ca**) for upcoming special events, including the annual Vancouver Pride Parade. Otherwise, here are some suggestions: Book a room at the West End Guest

House or the Sylvia Hotel (see chapter 3) and head over to the numerous West End and downtown clubs, such as the Odyssey and the Lava Lounge, or have coffee at Delaney's on Denman Street or at the Edge on Davie Street.

FOR SENIORS

Older travelers often qualify for discounts at hotels and attractions and on public transit throughout Vancouver. Make a habit of asking. You'll be pleasantly surprised at the number of discounts for which you're eligible. Discount transit passes for persons over 65 (with proof of age) may be purchased at shops in Vancouver that display a FAREDEALER sign (Safeway, 7-Eleven, and most newsstands). To locate a **FareDealer vendor,** contact BC Transit (☎ **604/521-0400**). If you or your mate is over 50 and you are not already a member of the **American Association of Retired Persons** (**AARP**), 3200 E. Carson, Lakewood, CA 90712 (☎ **800/424-3410**), consider joining. The AARP card is valuable for additional restaurant and travel bargains throughout North America.

FOR FAMILIES

Vancouver is one of the most child-friendly, cosmopolitan cities around. Where else would you find a Kids Market that's filled with children's stores and is located next to a free water park that's equipped with water guns and changing rooms? In addition to the standard attractions and sights, you'll find a lot of adventurous, outdoor, and free stuff that both you and your kids will enjoy (see "Especially for Kids," in chapter 5). You can try entertaining restaurants that aren't cafeteria-style or fast-food establishments but are decidedly kid-friendly (see "Family-Friendly Restaurants," in chapter 4).

Some hotels even offer milk and cookies to kids for evening snacks, plus special menus and child-size terry robes (see "Family-Friendly Hotels," in chapter 3).

FOR STUDENTS

This is definitely a student-oriented area. The University of British Columbia (UBC) in the Point Grey area, Burnaby's Simon Fraser University, and a number of smaller schools contribute to the enormous student population. Student travelers have a lot of free and inexpensive entertainment options, both day and night. The nightlife is active, centering around

Yaletown, Granville Street, the West End, and Kitsilano. Pick up a copy of *The Georgia Straight* to find out what's happening. Many attractions and theaters offer discounts if you have your student ID with you. While many establishments will accept a school ID, the surest way to obtain student discounts is with an International Student Identity Card (ISIC), which is available to any full-time high-school or college student from the **Council on International Educational Exchange** (**CIEE**), 205 E. 42nd St., New York, NY 10017 (☎ **212/ 822-2700**), or from your local campus student society. The CIEE has offices in major U.S. cities. To find the location nearest you, call ☎ **800/438-2643** or check the Web site at www.ciee.org.

5 Getting to Vancouver

BY PLANE

THE MAJOR AIRLINES   The Open Skies agreement between the United States and Canada has made flying to Vancouver easier than ever. Daily direct flights between major U.S. cities and Vancouver are offered by **Air Canada** (☎ **888/247-2262** or 800/661-3936), **Canadian Airlines** (☎ **800/363-7530**; though Air Canada and Canadian Airlines are in the process of merging, for the time being they maintain separate facilities, including telephone lines), **United Airlines** (☎ **800/241-6522**), **American Airlines** (☎ **800/433-7300**), **Continental** (☎ **800/231-0856**), and **Northwest Airlines** (☎ **800/447-4747**). Direct flights on major carriers serve Phoenix, Dallas, New York, Houston, Minneapolis, Reno, San Francisco, and many other cities.

FINDING THE BEST AIRFARE   The best advice we can give you on shopping for an airfare bargain is to call travel agencies or the major airlines 30 or more days before your departure. That's when you'll find the best discounted seats on flights. Most airlines offer restricted ticketing on these deals. You cannot change dates without paying extra, and the tickets are usually nonrefundable.

Non-U.S. and non-Canadian travelers can take advantage of the **Visit USA** air passes offered by **Continental** (☎ **800/ 231-0856**) and similar coupons from **Air Canada** (☎ **800/ 776-3000**). These tickets must be purchased outside North

America in conjunction with an international fare. For roughly an additional US$439, you can get three flight coupons that allow you to fly anywhere on the continent (price varies seasonally). You can buy up to a maximum of nine coupons for US$769. Low-season discounts are also available. **Canadian Airlines** (☎ 800/426-7000) offers a similar deal to every destination on its flight schedule, including Hawaii.

BY TRAIN

VIA Rail Canada, 1150 Station St. (☎ 800/561-8630; www.viarail.ca), connects with Amtrak at Winnipeg, Manitoba. From there, you travel on a spectacular route that runs between Calgary and Vancouver. Lake Louise's beautiful alpine scenery is just part of this enjoyable journey. **Amtrak** (☎ 800/872-7245; www.amtrak.com) has regular service from Seattle and also has a direct route from San Diego to Vancouver. It stops at all major U.S. West Coast cities, and takes a little under 2 days to complete the entire journey. Fares are US$190. Substantial seasonal discounts are available. Non-U.S. and non-Canadian travelers can buy a 15- to 30-day **USA Railpass** for US$440 to US$550 at peak season. The pass can be used for rail connections to Vancouver.

BC Rail, 1311 W. First St., North Vancouver (☎ 604/631-3500; www.bcrail.com), also connects Vancouver to other cities throughout the province, including Whistler. The trip to Whistler is 2½ hours each way, and the fare includes breakfast or dinner. A one-way ticket costs C$33 (US$22) for adults, C$29 (US$19) for seniors, and C$19 (US$13) for children 2 to 12. Children under 2 are free.

BY BUS

Greyhound Bus Lines (☎ 604/482-8747) and **Pacific Coach Lines** (☎ 604/662-8074) also have their terminals at the Pacific Central Station, 1150 Station St. Greyhound Canada's **Canada Pass** offers 15 or 30 days of unlimited travel for C$405 to C$480 (US$271 to US$322). **Quick Coach Lines** (☎ 604/940-4428) connects Vancouver to the Seattle-Tacoma International Airport. The bus leaves from Vancouver's Sandman Inn, 180 W. Georgia St., can pick up passengers from most major hotels, and stops at the Vancouver International Airport. The 4½ hour ride costs C$39 (US$26) one-way or C$70 (US$47) round-trip.

BY CAR

You'll probably be driving into Vancouver along one of two routes. **U.S. Interstate 5** from Seattle becomes **Highway 99** when you cross the border at the Peace Arch. The 210-kilometer (130-mile) drive takes about 2½ hours. You'll drive through the cities of White Rock, Delta, and Richmond, pass under the Fraser River through the George Massey Tunnel, and cross the Oak Street Bridge. The highway ends there and becomes Oak Street, a very busy urban thoroughfare. Turn left onto 70th Avenue. (A small sign suspended above the left lane at the intersection of Oak Street and 70th Avenue reads CITY CENTRE.) Six blocks later, turn right onto Granville Street. This street heads directly into downtown Vancouver on the Granville Street Bridge.

Trans-Canada Highway 1 is a limited-access freeway running all the way to Vancouver's eastern boundary, where it crosses the Second Narrows bridge to North Vancouver. When coming on Highway 1 from the east, exit at Cassiar Street and turn left at the first light onto Hastings Street (Hwy. 7A), which is adjacent to Exhibition Park. Follow Hastings Street 6.4 kilometers (4 miles) into downtown. When coming to Vancouver from Whistler or parts north, take Exit 13 (the sign says TAYLOR WAY, BRIDGE TO VANCOUVER) and cross the Lions Gate Bridge into Vancouver's West End.

BY SHIP & FERRY

The **Canada Place** cruise-ship terminal at the base of Burrard Street (☎ **604/665-9085**) is a city landmark. Topped by five eye-catching white Teflon sails, Canada Place Pier juts out into the Burrard Inlet and is at the edge of the downtown financial district. **Princess Cruises, Holland America, Royal Caribbean, Crystal Cruises, Norwegian Cruise Lines, World Explorer Majesty Cruise Line, Hanseatic, Seabourn,** and **Carnival Cruise** lines dock at Canada Place and the nearby Ballantyne Pier to board passengers headed for Alaska via British Columbia's Inside Passage. They carry approximately 700,000 passengers annually on their nearly 300 Vancouver-Alaska cruises. Public-transit buses and taxis greet new arrivals, but you can also easily walk to many major hotels, including the Pan-Pacific, Waterfront Centre, and Hotel Vancouver. (If you're considering an Alaska cruise, late May and all of June generally offer the best weather, the most daylight, and the best sightseeing opportunities.)

BY PACKAGE TOUR

Air Canada (☎ **888/247-2262**) offers a number of fly/drive packages. And **SNV International,** 402–1045 Howe St., Vancouver (☎ **604/683-5101**), specializes in vacation packages to Vancouver.

2

Getting to Know Vancouver

*L*osing yourself wandering around a fascinating new neighborhood is part of the joy of traveling. While that's certainly possible on a metaphorical level in Vancouver, getting physically lost is truly difficult—all you have to do to find your bearings is look up. The mountains are always in sight, and they're always north. If you're facing towards them, east is to your right, west is to your left, and the back of your head is pointing south. That one tip should keep you pointed in the right direction no matter where your exploration of the city takes you. The rest of this chapter offers more detailed information on how to find your way around town.

1 Orientation

ARRIVING

BY PLANE   **Vancouver International Airport** is 13 kilometers (8 miles) south of downtown Vancouver on uninhabited Sea Island, bordered on three sides by Richmond and the Fraser River delta. The International Terminal features an extensive collection of First Nations sculptures and paintings set amid grand expanses of glass under soaring ceilings. **Tourist Information Kiosks** on Level 2 of the Main and International arrival terminals (☎ **604/303-3601**) are open daily from 8am to 11:30pm.

Parking is available at the airport for both loading passengers and long-term stays (☎ **604/276-6106** for all airport services inquiries). **Courtesy buses** to the airport hotels are available, and a **shuttle bus** links the Main and International terminals to the South Terminal, where smaller and private aircraft are docked.

Leaving the Airport   The pale-green **YVR Airporter** (☎ **604/946-8866**) provides **airport bus service** to downtown Vancouver's major hotels. It leaves from Level 2 of the Main Terminal every 15 minutes daily from 6:30am to

10:30pm, and every 30 minutes from 10:30pm until mid-night, with a final run at 12:15am. The 30-minute ride to the downtown area whisks you through central Vancouver before taking the Granville Street Bridge into downtown Vancouver. The one-way fare is C$10 (US$7) for adults, C$8 (US$5) for seniors, and C$5 (US$3.35) for children; the round-trip fare is C$17 (US$11) for adults, C$16 (US$11) for seniors, and C$10 (US$7) for children. Bus service back to the airport leaves from selected downtown hotels every half hour between 5:35am and 10:55pm. Scheduled pickups serve the Bus Station, Four Seasons, Hotel Vancouver, Waterfront Centre Hotel, Georgian Court, Sutton Place, Landmark, and others. Ask the bus driver on the way in or ask your hotel concierge for the nearest pickup stop and time.

Getting to and from the airport with **public transit** is a pain. Buses are slow, and you have to transfer at least once to get downtown. Given that the YVR Airporter bus costs only C$10 (US$7), the hassle probably isn't worth the savings. If you insist, however, bus no. 100 stops at both terminals. At the Granville/West 71st Street stop, get off and transfer to bus no. 8 to downtown Vancouver. BC Transit fares are C$1.75 (US$1.15) during off-peak hours and C$2.50 (US$1.65) during weekdays until 6:30pm. But transfers are free in any direction within a 90-minute period.

The average **taxi** fare from the airport to a downtown Van-couver hotel is approximately C$25 (US$17) plus tip. Because the meter charges for time when the cab is stuck in traffic, and some hotels are closer to the airport than others, the fare can run up to C$40 (US$27). **AirLimo** (☎ **604/273-1331**) offers flat-rate stretch-limousine service. AirLimo charges C$29 (US$19) per trip to the airport (not per person), plus tax and tip. The drivers accept all major credit cards.

Most major **car-rental firms** have airport counters and shuttles. Make advance reservations for fast check-in and guaranteed availability—especially if you want a four-wheel-drive vehicle or a convertible (see "Rentals," below).

BY TRAIN & BUS   The main **Vancouver railway station** is at 1150 Station St., near Main Street and Terminal Avenue just south of Chinatown. You can reach downtown Vancouver from there by cab for about C$7 (US$4.70). There are plenty of taxis at the station entrance. One block from the station is

Greater Vancouver

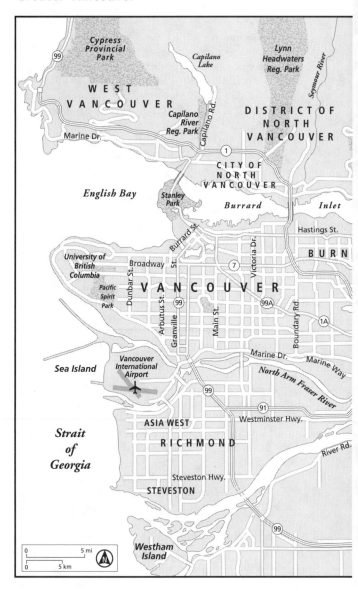

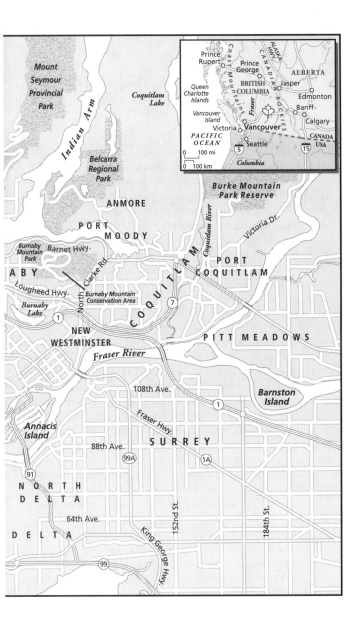

Mount
Seymour
Provincial
Park

Coquitlam
Lake

Indian Arm

Belcarra
Regional
Park

Burke Mountain
Park Reserve

ANMORE

PORT
MOODY

Burnaby
Mountain
Park

Barnet Hwy.

North Clarke Rd.

Coquitlam River

Victoria Dr.

PORT
COQUITLAM

ABY

Lougheed Hwy.

Burnaby Mountain
Conservation Area

C O Q U I T L A M

*Burnaby
Lake*

①

7

NEW
WESTMINSTER

PITT MEADOWS

Fraser River

108th Ave.

①

*Barnston
Island*

*Annacis
Island*

Fraser Hwy.

S U R R E Y

88th Ave.

99A

1A

91

N O R T H
D E L T A

64th Ave.

152nd St.

184th St.

D E L T A

King George Hwy.

99

Inset map:

Prince
Rupert

Prince
George

Coast Mountains

ALASKA HWY.

CANADIAN ROCKIES

ALBERTA

Jasper

Edmonton

*Queen
Charlotte
Islands*

BRITISH
COLUMBIA

Fraser

Banff

*Vancouver
Island*

Victoria

Vancouver

Calgary

CANADA

*PACIFIC
OCEAN*

Seattle

5

USA

15

0   100 mi

0   100 km

Columbia

the SkyTrain's Main Street Station. Within minutes, you're downtown. The Granville and Waterfront stations are two and four stops away, respectively.

Greyhound Bus Lines and **Pacific Coach Lines** also have their terminals at the Pacific Central Station, 1150 Station St.

For information on arriving **by ferry,** see "Getting to Vancouver," in chapter 1.

VISITOR INFORMATION

The Vancouver Tourist Info Centre, 200 Burrard St. (☎ **604/683-2000;** www.tourismvancouver.com), is your single best travel information source about Vancouver and the North Shore. If you've ever been to London, you'll be happy to know that Tourism Vancouver is similar to the British Tourist Authority. That means you can buy bus passes and pick up maps, brochures, and travel guides. The staff is outgoing and can be very helpful if you need directions or recommendations. If you have trouble finding accommodations, the office has catalogues of registered hotels and B&Bs; the staff will even make reservations for you. The Info Centre is open from May to Labour Day daily from 8am to 6pm; the rest of the year, it's open Monday to Friday from 8:30am to 5pm, and Saturday from 9am to 5pm.

Tourism Richmond, George Massey Tunnel (☎ **604/271-8280**), has information about the Richmond and Delta area, including the heritage fishing village of Steveston. It's open daily from 9am to 7pm in July and August and daily from 10am to 4pm September through June. The office is located north of the George Massey Tunnel and easily accessible when driving in from Delta. If you plan to see more of this beautiful province, **Super Natural British Columbia** (☎ **800/663-6000** or 604/663-6000) can help you.

Be sure to pick up a copy of the free weekly tabloid *The Georgia Straight* (☎ **604/730-7000**). It provides up-to-date schedules of concerts, lectures, art exhibits, plays, recitals, and other happenings. The *Straight* can be found all over the city in cafes, bookshops, and restaurants. Equally good—and with dollops more attitude—is the glossy city magazine *Vancouver* (☎ **604/877-7732**). "VanMag," as it's also known, is available on newsstands and on the Web at www.vanmag.com.

Coast: The Outdoor Recreation Magazine (☎ **604/876-4980**) publishes schedules of mountain biking, kayaking, skiing, hiking, and climbing events. Two free monthly tabloids, *BC Parent* (☎ **604/221-0366**) and *West Coast Families* (☎ **604/689-1331**), are geared for families with young children, listing many kid-friendly current events. Gay and lesbian travelers will want to pick up a copy of *Xtra! West* (☎ **604/684-9696**), a free biweekly tabloid available in shops and restaurants throughout the West End.

CITY LAYOUT

With four different bodies of water lapping at its edges and mile after mile of shoreline, Vancouver's geography can seem a bit convoluted. That's part of the city's charm, of course, and visitors normally don't find it too hard to get their bearings. Think of the downtown peninsula as being like an upraised thumb on the mitten-shaped Vancouver mainland. Stanley Park, the West End, Yaletown, and Vancouver's business and financial center are all located on the "thumb," which is bordered to the west by English Bay, to the north by Burrard Inlet, and to the south by False Creek. The mainland part of the city—the mitten—is mostly residential, with a sprinkling of businesses along main arterial streets. Both mainland and peninsula are covered by a simple rectilinear street pattern.

FINDING AN ADDRESS In many Vancouver addresses, the suite or room number precedes the building number. For instance, 100–1250 Robson St. is Suite 100 at 1250 Robson St.

In downtown Vancouver, Chinatown's **Carrall Street** is the east-west axis from which streets are numbered and designated. Westward, numbers increase progressively to Stanley Park; eastward, numbers increase heading toward Commercial Drive. For example, 400 W. Pender is about 4 blocks from Carrall Street heading toward downtown; 400 E. Pender is 4 blocks on the opposite side of Carrall Street.

Similarly, the low numbers on north-south streets start on the Canada Place Pier side and increase southward in increments of 100 per block (the 600 block of Thurlow Street is 2 blocks from the 800 block) toward False Creek and Granville Island.

Off the peninsula the system works the same, but **Ontario Street** is the east-west axis. Also, all east-west roads are avenues (for example, Fourth Avenue), while streets (for example, Main Street) run exclusively north-south.

STREET MAPS   The Travel Info Centres (see "Visitor Information," above) and most hotels can provide you with detailed downtown maps. A good all-around metropolitan area map is the Rand McNally Vancouver city map, which is available for C$3 (US$2) at the Vancouver Airport Tourism Centre kiosk. If you're an auto-club member, the Canadian Automobile Association (CAA) map is also good. It's not for sale, but is free to both AAA and CAA members and available at AAA offices across North America. **International Travel Maps and Books,** 552 Seymour St. (☎ **604/687-3320**), has the city's most extensive selection of Vancouver and British Columbia maps and specialty guide books.

THE NEIGHBORHOODS IN BRIEF

What's West   The thing to keep in mind, when figuring out what's where in Vancouver, is that this is a city where property is king, and the word "west" has such positive connotations that folks have always gone to great lengths to associate it with their particular patch of real estate. Thus we have the **West End,** and the **West Side,** and **West Vancouver,** which improbably enough is located immediately beside **North Vancouver.** It can be a bit confusing for newcomers, but fortunately each west has its own distinct character. The West End is a high-rise residential neighborhood located on the downtown peninsula. The West Side is one whole half of Vancouver, from Ontario Street west to the University of British Columbia. (The more working-class **East Side** covers the mainland portion of the city, from Ontario Street east to Boundary Road.) Very tony West Vancouver is a city to itself on the far side of Burrard Inlet. Together with its more middle-class neighbor, North Vancouver, it forms an area called the **North Shore.**

Downtown   Vancouver's commercial and office core runs from Nelson Street north to the harbor, with Homer as the eastern edge, and a more ragged boundary running roughly along Burrard Street forming the western border. The truly prime office space is on or near Georgia Street. Howe Street, home of the (in)famous Vancouver Stock Exchange, is the local synonym for flashy and slightly disreputable wealth. Hotels stick mostly to the northern third of downtown, clustering especially thickly near the water's edge. Restaurants are sprinkled throughout. Walking is a good bet for transport downtown, day and night. Unlike many North American cities, there are lots of people living in and around Vancouver's central business district, so the area is always populated.

The West End   A fascinating neighborhood of high-rise condos mixed with old Edwardian homes, the West End has within its borders all the necessities of life: great cafes, good nightclubs, many and varied bookshops, and some of the best restaurants in the city. That so many can live so well in such a small area is partially due to the interesting and eclectic architecture, but mostly it's thanks to the beautiful surroundings— the Pacific Ocean laps against the West End on two sides, Burrard Inlet to the north and English Bay to the south, while Stanley Park occupies the western edge. Burrard Street forms the West End's eastern border.

Gastown   The oldest section of Vancouver, Gastown was named after Vancouver's first settler, riverboat skipper and saloon keeper Jack Deighton, nicknamed "Gassy" thanks to his long-winded habits of speech. It was rebuilt in brick after the 1886 fire wiped out the original wooden city. Gastown's cobblestone streets and late Victorian architecture make it well worth a visit, despite a rather heavy infestation of curio shops and souvenir stands. It lies to the east of downtown, in the 6 square blocks between Water and Hastings Streets, and Cambie and Columbia Streets.

Chinatown   Located south of Hastings Street, between Gore and Carrall to the east and west, and Keefer Street to the south, Vancouver's Chinatown is not large, but it is intense. Fishmongers stand calling out their wares in Cantonese before a shop filled with crabs, eels, geoducks, and bullfrogs. Elderly Chinese women haggle over produce, while their husbands hunt for deer antler or dried sea horse at a traditional Chinese apothecary. Inside any one of a dozen restaurants, meanwhile, entire extended families—father, mother, grandparents, grown children, and grandkids—sit at a single big round table, consuming a half-dozen plates of succulent Cantonese cooking.

Yaletown   Vancouver's former warehouse district—located below Granville Street and above Pacific Boulevard, from Davie Street over to Smithe Street—Yaletown has long since become an area of apartment lofts, nightclubs, restaurants, high-end furniture shops, and a fledgling multimedia biz. The conversion was less an organic occurrence than a calculated agreement between City Hall and area landowners. It took a long while to work (15 years), but the area is finally coming into its own.

False Creek North (Concorde Pacific)   Stretching along Pacific Boulevard on the north shore of False Creek, Concorde's 30-odd high-rise towers are bright, shiny, and brand-spanking new. Perhaps a bit too new—like a pair of runners that need to lose a little gloss before they'll really be comfortable. The area's worth visiting though, if only to admire one of the largest—and so far most successful—urban redevelopment projects on the continent.

Granville Island   Some 20 years ago, some clever lad in the federal government had the bright idea of redeveloping this former industrial site into something more people-oriented. The result would not be a park, though there are parks on the island. Nor would it be offices, though there are those too. In fact, there's a bit of everything, including crafts shops, a boatyard, an art school, a public market, a pair of theaters, a hotel, and several pubs and restaurants. There's even a bit of heavy industry. The result is hard to describe, but well worth a visit. Just don't bring a car. There are 97,000 visitors every day, and only three parking spaces. Or that's what it feels like, anyway.

Kitsilano   Back in the '60s, Kitsilano was Canada's Haight-Ashbury, a slightly seedy enclave of coffeehouses, head shops, and lots of long-haired hippies. Its days as a counterculture hotbed have long since drifted away on a wave of fragrant smoke, but the area—known as Kits—remains one of Vancouver's most popular and sought-after neighborhoods. The attraction is the mixture of affordable apartments and 1920s Craftsman homes, together with funky shops, great restaurants, and pleasant walkable streets. And then, of course, there's Kits Beach, that bastion of bronzed skin and supple spandex. Less sought-after surrounding areas have recently taken to calling themselves "Upper Kits," making a precise definition of Kitsilano's borders problematic. Roughly speaking, Alma Street and Burrard Street form Kitsilano's east and west boundaries, with West 16th Avenue to the south and the ocean to the north.

Shaughnessy   Designed in the 1920s as an enclave for Vancouver's budding elite, Shaughnessy for the longest time refused even to admit that it was part of the city of Vancouver. Even today, traffic is carefully diverted away from the area, and it takes a concerted effort to see the stately homes and monstrous mansions, many of which are now featured in film shoots. To find the neighborhood, look on a map for the area of curvy and convoluted streets between Cypress and Oak Streets and 12th and 32nd Avenues. The center of opulence is the Crescent, an elliptical-shaped street to the southwest of Granville and 16th Avenue.

Richmond   Twenty years ago Richmond was mostly farmland, with a bit of sleepy suburb. Now it's Asia West, an agglomeration of shopping malls geared to the new—read: rich, educated, and successful—Chinese immigrant. The residential areas of the city are not worth visiting (unless tract homes are your thing), but malls like the Aberdeen Mall or the Yao Han Centre are something else. It's like getting into your car in Vancouver and getting out in Singapore.

Steveston   Steveston once existed for nothing but salmon. Located at the southwest corner of Richmond by the mouth of the Fraser River, Steveston was where the boats left to catch the migrating sockeye, returning with loads of fish to be cleaned and canned. In the huge processing plants covering its waterfront, thousands of workers gutted millions of fish. The catch has since declined, and the industry has automated, leaving Steveston a smaller and more pleasant place. The fixed-up waterfront is now an interesting place to stroll. There are public fish sales, a cannery museum, and charter trips up the river or out to the Fraser delta. Above all, there's a pleasant, laid-back, small-town atmosphere.

Commercial Drive   Every immigrant group that ever passed through the city left its mark on the "Drive." First came the Italians—who left quality espresso—then the Portuguese, the Hondurans and Guatemalans, the leftist alternative vegetarians, the artists, and finally the last wave of immigrants, the yuppies. The result is a peculiar but endearing mix: the Italian cafe next to the Marxist bookstore across from the vegetarian deli that has lately taken to selling really expensive yeast-free Tuscan bread.

Punjabi Market   India imported. For reasons still unknown, many of the businesses catering to Vancouver's sizable Punjabi population set up shop on a 4-block stretch of Main Street, from 48th up to 52nd Avenue. The area is best seen during business hours, when the fragrant scent of spices wafts from food stalls, while Hindi pop songs blare from hidden speakers. Young brides hunt through sari shops, or seek out suitable material in discount textile outlets. Shopping here is like sipping from the distilled essence of the Indian subcontinent.

The North Shore (North Vancouver & West Vancouver) The most impressive thing about the North Shore is its mountain range. Huge, wild, and compellingly beautiful, the mountains are responsible for much of Vancouver's vaunted reputation for physical beauty. They are certainly worth a visit. But the two cities on the North Shore are not without their charms. West Vancouver has the distinction of being the richest city in Canada. That doesn't mean much to visitors, of course, but there are some worthwhile restaurants in the Dundarave area on the West Van waterfront. (Roughly speaking, West Vancouver is everything west of the Lions Gate Bridge.) Better from a visitor's point of view is North Vancouver. It's easily reached by public transit, and the Lonsdale Quay public market—where the SeaBus docks—makes a pleasant afternoon's outing.

2 Getting Around

BY PUBLIC TRANSPORTATION

The **Translink** (otherwise known as BC Transit; ☎ 604/ 521-0400; www.translink.bc.ca) system includes electric buses, SeaBus catamaran ferries, and the magnetic-rail Sky-Train. It's an ecologically friendly, highly reliable, and inexpensive system that allows you to get everywhere, including the beaches and ski slopes. Regular service on the main routes runs from 5am to 2am, and less frequent "Owl" service operates on several downtown and suburban routes until 4:20am.

Schedules and routes are available at the Travel Info Centres, at many major hotels, online, and on buses. Pick up a copy of *Discover Vancouver on Transit* at one of the Travel Info Centres (see "Visitor Information," above). This publication gives transit routes for many city neighborhoods, landmarks, and attractions, including numerous Victoria sites.

FARES   Fares are the same for the buses, SeaBus, and Sky-Train. One-way, all-zone fares are C$1.75 (US$1.15) after 6:30pm on weekdays, and all day on weekends and holidays. At other times, a one-zone fare costs C$1.75 (US$1.15) and covers the entire city of Vancouver. A two-zone fare—C$2.50 (US$1.65)—is required to travel to nearby suburbs such as Richmond or North Vancouver, while a three-zone fare—C$3.50 (US$2.35)—is required for travel to the far-off edge city of Surrey. Free transfers are available on boarding and are good for travel in any direction and for the SkyTrain and SeaBus, but they do have a 90-minute expiration. **DayPasses,** which are good on all public transit, are C$7 (US$4.70) for adults and C$5 (US$3.35) for seniors, students, and children. They can be used for unlimited travel on weekdays or week-ends and holidays. Tickets and passes are available at Travel Info Centres, both SeaBus terminals, convenience stores, drugstores, credit unions, and other outlets displaying the "FareDealer" symbol.

BY SKYTRAIN   The SkyTrain is a computerized, magnetic-rail train that services 20 stations along its 35-minute trip from downtown Vancouver east to Surrey through Burnaby and New Westminster.

BY SEABUS   The SS *Beaver* and SS *Otter* catamaran ferries annually take more than 700,000 passengers, cyclists, and wheelchair riders on a scenic 12-minute commute between downtown's Waterfront Station and North Vancouver's Lonsdale Quay. On weekdays, a SeaBus leaves each stop every 15 minutes from 6:15am to 6:30pm, then every 30 minutes until 1am. SeaBuses depart on Saturdays every half hour from 6:30am to 12:30pm, then every 15 minutes until 7:15pm, then every half hour until 1am. On Sundays and holidays, runs depart every half hour from 8:30am to 11pm.

BY BUS   There are some key routes to keep in mind if you're touring the city by bus: **no. 5** (Robson Street), **no. 22** (Kitsilano Beach to downtown), **no. 50** (Granville Island), **no. 35** or **135** (to the Stanley Park bus loop), **no. 240** (North Vancouver), **no. 250** (West Vancouver–Horseshoe Bay), and buses **no. 4** and **10** (UBC to Exhibition Park via Granville Street downtown). In the summer, the **Vancouver Parks Board** operates a bus route through Stanley Park (☎ **604/ 257-8400**).

BY TAXI

Cab fares start at C$2.30 (US$1.55) and increase at a rate of C$1.25 (US85¢) per kilometer, plus C30¢ (US20¢) per minute at stoplights. It's a little less than in most other major cities, but it still adds up pretty quickly. In the downtown area, you can expect to travel for less than C$6 (US$4) plus tip. The typical fare for the 13-kilometer (8-mile) drive from downtown to the airport is C$25 (US$17).

Taxis are easy to find in front of major hotels, but flagging one can be tricky. Most drivers are usually on radio calls. But thanks to built-in satellite positioning systems, if you call for a taxi, it usually arrives faster than if you go out and hail one. Call for a pickup from **Black Top** (☎ **604/731-1111**), **Yellow Cab** (☎ **604/681-1111**), or **MacLure's** (☎ **604/ 731-9211**). **AirLimo** (☎ **604/273-1331**) offers flat-rate stretch limousine service. AirLimo charges C$29 (US$19) per trip to the airport (not per person), plus tax and tip. The drivers accept all major credit cards.

BY CAR

Vancouver has nowhere near the near-permanent gridlock of northwest cities like Seattle, but neither are the roads exactly empty. Fortunately, if you're just sightseeing around town or heading up to Whistler (a car is unnecessary in Whistler), public transit and cabs should see you through. However, if you're planning to visit the North Shore mountains or pursue other out-of-town activities, then by all means rent a car or bring your own. Gas is sold by the liter, averaging around C65¢ (US45¢) per liter. This may seem inexpensive until you consider that a gallon of gas costs about C$2.70 (US$1.80). Also, speeds and distances are posted in kilometers.

RENTALS   Rates vary widely depending on demand and style of car. If you're over 25 and have a major credit card, you can rent a vehicle from **Avis,** 757 Hornby St. (☎ **800/ 879-2847** or 604/606-2847); **Budget,** 501 W. Georgia St. (☎ **800/472-3325,** 800/527-0700, or 604/668-7000); **Enterprise,** 585 Smithe St. (☎ **800/736-8222** or 604/ 688-5500); **Hertz Canada,** 1128 Seymour St. (☎ **800/ 263-0600** or 604/688-2411); **National/Tilden,** 1130 W. Georgia St. (☎ **800/387-4747** or 604/685-6111); or **Thrifty,** 1015 Burrard St. or 1400 Robson St. (☎ **800/ 847-4389** or 604/606-1666). These firms all have counters and shuttle service at the airport as well. To rent a recreational vehicle, contact **CC Canada Camper RV Rentals,** 4431 Vanguard Rd., Richmond (☎ **604/270-1833;** www.canada-camper.com). At **Exotic Motorcycle & Car Rentals,** 1820 Burrard St. (☎ **604/644-9128;** www.exoticcars.com), you can rent a Ferrari, Viper, Porsche, Hummer, Jaguar, Lotus, Volkswagen Beetle, or Corvette. A wide selection of Harley-Davidson motorcycles is also available; rental (C$239/US$160 per day) includes helmets, gloves, and leather jackets for two.

PARKING   All major downtown hotels have guest parking; rates vary from free to C$20 (US$13) per day. There's public parking at **Robson Square** (enter at Smithe and Howe Streets), the **Pacific Centre** (Howe and Dunsmuir Streets), and **The Bay** department store (Richards near Dunsmuir Street). You'll also find **parking lots** at Thurlow and Georgia Streets, Thurlow and Alberni Streets, and Robson and Seymour Streets.

Metered **street parking** isn't impossible to come by, but it may take a trip or three around the block to find a spot. Rules are posted on the street and are invariably strictly enforced. Unmetered parking on side streets is often subject to neighborhood residency requirements. Check the signs. If your car is towed away or if you need a towing service and aren't a member of AAA, call **Unitow** (☎ **604/251-1255**) or **Busters** (☎ **604/685-8181**).

SPECIAL DRIVING RULES   Canadian driving rules are similar to those in the United States. Unlike in the United States, however, daytime headlights are mandatory. Also, the police have recently discovered the joys of automated ticketing: Photo radar is used extensively in Vancouver, and photo-monitored intersections are quickly coming into vogue. If you speed or go through a red light, you may get an expensive picture of your vacation from the Royal Canadian Mounted Police. Fines start at C$100 (US$67).

AUTO CLUB   Members of the American Automobile Association (AAA) can get assistance from the **Canadian Automobile Association** (**CAA**), 999 W. Broadway, Vancouver (☎ **604/268-5600,** or for road service 604/293-2222).

BY BIKE

Vancouver is decidedly bicycle-friendly. There are plenty of places to rent a bike along Robson and Denman Streets near Stanley Park. (For specifics, see "Outdoor Activities" in chapter 5.) Bike routes are designated throughout the city. Paved paths crisscross through parks and along beaches (see chapter 5), and new routes are constantly being added. Helmets are mandatory, and riding on sidewalks is illegal except on designated bike paths.

Cycling BC (☎ **604/737-3034;** www.cycling.bc.ca) accommodates cyclists on the SkyTrain and buses by providing "Bike & Ride" lockers at all "Park & Ride" parking lots. The department also dispenses loads of information about events, bike touring, and cycle insurance. Many downtown parking lots and garages also have no-fee bike racks.

You can take your bike on the SeaBus anytime at no extra charge. Bikes are not allowed in the George Massey Tunnel, but a tunnel shuttle operates four times daily from mid-May through September to transport you across the Fraser River. From May 1 to Victoria Day (the third weekend of May), the service operates on weekends only.

All the West Vancouver blue buses (including the bus to the Horseshoe Bay ferry terminal) can carry two bikes, first-come, first-served, free of charge. In Vancouver, only a limited number of suburban routes allow bikes on the bus; bus 351 to White Rock, bus 601 to South Delta, bus 404 to the airport, and the 99 Express to UBC.

BY FERRY

Crossing False Creek to Vanier Park or Granville Island on one of the blue miniferries is cheap and fun. The **Aquabus** docks at the foot of Howe Street. It takes you either to Granville Island's public market or east along False Creek to Science World and Stamps Landing. The **Granville Island Ferry** docks at Sunset Beach below the Burrard Street Bridge and the Aquatic Centre. It goes to Granville Island and Vanier Park. Ferries to Granville Island leave every 5 minutes from 7am to 10pm. Ferries to Vanier Park leave every 15 minutes from 10am to 8pm. One-way fares on all routes are $2 (US$1.35) for adults and C75¢ (US50¢) for seniors and children.

FAST FACTS: Vancouver

American Express   666 Burrard St. (☎ **604/669-2813**). It's open Monday to Friday from 8am to 5:30pm, Saturday from 10am to 4pm.

Baby-Sitters   Most major hotels can arrange baby-sitting service and have cribs available. If you need cribs, car seats, play pens, or other baby accessories, **Cribs and Carriages** (☎ **604/988-2742**) delivers them right to your hotel.

Business Hours   Vancouver **banks** are open Monday to Thursday from 10am to 5pm and Friday from 10am to 6pm. Some banks, like Canadian Trust, are also open on Saturday. **Stores** are generally open Monday to Saturday from 10am to 6pm. Last call at the city's **restaurant bars** and **cocktail lounges** is 2am.

Consulates   The **U.S. Consulate** is at 1095 W. Pender St. (☎ **604/685-4311**). The British Consulate is at 800–1111 Melville St. (☎ **604/683-4421**). The Australian Consulate is at 1225–888 Dunsmuir St. (☎ **604/684-1177**). Check the Yellow Pages for other countries.

Dentist   Most major hotels have a dentist on call. **Vancouver Centre Dental Clinic,** Vancouver Centre Mall, 11–650 W. Georgia St. (☎ **604/682-1601**), is another option. You must make an appointment. The clinic is open Monday to Wednesday 8:30am to 6pm, Thursday 8:30am to 7pm, Friday 9am to 6pm, and Saturday 9am to 4pm.

Doctor   Hotels usually have a doctor on call. **Vancouver Medical Clinics,** Bentall Centre, 1055 Dunsmuir St. (☎ **604/683-8138**), is a drop-in clinic open Monday to Friday 8am to 4:45pm. Another drop-in medical center, **Carepoint Medical Centre,** 1175 Denman St. (☎ **604/ 681-5338**), is open daily from 9am to 9pm. See also "Emergencies," below.

Electricity   As in the United States, electric current is 110 volts AC (60 cycles).

Emergencies   Dial ☎ **911** for fire, police, ambulance, and poison control.

Hospitals   **St. Paul's Hospital,** 1081 Burrard St. (☎ **604/ 682-2344**), is the closest facility to downtown and the West

End. West Side Vancouver hospitals include **Vancouver General Hospital Health and Sciences Centre,** 855 W. 12th Ave. (☎ **604/875-4111**), and **British Columbia's Children's Hospital,** 4480 Oak St. (☎ **604/875-2345**). In North Vancouver, there's **Lions Gate Hospital,** 231 E. 15th St. (☎ **604/ 988-3131**).

Hot Lines Emergency numbers include **Crisis Centre** (☎ 604/872-3311); **Rape Crisis Centre** (☎ 604/255-6344); **Rape Relief** (☎ 604/872-8212); **Poison Control Centre** (☎ 604/682-5050); **Crime Stoppers** (☎ 604/669-8477); **SPCA** animal emergency (☎ 604/879-7343); **Vancouver Police** (☎ 604/717-3535); **Fire** (☎ 604/665-6000); and **Ambulance** (☎ 604/872-5151). See also "Emergencies," above.

Liquor Laws The legal drinking age in British Columbia is 19. Spirits are sold only in government liquor stores, but beer and wine can be purchased from specially licensed, privately owned stores and pubs. There are 22 LCBC (Liquor Control of British Columbia) stores scattered throughout Vancouver. Most are open Monday to Saturday from 10am to 6pm, but some are open to 11pm.

Lost Property The **Vancouver Police** have a lost-property room (☎ **604/717-2726**), open during office hours Monday to Saturday. If you think you may have lost something on public transportation, call **Translink** (BC Transit) during office hours at ☎ **604/682-7887.**

Luggage Storage & Lockers Most downtown hotels will gladly hold your luggage before or after your stay. Just ask at the front desk. Lockers are available at the main Vancouver railway station (which is also the main bus depot), **Pacific Central Station,** 1150 Station St., near Main Street and Terminal Avenue south of Chinatown (☎ **604/661-0328**), for C$2 (US$1.35) per day.

Maps See "City Layout," earlier in this chapter.

Newspapers & Magazines The two local papers are the *Vancouver Sun* (published Monday to Saturday) and *The Province* (published Sunday to Friday mornings). The free weekly entertainment paper *The Georgia Straight* comes out on Thursday. Other newsworthy papers are the national *Globe and Mail* or the *National Post,* the *Chinese Oriental Star,* the

Southeast Asian *Indo-Canadian Voice,* and the *Jewish Western Daily. Where Vancouver,* a shopping and tourist guide, is usually provided in your hotel room or can be picked up from Tourism Vancouver. See "Visitor Information," earlier in this chapter, for more information.

Pharmacies   **Shopper's Drug Mart,** 1125 Davie St. (☎ **604/ 685-6445**), is open 24 hours a day. Several Safeway supermarkets have late-night pharmacies, including the one at the corner of Robson and Denman streets, which is open until midnight.

Police   For emergencies, dial ☎ **911.** Otherwise, the **Vancouver City Police** can be reached at ☎ **604/717-3535.**

Post Office   The **main post office** (☎ **604/662-5722**) is at West Georgia and Homer Streets (349 W. Georgia St.). It's open Monday to Friday from 8am to 5:30pm. Postal outlets are usually open Saturday and Sunday as well as later in the evening and can be found in souvenir stores, 7-11 stores, and drugstores displaying the red-and-white CANADA POST emblem. Letters and postcards cost C50¢ (US35¢) to mail outside Canada, C45¢ (US30¢) within Canada, and C90¢ (US60¢) overseas.

Rest Rooms   Hotel lobbies are your best bet for downtown facilities. The shopping centers like Pacific Centre and Sinclair Centre, as well as the large department stores like the Bay, also have rest rooms.

Safety   Overall, Vancouver is a safe city; violent-crime rates are quite low. However, property crimes and crimes of opportunity (such as items being stolen from unlocked cars) do occur with troubling frequency, particularly downtown. Vancouver's Downtown East Side, between Gastown and Chinatown, is a troubled neighborhood and should be avoided at night.

Taxes   Hotel rooms are subject to a 10% tax. The provincial sales tax (PST) is 7% (excluding food, restaurant meals, and children's clothing). For specific questions, call the **B.C. Consumer Taxation Branch** (☎ **604/660-4500**).

Most goods and services are subject to a 7% federal goods and services tax (GST). You can get a refund on short-stay accommodations and all shopping purchases that total at least C$100 (US$67). (This refund doesn't apply to car rentals, parking, restaurant meals, room service, tobacco, or alcohol.)

Hotels and the Info Centres can give you application forms. Save your receipts. For details on the GST, call ☎ **800/ 668-4748** in Canada or 902/432-5608 outside Canada (www.ccra-adrc.gc.ca/visitors).

Telephone   Phones in British Columbia are identical to U.S. phones. The country code is the same as the U.S. code (1). Local calls normally cost C25¢ (US15¢). Many hotels charge up to C$1 (US65¢) per local call and much more for long-distance calls. You can save considerably by using your calling card. You can also buy prepaid phone cards in various denominations at grocery and convenience stores. If you need a cellular phone, **Cell City,** 105–950 W. Broadway (☎ **604/656-2311**), rents them for C$19 (US$13) per day, plus C70¢ (US45¢) per minute, or C$39 (US$26) per week, plus C65¢ (US45¢) per minute.

Time Zone   Vancouver is in the Pacific time zone, as are Seattle and San Francisco. Daylight saving time applies from April through October.

Tipping   Tipping etiquette is the same as in the United States: 15% in restaurants, C$1 (US65¢) per bag for bellboys and porters, and C$1 (US65¢) per day for the hotel house-keeper. Taxi drivers get a sliding-scale tip—fares under C$4 (US$2.70) deserve a C$1 (US65¢) tip; for fares over C$5 (US$3.35), tip 15%.

Weather   Call ☎ **604/664-9010** or 604/664-9032 for weather updates; dial ☎ **604/666-3655** for marine forecasts.

3

Accommodations

*T*he past few years have seen a lot of activity in the Vancouver hotel business. Lots of new rooms have opened up, some in the high end, and a lot more in the moderate-to-budget range. Other hotels have undergone extensive renovations, and good-natured competition has flourished among all the city's hostelries. So no matter what your budget, there's no reason to settle for second best. Most of the hotels are in the downtown/Yaletown area, or else in the West End. Both neighborhoods are close to major sites and services. The West Side of Vancouver has a few hotels, plus many pleasant bed-and-breakfasts. Other good accommodations are found across Burrard Inlet on the North Shore.

Whichever area you choose, here are some tips for a more pleasant and possibly more affordable stay:

- Quoted prices don't include the 10% provincial accommodations tax or the 7% goods and services tax (GST). Non-Canadian residents can get a GST rebate on short-stay accommodations by filling out the Tax Refund Application (see "Taxes" under "Fast Facts: Vancouver" in chapter 2).

- The prices listed are the "rack rates"—the one listed on the door and given to the public. Always ask about discounts (AAA, corporate, military) or vacation packages, particularly in the October through April low season. A simple inquiry could save you up to 50%. In the summer high season, however, prices are much less flexible.

- Beware the incidentals. Though competition is making the practice less common, many establishments still tack on a $1 surcharge each time you make a local call. To avoid unpleasant surprises, ask beforehand what kinds of surcharges exist. If presented with a sizable surcharge bill upon checkout, complain loudly. Local telephone fees have a way of magically evaporating.

• There are only a few small areas to avoid when booking a room. Granville Street offers location without the price, but, though the area has improved considerably, it's still the hangout for panhandling teenagers. Hotels on E. Hastings Street or E. Cordova Street are not worth the savings. These streets are in Vancouver's East Side skid row, which has some of Canada's highest property-crime rates.

RESERVATIONS   Reservations are highly recommended from June through September and over the holidays. If you arrive without a reservation or have trouble finding a room, call **Super Natural British Columbia's Discover British Columbia** hot line at ☎ **800/663-6000,** or **Tourism Vancouver's** hot line at ☎ **604/683-2000.** Specializing in last-minute bookings, either organization can make arrangements using its large daily listing of hotels, hostels, and B&Bs.

1 Downtown & Yaletown

All downtown hotels are within 5 to 10 minutes' walking distance of shops, restaurants, and attractions. Hotels in this area lean more toward luxurious than modest, a state of affairs reflected in their prices.

You can reach the downtown hotels by taking the **SkyTrain** to the **Granville** or **Burrard** stops, which are just a few blocks apart. The **Waterfront station** is close to the Pan-Pacific Hotel. The **Stadium station** is just a few blocks from the Georgian Court Hotel, Rosedale on Robson, and the YWCA. The **no. 1 or 5 bus** will take you to the West End hotels; the **no. 4 or 10 bus** will get you to hotels near False Creek.

VERY EXPENSIVE

✪ **Crowne Plaza Hotel Georgia.** 801 W. Georgia St., Vancouver, B.C. V6C 1P7. ☎ **800/663-1111** or 604/682-5566. Fax 604/642-5579. www. hotelgeorgia.bc.ca. E-mail: reservations@hotelgeorgia.bc.ca. 313 units. A/C TV TEL. May–Oct C$299–C$399 (US$200–US$267) double; Nov–Dec C$219–C$279 (US$147–US$187) double; Jan–Apr C$209–C$269 (US$140–US$180) double. Children under 16 stay free in parents' room. AE, CB, DC, DISC, MC, V. Parking C$18 (US$12).

Built in 1927, the Crowne Plaza Hotel Georgia has just recently undergone major renovations to restore it to its 1920s glory. The dark wood–paneled lobby is decorated with brass elevator doors, a black marble fireplace in the cozy sitting area, and original terrazzo tiles. Upstairs, the rooms have custom-designed art deco–style furniture. The rooms are comfortable with adequate workspace, modem access, coffee- and tea-making service, and two phone lines. The entire 12th floor consists of Club Level rooms, well worth the C$30 (US$20) surcharge. In addition to all the standard features, Club Level rooms have CD players, speakerphones, and robes. All Club Level guests also have access to the "Elvis Room" (Elvis stayed in this room when it used to be a suite, hence the blue suede lounge chairs). The rooms include complimentary breakfast, hors d'oeuvres, and drinks in the afternoon, a workstation with computer and office supplies, business publications, and meeting space.

Dining/Diversions: The Casablanca lounge, complete with leopard-skin wallpaper, is open for drinks, light lunches, and snacks. The As Time Goes By restaurant serves breakfast, lunch, dinner, and afternoon tea. Also housed in the hotel is the funky downstairs Chameleon Urban Lounge (see "Vancouver After Dark," chapter 7) and the street-level Georgia Street Bar and Grill.

Amenities: Concierge, 24-hour room service, dry cleaning, laundry service, newspaper delivery, express checkout, valet parking, free coffee, health club, business center, conference rooms, and beauty salon.

✪ **Four Seasons Hotel.** 791 W. Georgia St., Vancouver, B.C. V6C 2T4. ☎ **800/332-3442** in the U.S. or 604/689-9333. Fax 604/684-4555. www.fourseasons.com. 385 units. A/C MINIBAR TV TEL. C$290–C$450 (US$194–US$302) double, C$340–C$500 (US$228–US$335) junior suite, C$375–C$570 (US$251–US$382) executive suite. Wheelchair-accessible units available. AE, DC, ER, MC, V. Parking C$20 (US$13). Pets are welcome.

This modern 28-story palace sits atop the Pacific Centre's 200 retail stores and is only a few blocks from the financial district. It's a particularly appealing location for both shoppers and business travelers. From the street, the hotel is so well hidden you could walk right past without noticing the enclosed driveway. Once inside, however, you are instantly immersed in understated luxury: wood paneling, Asian accessories, and subdued lighting. The guest rooms are tastefully appointed with French provincial furniture and marble bathrooms. The rooms aren't large, however, so for more space try a deluxe room on one of the building's corners; a deluxe "Four

Downtown Vancouver Accommodations

Barclay House in the West End **10**
Best Western Downtown Vancouver **16**
Blue Horizon **23**
Buchan Hotel **3**
Canadian-Pacific Hotel Vancouver **30**
Coast Plaza at Stanley Park **4**
Days Inn Downtown **26**
Delta Vancouver Suite Hotel **27**
Empire Landmark Hotel & Conference Centre **7**
Executive Inn **14**
Four Seasons Hotel **33**
Georgian Court Hotel **37**
Granville Island Hotel **13**
Hostelling International Downtown **12**
Hotel Georgia **32**
Howard Johnson Hotel **18**
Hyatt Regency Vancouver **29**
Kingston Hotel **34**
Le Soleil (Sheraton Suites) **28**
Listel Vancouver **9**
Metropolitan Hotel Vancouver **31**
Pacific Palisades Hotel **24**
Pan-Pacific Hotel Vancouver **25**
Parkhill Hotel **11**
Quality Hotel Downtown/The Inn at False Creek **15**
Ramada Inn & Suites **17**
Rosedale on Robson Suite Hotel **36**
Rosellen Suites **2**
Sheraton Wall Centre Vancouver **19**
Sunset Inn Travel Apartments **6**
Sutton Place Hotel **22**
Sylvia Hotel **5**
Wedgewood Hotel **20**
West End Guest House **8**
Westin Bayshore **1**
Westin Grand **35**
YMCA **21**
YMCA Hotel/Residence **38**

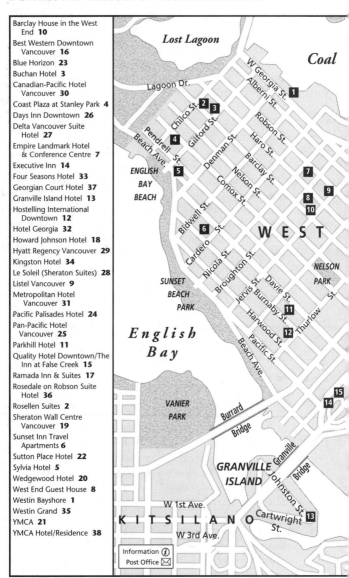

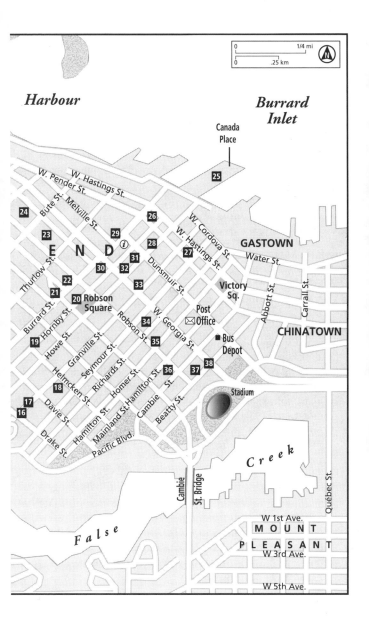

Harbour

Burrard Inlet

Canada Place

25

W. Pender St.
W. Hastings St.

Bute St. Melville St.

24

23

E N D

Thurlow St.

22

21

20 Robson Square

19

Hornby St.
Howe St.
Burrard St.

Granville St.
Seymour St.
Helmcken St.
Richards St.
Homer St.
Hamilton St.
Mainland St.
Cambie St.
Beatty St.

18

17
16

Davie St.

Drake St.

Pacific Blvd.

False

30
31
32
33

29
ⓘ

28

26

W. Cordova St.

W. Hastings St.

27

GASTOWN

Water St.

Dunsmuir St.

Victory Sq.

Abbott St.

Carrall St.

CHINATOWN

34
35

W. Georgia St.

Robson St.

Post Office

■ Bus Depot

36
37 38

Stadium

C r e e k

Québec St.

Cambie
St. Bridge

W 1st Ave.
M O U N T
P L E A S A N T
W 3rd Ave.
W 5th Ave.

0   1/4 mi
0   .25 km

Seasons" room (they have a separately partitioned sitting area); or a spacious suite or junior suite.

Dining: Chartwell's serves an eclectic blend of continental, West Coast, and Asian dishes. The Garden Terrace and the Terrace Bar offer more casual dining.

Amenities: 24-hour room service, concierge, laundry and valet service, twice-daily housekeeping, limo service. Children get cookies and milk in the evening as well as special room-service menus and terry robes. There's an indoor/outdoor pool, weight and exercise room, whirlpool and saunas, sundeck, florist, and cigar store.

✪ **Hotel Vancouver.** 900 W. Georgia St., Vancouver, B.C. V6C 2W6. ☎ **800/866-5577** or 604/684-3131. Fax 604/662-1929. www.fairmont. com. E-mail: reserve@hvc.cphotels.ca. 556 units. A/C MINIBAR TV TEL. High-season rates C$259–C$489 (US$174–US$328) double, C$419–C$1,899 (US$281–US$1,272) suite. Low-season rates from C$179 (US$120) double, from C$339 (US$227) suite. AE, DC, DISC, MC, V. Parking C$19 (US$13). Small pets are welcome for a C$25 (US$17) charge.

With a C$65-million renovation completed recently, the grande dame of Vancouver's hotels has been restored beyond her former glory. The Hotel Vancouver evokes a feeling of luxury and spaciousness. The bedrooms have marble bathrooms and mahogany furnishings and offer city, harbor, and mountain views. Most of the rooms have been specially equipped for business travelers: dedicated fax and modem lines, speakerphones, coffeemakers, and desk supplies. The best rooms are on the Entrée Gold floors. Offering upgraded furniture, these rooms include a private concierge, check-in/out service, continental breakfast, free local calls, shoeshine, and afternoon tea with hors d'oeuvres.

Dining: Serving West Coast cuisine, 900 West is one of Vancouver's best spots for fine dining. Griffins is the casual, brasserie-style restaurant. The Lobby Bar also serves a light menu.

Amenities: 24-hour room service; concierge; valet; laundry; indoor pool; wading pool; Jacuzzi; health club with weight room; sauna; tanning salon; day spa; shops, including Louis Vuitton, Bally, and Aquascutum.

✪ **Metropolitan Hotel Vancouver.** 645 Howe St., Vancouver, B.C. V6C 2Y9. ☎ **800/667-2300** or 604/687-1122. Fax 604/643-7267. www. metropolitan.com. For reservations: reservations@metropolitan.com. 197 units. A/C MINIBAR TV TEL. Apr–Oct C$229–C$385 (US$153–US$258) double;

Nov–Mar C$209–C$335 (US$140–US$224) double; C$1,500 (US$1,005) suite. Business Class C$30 (US$20) extra per unit. Children under 18 stay free in parents' room. AE, DC, MC, V. Underground valet parking C$18 (US$12).

The luxurious Metropolitan is centrally situated between the financial district and downtown shopping areas, and caters to business travelers on weekdays. A very clever design has rendered the tiny lobby quite elegant—it's furnished with overstuffed armchairs and dominated by a huge, hand-carved, gilded Chinese screen. Most units in the 18-story hotel have small balconies. All rooms have stately dark-wood furnishings, queen-size beds, marble bathrooms, fluffy bathrobes, complimentary in-room coffee, and morning paper delivery. We recommend the studio suites, which are much roomier and only slightly more expensive. Each of the Business Class rooms and studio suites has a fax machine, printer, modem hookup, cordless speakerphone, power strip, and other home-office amenities.

Dining/Diversions: Diva at the Met is one of Vancouver's finest restaurants, serving innovative Pacific Northwest cuisine until 1am; the bar serves excellent martinis.

Amenities: Concierge, 24-hour room service, dry cleaning, newspaper delivery, baby-sitting, secretarial services, express checkout, valet parking, courtesy car or limo, free coffee, in-room movies. Facilities include business center, lap pool, health club, Jacuzzi, men's steam room, squash and racquetball courts, saunas, sundeck.

✪ **Pan-Pacific Hotel Vancouver.** 300–999 Canada Place, Vancouver, B.C. V6C 3B5. ☎ **800/937-1515** in the U.S. or 604/662-8111. Fax 604/685-8690. www.panpac.com. E-mail: reservations@panpacific-hotel.com. 504 units. A/C MINIBAR TV TEL. May–Oct C$465–C$545 (US$312–US$365) double; Nov–Apr C$380–C$430 (US$255–US$288) double; C$565–C$3,000 (US$379–US$2,010) suite year-round. AE, DC, DISC, JCB, MC, V. Parking C$21 (US$14).

Apart from Vancouver's natural surroundings, the city's most distinctive landmark is Canada Place Pier. Its five gleaming-white Teflon sails are reminiscent of a giant sailing vessel. Atop this busy complex is a spectacular 23-story hotel (if you're taking an Alaskan cruise, this is the closest accommodation available). An escalator lifts arriving guests to the third-floor lobby. The lobby lounge has a full menu, huge picture windows, and a fountain that flows from outside into an ornate channel that runs through the lobby. Upstairs, all of the guest rooms are modern, spacious, and comfortably furnished with soft colors, down duvets on king-size beds, and elegant marble bathrooms. Many of the rooms look out over the harbor and up to the mountains; they have some of the most spectacular views in town.

Dining: Whether you stay here or not, the Five Sails restaurant is worth a visit. It's one of the city's best. (See chapter 4.)

Amenities: 24-hour room service, concierge, valet, limo service. There's an outstanding health club, which guests can use for an additional C$10 (US$7). The outdoor pool and terrace overlook the cruise ships. Wheelchair-accessible rooms are available.

Sheraton Suites Le Soleil-Vancouver. 567 Hornby St., Vancouver, B.C. V6C 2E8. ☎ **604/632-3000.** Fax 604/632-3001. www.lesoleilhotelcom. 122 units. MINIBAR TV TEL. May 1–Oct 15 C$350 (US$235) double, C$400 (US$268) suite, C$600 (US$402) penthouse; Oct 16–Apr 30 C$250 (US$168) double, C$300 (US$201) suite, C$500 (US$335) penthouse. AE, DC, ER, MC, V. Valet parking C$20 (US$13).

Stepping into Le Soleil is like entering a European luxury hotel. The uniformed doorman will welcome you into the lobby decorated with crystal chandeliers, Italian marble, plush carpeting, and gilded, vaulted ceilings. The opulence of the hotel can get a bit overwhelming in the narrow guest hallways, where a mix of prints and colors seems, at times, like too much of a good thing. In the suites (all units except 10 doubles are suites), however, the luxury comes off about right. Interiors are decorated in either crimson or gold color schemes, with maple-finished Biedermeier-style furniture. The sitting areas are comfortable; the sofas can convert into beds. As you would expect, all the little touches are there—the fruit plate upon check-in, the turndown service with Godiva chocolates. Rooms also include two-line speakerphones, data ports, cordless phones, in-room safes, and coffee and tea makers. Because the hotel is right downtown, nearly all suites feature skyline views—you get to look at surrounding buildings. However, for good views, not to mention ultimate luxury, you could try one of the Penthouse suites. The Versace-inspired bedroom-and-den Penthouse has a black Jacuzzi tub in the living room and 18-foot floor-to-ceiling windows.

Dining: The Oritalia restaurant serves up Italian-inspired West Coast fusion.

Amenities: 24-hour room service, concierge, twice-daily maid service, business center, health-club facilities available nearby.

The Sutton Place Hotel. 845 Burrard St., Vancouver, B.C. V6Z 2K6. ☎ **800/961-7555** or 604/682-5511. Fax 604/682-5513. www.suttonplace. com. E-mail: info@vcr.suttonplace.com. 397 units. A/C MINIBAR TV TEL. Nov–Apr C$189–C$299 (US$127–US$200) double, C$289–C$1,500 (US$194–US$1,005) suite; May–Oct C$269–C$439 (US$180–US$294) double, C$375–C$1,700 (US$251–US$1,139) suite. AE, CB, DC, DISC, ER, JCB, MC, V. Underground valet parking C$17 (US$11). Pets accepted C$150 (US$100), non-refundable, per stay.

Don't let the big pink hospital-like exterior fool you. Once you enter the lobby of this centrally located five-diamond hotel, it's pure luxury. The grand lobby is elegantly decorated with beige marble, fresh flowers, chandeliers, and European artwork. All standard rooms are tastefully decorated in a classic European style with a maroon and gold color scheme. In-room amenities include bathrobes, ice dispensers, mini-bars, umbrellas, newspapers, and desks with data ports and two phone lines. The one- or two-bedroom junior suites have a small parlor. In larger suites, double French doors separate the bedroom from the large sitting area.

Your four-legged furry friend will also receive five-diamond treatment at the Sutton Place: Your pet will be registered and photographed at the Sit & Stay check-in while all its pet-icular preferences are noted. For C$95 (US$64), you can purchase the VIP program which comes with gourmet dinner (T-bone or seared fresh tuna) and turndown service with doggie treats.

Dining/Diversions: The Fleuri Restaurant serves three meals daily, Sunday jazz brunch, and a seafood buffet on Friday and Saturday evenings. It also features an extensive "chocoholic" dessert bar Thursday to Saturday evenings. La Promenade offers light snacks and live piano music. The dark wood–paneled Gerard Lounge has oversized armchairs, a fireplace, and light snacks.

Amenities: Concierge, 24-hour room service, dry cleaning, laundry service, newspaper delivery, in-room massage, twice-daily maid service, baby-sitting, secretarial services, express checkout, valet parking, courtesy car and limo, free coffee and refreshments, video rentals, bike rental, indoor heated pool, children's programs, health club, Jacuzzi, sauna, sundeck, business center, conference rooms, and tour desk.

EXPENSIVE

Delta Vancouver Suite Hotel. 550 W. Hastings St., Vancouver, B.C. V6B 1L6. ☎ **800/268-1133** or 604/689-8188. Fax 604/605-8881. www.deltahotels. com. E-mail: vancouversuite@deltahotels.com. 226 units. A/C MINIBAR TV TEL. Jan–Apr C$185–C$370 (US$124–US$248) double; May–Oct C$245–C$400 (US$164–US$268) double; Nov–Dec C$195–C$370 (US$131–US$248) double. Children under 18 stay free in parents' room. AE, CB, DC, JCB, MC, V. Valet parking C$15 (US$10).

The Delta Vancouver Suite Hotel considers itself a Manhattan-style hotel. The spacious and bright lobby is decorated with black marble, cherry-colored wood, and stone white walls. The indoor atrium extends up to the third floor and connects to Simon Fraser University's conference space in the adjacent building. Note that none of the suites have kitchen facilities. Each suite does have a living room and bedroom with queen, king, or two double beds. The layout allows for a lot of natural light and, wherever possible, floor-to-ceiling windows. For more comfort, ask for a suite with a sofa, chair, and ottoman; some suites only come with two chairs. Designed for business travelers, the rooms provide a large workspace, with voice mail, two phone lines, and speakerphone. Internet access is available in the room for a maximum of C$10 (US$7) for 24 hours. The top three floors are reserved for Signature Club guests. The C$30 (US$20) premium upgrades you to a great view, down duvets, CD players, and access to the Signature Lounge with complimentary breakfast and afternoon cocktails.

Dining: Manhattan, located on the first floor, is becoming popular with the lunch crowd from the surrounding offices. It's open for breakfast, lunch, and dinner.

Amenities: Indoor pool, fitness center with sauna and whirlpool, full-service business center.

✪ Georgian Court Hotel. 773 Beatty St., Vancouver, B.C. V6B 2M4. ☎ **800/663-1155** or 604/682-5555. Fax 604/682-8830. www.georgiancourt. com. E-mail: info@georgiancourt.com. 180 units. A/C MINIBAR TV TEL. May 1–Oct 15 C$210–C$275 (US$141–US$184) double; Oct 16–Apr 30 C$125–C$215 (US$84–US$144) double. AE, CB, DC, MC, V. Parking C$8 (US$5).

This modern, 14-story brick hotel is extremely well located—it's a block or two from B.C. Place Stadium, G.M. Place Stadium, the Queen Elizabeth Theatre, the Playhouse, and the Vancouver Public Library, making it ideal for sports fans, trade-show attendees, and culture vultures. The guest rooms are large and attractively decorated with crown moldings and wooden baseboards. Especially welcome for business travelers, each room comes equipped with a writing desk, cordless phone, three phone lines, and voice mail.

Dining/Diversions: The William Tell Restaurant serves classic Swiss dishes prepared by 1995 Restaurateur of the Year Erwin Doebeli (see chapter 4). If you don't have tickets to a local game, you can always catch the action on one of 15 TVs in the Beatty St. Bar & Grill.

Amenities: Concierge, room service until 11pm, dry cleaning, laundry service, newspaper delivery, baby-sitting, secretarial services. A small health club is equipped with weights, LifeCycle, StairMaster, whirlpool, and sauna.

Hyatt Regency Vancouver. 655 Burrard St., Vancouver, B.C. V6C 2R7. ☎ **800/233-1234** or 604/683-1234. Fax 604/643-5812. www.hyatt.com. 644 units. A/C MINIBAR TV TEL. Apr 16–Oct 31 C$230–C$465 (US$154–US$312) double; Nov 1–Apr 15 C$119–C$320 (US$80–US$214) double. C$680–C$1,250 (US$456–US$838) suite. Regency Club rooms C$50 (US$34) extra. Weekend discounts available. AE, DC, DISC, ER, JCB, MC, V. Parking C$19 (US$13).

The Hyatt is an ultramodern white tower built over the huge Royal Centre Mall, which contains 60 specialty shops. The chandeliered atrium lobby reflects Vancouver's verdant outdoors, filled with trees and flowerbeds in marble planters. The very large guest rooms are tastefully decorated with understated yet comfortable furnishings. Corner rooms on the north and west sides have balconies with lovely views. Rooms on the Regency Club floors have a separate keyed elevator, concierge, continental breakfast, 5pm hors d'oeuvres service, and evening pastries, coffee, tea, and soda in a private lounge with a stereo and large-screen TV.

Dining/Diversions: Fish and Co. offers upscale seafood and continental cuisine at lunch and dinner and a Sunday brunch buffet. The Café serves casual breakfast and lunch. Peacocks Lounge offers an à la carte menu. The Gallery Bar serves a weekly lunch buffet and features big-screen sports.

Amenities: Room service, concierge, laundry, valet service, doctor and dentist on call, in-room coffeemaker, in-room iron and ironing board, heated outdoor pool, health club, saunas, access to squash and racquetball courts, business center, 26 meeting rooms.

✪ **The Sheraton Vancouver Wall Centre Hotel.** 1088 Burrard St., Vancouver, B.C. V6Z 2R9. ☎ **800/325-3535** or 604/331-1000. Fax 604/331-1001. www.sheratonvancouver.com. 735 units. A/C MINIBAR TV TEL. Oct 23–May 14 C$129–C$249 (US$86–US$167) double, C$179–C$399 (US$120–US$267) suite; May 15–Oct 22 C$199–C$399 (US$133–US$267) double, C$249–C$549 (US$167–US$368) suite. AE, DC, MC, V. Valet parking C$19 (US$13).

The Wall Centre is hard to miss. Look for the towering two-tone oval spire, the result of a strange compromise between city hall—which wanted the tower to have clear glass—and the developer, who preferred his glass opaque and black. Set together with two other sizable towers on one of the downtown area's highest points, the Wall Centre is development mogul Peter Wall's personal tribute to everything he has ever liked in the world's finest accommodations.

The opulent decor would not look out of place in a modern-art gallery, from the lobby's gold-leaf staircase, custom-designed furniture, and handblown glass chandeliers, to the half dozen peepholes on each guest room door. The guest rooms are elegantly appointed with blond wood furnishings, luxury bathrooms, heated floors, and king-size or double beds with down duvets and Egyptian cotton sheets. Every room has stunning floor-to-ceiling windows. In-room amenities include video checkout in five languages, in-room safes, and three two-line phones. For an additional C$25 to C$40 (US$17 to US$27) fee, you can upgrade to one of the 25th- or 26th-floor Crystal Club rooms, which brings added room amenities as well as access to the two-level Crystal Club lounge. Not only does the lounge serve complimentary breakfast and afternoon appetizers and drinks, it is also one of the nicest spaces to relax, with comfortable sitting areas and a north-facing (mountain view) terrace.

Dining/Diversions: Indigo features innovative West Coast cuisine in modern decor. Patio seating is also available. The hotel's bar, Cracked Ice, offers deep club chairs, an intimate atmosphere, and a lighter menu.

Amenities: Concierge, 24-hour room service, dry cleaning, laundry service, newspaper delivery, in-room massage service available, baby-sitting, secretarial services, express checkout, valet parking, courtesy car or limo, indoor heated pool, health club, Jacuzzi, sauna, business center, conference rooms, beauty salon.

✪ **Wedgewood Hotel.** 845 Hornby St., Vancouver, B.C. V6Z 1X1. ☎ **800/663-0666** or 604/689-7777. Fax 604/608-5349. www.wedgewoodhotel.com. E-mail: info@wedgewoodhotel.com. 89 units. A/C MINIBAR TV TEL. C$200–C$380 (US$134–US$255) double, C$480 (US$322) suite, C$680 (US$456) penthouse. AE, CB, DC, DISC, JCB, MC, V. Underground valet parking C$15 (US$10).

The romance, elegance, and opulence of this European-style hotel are personal touches created by owner and general manager Ileni Skalbania. In 1984, she acquired the failing 13-story Mayfair Hotel, and then completely gutted and rebuilt the interior, furnishing the public spaces with many pieces from her own art and antique collection. The result is a four-diamond hotel with an eclectic decor that blends French Provincial, Italianate, and Edwardian styles. On weekdays, the hotel draws a corporate crowd. On weekends, it's transformed into a romantic getaway. All guest rooms have balconies with flower beds overlooking Robson Square. Terry robes, room-darkening drapes, a morning paper, and a box of chocolates are just a few of the hotel's special touches.

Dining/Diversions: Bacchus Restaurant, well known for its fine dining, recently hired chef Robert Sulatycky, who specializes in modern French cuisine. The Bacchus Lounge features live jazz Monday to Saturday nights (see chapter 7). The restaurant also serves breakfast, lunch, afternoon tea (Sat and Sun from 2 to 4pm), cocktails, and snacks.

Amenities: Concierge, 24-hour room service, dry cleaning, laundry service, newspaper delivery, in-room massage service available, twice-daily maid service, baby-sitting, secretarial services, express checkout, valet parking, health club, sauna, business center, conference rooms.

✪ **The Westin Grand.** 433 Robson St., Vancouver, B.C. V6B 6L9. ☎ **888/680-9393** or 604/602-1999. Fax 604/647-2502. www.westingrandvancouver. com. E-mail: play@westingrandvancouver.com. 207 suites. A/C MINIBAR TV TEL. May 16–Oct 14 C$199–C$349 (US$133–US$234) suite. Oct 15–May 15 C$149–C$299 (US$100–US$200) suite. Children under 17 stay free in parents' room. AE, DC, DISC, JCB, MC, V. Parking: C$15 (US$10) self, C$19 (US$13) valet.

Showbiz can be such a headache. The luxurious Westin Grand opened in April 1999, right next to Vancouver's new Broadway-style music hall, the Ford Centre for the Performing Arts. The location was considered a key selling feature—the building itself was shaped to look like a grand piano.

Unfortunately, shortly after the Grand opened, Livent—the company producing the musicals—went bankrupt, leaving the Grand all alone. Fortunately, the fundamentals are still good. The Grand is also across from the public library (could have shaped the hotel like a great big book, eh guys?) and within easy walking distance of Yaletown, GM Place, and the Robson shopping area. The 207 spacious suites are brightened by lots of natural light and decorated in mahogany and elegant earth tones. Sitting rooms come with a kitchenette tucked away behind the blond wood cabinet doors (no stove but a microwave, toaster, coffee/tea maker, mini-dishwasher, and all utensils). Bedrooms have either queen or king beds, and for the corporate traveler, there are big work spaces, data ports, and lots of electrical plugs. Some 40 of the Guest Office suites also have speakerphones, cordless phones, and combo fax/laser printer/photocopiers. Rooms for travelers with disabilities include safety bars in the bathrooms, handheld showers, and safety/emergency flashing lights.

Dining/Diversions: The Aria restaurant has received great reviews from local food critics and Club Voda offers live and canned music.

Amenities: 24-hour room service, outdoor pool, sundeck, Jacuzzi, health club, business center, meeting rooms, valet parking.

MODERATE

Best Western Downtown Vancouver. 718 Drake St., Vancouver, B.C. V6Z 2W6. ☎ **888/669-9888** or 604/660-9888. Fax 604/669-3440. www. bestwesterndowntown.com. E-mail: welcome2@bestwesterndowntown.com. 143 units. A/C TV TEL. C$139–C$209 (US$93–US$140) double, C$280–C$350 (US$188–US$235) penthouse. AE, DC, DISC, MC, V. Parking C$5 (US$3.35).

The 12-story Best Western is located on Granville and Drake, a 5-block walk from the theater area on Granville Street at the south end of downtown. Of the 143 rooms, 32 have full kitchens, available for an additional C$20 to C$25 (US$13 to US$17). The rooms are comfortable; the corner rooms are a bit smaller than the rest, but they do have more light. Some rooms have harbor views. This hotel is not overflowing with facilities, but the rooms are well furnished and the location is convenient. If you need a workspace, ask for a corporate room, which includes a full-size desk and activities table. All rooms have voice-mail phones and data ports. In addition,

---

🏨 Family-Friendly Hotels

Vancouver hotels offer a wide range of choices if you're bringing your kids, and you don't have to sacrifice service or quality. To add to their appeal, a lot of the downtown hotels offer baby-sitting.

Four Seasons Hotel *(see p. 39)*   Kids get cookies and milk in the evening as well as special room-service menus and warm terry robes.

Westin Bayshore *(see p. 58)*   Its Coal Harbour location makes this a great family hotel. Guests can walk to Stanley Park, the Vancouver Aquarium, the Nature House, and other park attractions without even crossing a street.

Quality Hotel Downtown/The Inn at False Creek *(see p. 52)* Family suites in this hotel are spacious and well designed. Some upper-floor suites even have glass-enclosed balconies. The full kitchen facilities, casual restaurant, and off-season "Adventure Passport" discounts also make this an excellent deal for families.

Rosellen Suites *(see p. 61)*   This is the perfect place if you're looking for a homelike atmosphere in fully equipped apartment accommodations. It's conveniently located near grocery shopping and play areas. Stanley Park, the beaches, and Denman Street are only a block away.

---

there's a rooftop exercise room, game area, Ping-Pong table, VCR and movies, sauna, Jacuzzi, and sundeck. Complimentary deluxe continental breakfast is served in the breakfast lounge in the lobby.

Days Inn Downtown. 921 W. Pender St., Vancouver, B.C. V6C 1M2. ☎ **800/ 329-7466** or 604/681-4335. Fax 604/681-7808. www.daysinnvancouver. com. E-mail: welcome2@daysin-van.com. 85 units. TV TEL. May–Oct C$149–C$189 (US$100–US$127) double, C$209 (US$140) suite; Nov–Apr C$105–C$125 (US$70–US$84) double, C$155 (US$104) suite. AE, CB, DC, DISC, JCB, MC, V. Valet parking C$10 (US$7).

Situated in a heritage building dating back to 1910, Days Inn Downtown provides a central location for exploring Vancouver. The building is well-maintained—all the rooms were refurbished in 1998, and the lobby underwent complete renovations in the summer of 1999. For travelers who don't need all the amenities of a large hotel, these rooms are comfortable and simply furnished. Each has a minifridge, ceiling fan, desk, data port, voice mail, and safe. Ten of the rooms have stand-up showers only. Rooms facing east stare directly at the concrete walls of the building next door, so ask for a water view or consider a harbor-facing suite. The Chelsea Restaurant serves three meals daily. The English-pub–style Bombay Bicycle Club lounge and the Bull and Bear Sports Lounge— featuring a large-screen TV—are popular spots with local businesspeople. Facilities include a coin laundry and refrigerators. The front desk will provide photocopying, faxing, and secretarial services for a nominal charge.

The Executive Inn. 1379 Howe St., Vancouver, B.C. V6Z 2R5. ☎ **800/ 570-3932** or 604/688-7678. Fax 604/688-7679. www.executiveinnhotels. com. 134 units. A/C TV TEL. May–Oct C$179 (US$120) standard double, C$199 (US$133) deluxe double, C$295 (US$198) 1-bedroom suite, C$395 (US$265) 2-bedroom suite; Nov–Apr C$119 (US$80) standard double, C$139 (US$93) deluxe double, C$255 (US$171) 1-bedroom suite, C$355 (US$238) 2-bedroom suite. AE, DC, MC, V. Parking C$6 (US$4).

Located at the on-ramp to the Granville Street Bridge, next to the Inn at False Creek, The Executive Inn lacks a bit of character. The hotel focuses mainly on business travelers. The rooms are well furnished, with lots of light, as many have floor-to-ceiling windows. Desks, data ports, safes, and sitting areas are standard in all rooms. For rooms with a view, ask for south or southwest facing rooms looking towards English Bay. The one- and two-bedroom suites are excellent, containing all the conveniences of an apartment: comfortable furniture, TV, VCR, stereo with CD player, dining area, full luxury kitchen, large storage space, in-suite laundry, Jacuzzi tub, desk, and separate bedroom. The hotel also has an in-house business center, fitness center, laundry, restaurant, and lounge.

✪ **Quality Hotel Downtown/The Inn at False Creek.** 1335 Howe St. (at Drake St.), Vancouver, B.C. V6Z 1R7. ☎ **800/663-8474** or 604/682-0229. Fax 604/662-7566. www.qualityhotelvancouver.com. E-mail: quality@ qualityhotelvancouver.com. 157 units. A/C TV TEL. May 1–Oct 12 C$169 (US$113) double, C$189–C$209 (US$127–US$140) suite; Oct 13–Apr 30 C$99 (US$66) double, C$99–C$109 (US$66–US$73) suite. AE, CB, DC, DISC, ER, MC, V. Parking C$8 (US$5).

Strange to have a hotel with a Tex-Mex theme in Vancouver, but surprisingly, it works. The Inn at False Creek is a boutique hotel decorated with Mexican art, pottery, and rugs, all in a kind of Santa Fe style. Room decor consists of dark green, terra-cotta, and earth tones, and brick for a touch of authenticity. The spacious suites are great for families—15 have full kitchens, and a number of others have glassed-in balconies, which double as enclosed play areas (the hotel staff keeps a supply of board games and puzzles behind the front desk). Rooms on the back side are preferable because the hotel is situated beside the Granville Bridge on-ramp. The traffic noise is minimized in the front, however, by double-pane windows and dark-out curtains. In the low season, the hotel's "City Passport" entitles guests to two-for-one discounts at numerous attractions, theaters, and restaurants.

On the lobby level, the Creekside Café serves decent basics at reasonable prices throughout the day; the Sports Lounge offers a relaxed atmosphere, friendly service, and a full bar. The hotel has laundry and valet services. There's an outdoor pool, plus you have complimentary use of the extensive fitness facilities at Fitness World, a block away.

Rosedale on Robson Suite Hotel. 838 Hamilton (at Robson St.), Vancouver, B.C. V6B 6A2. ☎ **800/661-8870** or 604/689-8033. www.rosedaleonrobson. com. E-mail: reserve@direct.ca. 275 units. A/C TV TEL. May–Sept C$205–C$285 (US$137–US$191) suite; Oct–Apr C$125–C$185 (US$84–US$124) suite. Additional adult C$20 (US$13). Kitchen utensils C$5 (US$3.35). AE, DC, ER, JCB, MC, V. Parking C$8 (US$5).

The Rosedale has a tower capped by a 15-foot-tall rose emblem and is located directly across the street from Library Square. Guests arrive through a covered driveway and are welcomed in a large marble lobby. The one- and two-bedroom suites feature separate living rooms, two TVs each, and full kitchenettes equipped with microwaves, stoves, ovens, sinks, and half-size refrigerators. Dishes and cooking utensils are available on request. The rooms are rather small, but ample bay windows and light wood furnishings create a feeling of spaciousness. Corner suites have more windows. Upper-floor suites have furnished terraces and great city views. Guests on executive floors get bathrobes, free local calls, a daily newspaper, nightly turndown service, in-room movies, Nintendo games, and modem and fax access lines. This end of Robson Street is a few minutes' stroll from most shops and restaurants, and the Pacific Centre Mall, Library Square, the Queen Elizabeth Theatre, and B.C. Place and General Motors Place stadiums are only a block or two away.

Rosie's is a New York-style deli (without the attitude, of course). It's a rarity in this city filled with West Coast and Pacific Northwest cuisine. There's also a lounge off the lobby. The hotel also has an indoor pool, a Jacuzzi, a sauna, a weight- and exercise-room, and a gift shop.

INEXPENSIVE

The Howard Johnson Hotel. 1176 Granville St., Vancouver, B.C. V6Z 1L8. ☎ **888/654-6336** or 604/688-8701. Fax 604/688-8335. www.hojovancouver. com. E-mail: info@hojovancouver.com. A/C TV TEL. May 1–Oct 15 C$129– C$149 (US$86–US$100) double, C$149–C$169 (US$100–US$113) suite; Oct 16–Apr 30 C$69–C$89 (US$46–US$60) double, C$99–C$119 (US$66– US$80) suite. Children under 17 stay free in parents' room. AE, MC, V. Parking C$6 (US$4).

Yet another sign of south Granville's rapid gentrification, this formerly down-at-the-heels hotel was bought, gutted, reno- vated, and reopened in 1998 with an eye to the budget- conscious traveler. Hallways are decorated with photographs of Vancouver's early days, while the rooms themselves are comfortably if simply furnished. Some rooms have mini- kitchenettes, and the suites provide sofa beds, convenient for those traveling with children. If you need a desk, fax machine, and e-mail and Internet access, book a home-office suite. A continental breakfast is included and served in the lounge on the mezzanine. The hotel also houses the Lava Lounge, a popular gay Vancouver nightspot.

The Kingston Hotel. 757 Richards St., Vancouver, B.C. V6B 3A6. ☎ **604/ 684-9024.** Fax 604/684-9917. www.kingstonhotelvancouver.com. 57 units, 9 with bathroom. TEL. C$55–C$105 (US$37–US$70) double. Extra person C$10 (US$7). Continental breakfast included. AE, MC, V. Parking C$10 (US$7) per day, half a block away.

An affordable downtown hotel is a rarity for Vancouver. If all you need is a clean and comfortable place to sleep and a cup of coffee and breakfast to start your day, then the Kingston is your place. Called a European-style hotel, it is indeed reminiscent of the small Parisian or Roman pensiones: no elevators, very small rooms, and only 9 of the 57 rooms have private bathrooms and TVs. The rest have hand basins and the use of shared showers and toilets on each floor. However, you will not find a cheaper hotel so close to all the downtown action.

The Ramada Inn and Suites. 1221 Granville St., Vancouver, B.C. V6Z 1M6. ☎ **888/835-0078** or 604/685-1111. Fax 604/685-0707. www. ramadavancouver.com. E-mail: ramada@intergate.bc.ca. 133 units. TV TEL. May–June C$99–C$129 (US$66–US$86) double; July–Sept C$125–C$169 (US$84–US$113) double; Oct–Apr C$69–C$99 (US$46–US$66) double. Suite C$20–C$40 (US$13–US$27) more than a standard room. AE, MC, V. Valet parking C$10 (US$7). Pets are welcome.

The Ramada was recently converted from a rooming house into a tourist hotel. The bright lobby and the guest rooms are all decorated in an art deco theme. The rooms are pleasant, with dark wood furniture, everything very new. Small desks, TV, and a coffee/tea maker are standard in all. Suites feature a pull-out sofa bed, kitchenette, and small dining area, making them very attractive for families. The location is convenient for exploring downtown and Yaletown, as well as hopping over to Granville Island or Kitsilano. A restaurant and Irish pub are located downstairs.

YMCA. 955 Burrard St., Vancouver, B.C. V6Z 1Y2. ☎ **604/681-0221.** Fax 604/681-1630. www.ymca.vancouver.bc.ca. E-mail: vancouver.hotel@ vanymca.org. 113 units, all with shared bathroom. May–Sept C$59 (US$40) double; Oct–Apr C$49 (US$33) double. Cot C$8 (US$5) extra. MC, V. Parking C$6 (US$4).

Male and female guests here are mostly a mixture of new arrivals, businesspeople with limited expense accounts, and budget-minded travelers seeking an alternative to youth hostels. The building is not nearly as new as the YWCA, but it's as conveniently located. Rooms are small, simply furnished, and spotless. Some include private TVs for C$2 (US$1.35) extra. The bathrooms are shared, as are the pay phones. Guests have use of the extensive facilities, including two swimming pools, LifeCycles, Nautilus and Universal equipment, a rooftop running track, racquetball courts, and a coin laundry. The restaurant, Jonathan T's, is open Monday to Saturday for breakfast and lunch. No alcoholic beverages are permitted in the building. The facility is not wheelchair accessible.

✪ **The YWCA Hotel/Residence.** 733 Beatty St., Vancouver, B.C. V6B 2M4. ☎ **800/663-1424** or 604/895-5830. Fax 604/681-2550. www.ywcahotel. com. E-mail: hotel@ywcavan.org. 155 units, 53 with bathroom. A/C TEL. C$68–C$88 (US$46–US$59) double with shared bathroom; C$74–C$112 (US$50–US$75) double with private bathroom. Weekly, monthly, group, and off-season discounts available. AE, DC, MC, V. Parking C$5 (US$3.35) per day.

Built in 1995, this attractive 12-story residence is next door to the Georgian Court Hotel. It's an excellent choice for male and female travelers as well as families with limited budgets. Bedrooms are simply furnished; some have TVs. There are quite a few reasonably priced restaurants nearby (but none in-house). All guest rooms do have mini-refrigerators, and three communal kitchens are available for guests' use. (There are a number of small grocery stores nearby, as well as a Save-On Foods Supermarket a 10-minute walk west on Davie Street.) There are also three TV lounges, a coin laundry, and free access to the best gym in town at the nearby co-ed YWCA Fitness Centre.

2 The West End

About a 10-minute walk from the downtown area, the West End's hotels are nestled amid the tree-lined residential streets bordering Stanley Park, within close proximity to Robson Street's many shops, restaurants, and attractions, as well as the natural beauty of the park itself and the surrounding beaches. Though there are fewer hotels here than downtown, there's a wider variety of accommodations.

EXPENSIVE

Empire Landmark Hotel & Conference Centre. 1400 Robson St., Vancouver, B.C. V6G 1B9. ☎ **800/830-6144** or 604/687-0511. Fax 604/687-2801. www.asiastandard.com. E-mail: ehlsales@asiastandard.com. 357 units. A/C TV TEL. C$210–C$240 (US$141–US$161) double. AE, CB, DC, JCB, MC, V. Parking C$7 (US$4.70).

If you are looking for a room with a view, this is the place to be. The 42-story Landmark stands taller than all the surrounding buildings, near the peak of a small rise at the western end of Robson Street. Stanley Park, the beaches of English Bay, and Denman Street are all within walking distance. The rooms make the most of the location—all have balconies, and the higher you go the more you see. Thanks to a recent renovation, which brought in new carpets, wallpaper, beds, and lighting, the view of the room now matches the view from the room. Standard rooms are comfortable and bright, decorated in burgundy tones with dark-wood furnishings. Above the 33rd floor, the Emily Carr rooms—named for the B.C. artist whose art graces the walls—expand out to include a sitting area and wet bar.

Dining/Diversions: The Spice Gallery Cafe & Bar on the lobby level serves a fusion of Western and Asian cuisine in tapas-sized portions. For those who can't get enough of the vistas, take the elevator to the 42nd floor to the rotating Cloud 9 Lounge and Restaurant (see chapter 4).

Amenities: Concierge, limited-hour room service, dry cleaning, laundry service, baby-sitting, secretarial services, express checkout, health club, Jacuzzi, sauna, business center, conference rooms, self-service Laundromat, and car-rental desk.

Listel Vancouver. 1300 Robson St., Vancouver, B.C. V6E 1C5. ☎ **800/ 663-5491** or 604/684-8461. Fax 604/684-8326. www.listel-vancouver.com. 130 units. A/C MINIBAR TV TEL. May–Sept C$240–C$300 (US$161–US$201) double, C$260–C$320 (US$174–US$214) suite; Oct–Apr C$150–C$190 (US$101–US$127) double, C$170–C$210 (US$114–US$141) suite. AE, DC, DISC, ER, JCB, MC, V. Parking C$14 (US$9).

This hotel has always had a killer location—right at the western end of the Robson Street shopping strip. Recently, the owners have been putting a lot of effort—and money—into making the interior match the address. A recent renovation turned the lobby from a rather plain space to something modern and elegant, if still diminutive. Rooms now feature top-quality bedding and cherry-wood furnishings, including little window-banquettes on which to sit and read or relax. Particularly noteworthy are the Gallery Rooms on the top two floors. Each of these rooms and suites is like a small art gallery, hung with original art works borrowed from the Buschlen Mowatt Gallery, one of the city's leading private art dealers. On a more practical note, these rooms feature upgraded amenities—including Aveda toiletries—and better views. The upper-floor rooms facing Robson Street, with glimpses of the harbor and the mountains beyond, are worth the price. (The others face the alley and nearby apartment buildings.) Soundproof windows eliminate traffic noise, which can be pretty loud on summer weekends.

Dining: With sidewalk tables and picture windows all around, O'Doul's restaurant is a good spot for people-watching. And despite the sports-bar name (and history), the restaurant has been slowly reinventing itself as a spot for fine dining. Breakfast, lunch, and dinner are served all day.

Amenities: Room service, concierge, valet, laundry, secretarial services, newspaper delivery, express checkout, exercise room, whirlpool, meeting and banquet space, two-line phones.

Pacific Palisades Hotel. 1277 Robson St., Vancouver, B.C. V6E 1C4. ☎ **800/663-1815** or 604/688-0461. Fax 604/688-4374. www.pacificpalisadeshotel. com. E-mail: reservations@pacificpalisadeshotel.com. 233 units. A/C MINIBAR TV TEL. May 1–Oct 15 C$275 (US$184) double, C$325 (US$218) suite; Oct 16–Apr 30 C$200 (US$134) double, C$250 (US$168) suite. Full kitchens C$10 (US$7) extra. AE, DC, DISC, JCB, MC, V. Parking C$15 (US$10).

The Pacific Palisades is a luxury hotel in every respect but price. Standing on the crest of Robson Street, it was converted from two luxury apartment towers in 1991. It's popular with visiting film and TV production companies who demand sterling service, privacy, spacious accommodations, and more-than-great value. The intimate lobby and side-street entrance are more discreet than grand. Accommodations come in studio suites (i.e., rooms) and one-bedroom suites. All are spacious, and come equipped with sinks, microwave ovens, coffeemakers, and minibars. Most have panoramic views and private terraces. Thanks to a recent full renovation, decor is now an elegant new update on '50s Moderne, with blond-wood tables, bright walls, and simple, comfortable couches, beds, and chairs. For business travelers, all rooms come equipped with writing desks, two phone lines, and voice mail. As of press time, a next-door restaurant has been promised but not yet delivered.

Amenities: 24-hour room service; concierge; twice-daily maid service; complimentary tea and coffee; laundry; business center; voice-mail message service; daily newspaper; in-room movies; complete fitness center with whirlpool, sauna, and indoor lap pool; bicycle rentals (mountain bikes available); meeting and banquet rooms.

✪ **Westin Bayshore Resort & Marina.** 1601 Bayshore Dr., Vancouver, B.C. V6G 2V4. ☎ **800/228-3000** or 604/682-3377. Fax 604/687-3102. www. westinbayshore.com. E-mail: bayshorereservations@westin.com. 510 units. A/C MINIBAR TV TEL. Mid-Apr to Oct C$289 (US$194) double, C$450–C$700 (US$302–US$469) suite; Nov to mid-Apr C$195 (US$131) double, C$370–C$420 (US$248–US$281) suite. Children under 19 stay free in parents' room. AE, CB, DC, ER, MC, V. Self-parking C$10 (US$7), valet parking C$15 (US$10).

Thanks to a C$50-million renovation, this venerable '60s resort hotel looks better than ever. The lobby has been completely redesigned to show off the surrounding park and mountains; achieving much the same thing are two new restaurants and a coffee bar, one of which has a huge outdoor deck overlooking the harbor. Perched on the water's edge overlooking Coal Harbour at Stanley Park's eastern entrance, the Bayshore is still just a short stroll along the seawall from the Canada Place Pier and downtown. Rooms in the original 1961 building have been completely refurbished with classic-looking decor. In the newer tower, the rooms are spacious and come with balconies and large windows. Both towers offer unobstructed views of the harbor's dazzling array of sailboats, fishing boats, and luxury yachts. (Many crafts are available for charter through the hotel's on-site charter service.) The hotel's Guest Office rooms include a fax/copier/printer, speakerphone, and other business amenities. Two floors of the hotel are wheelchair accessible.

Dining: Currents At Bayshore offers three meals daily. The Seawall Bar & Bistro is open for lunch and dinner. The coffee bar, Stanley Perks, is open for breakfast and lunch.

Amenities: 24-hour room service, concierge, laundry, business center, boat charters, bicycle and car rentals, free shuttle service to the downtown area, indoor and outdoor pools, a complete health club, nine retail shops, barber shop, beauty salon.

MODERATE

✪ **Barclay House in the West End.** 1351 Barclay St., Vancouver, B.C. V6E 1H6. ☎ **800/971-1351** or 604/605-1351. Fax 604/605-1382. www. barclayhouse.com. 5 units. TV/VCR TEL. C$145–C$225 (US$97–US$151) double. MC, V. Free parking.

Barclay House in the West End is located just one block from the heritage Barclay square, on one of the West End's quiet maple-lined streets. Open as a bed-and-breakfast since 1999, this beautiful house built in 1904 by Thomas Hunter, a local developer, can be a destination on its own. The elegant parlors and dining rooms are perfect for lounging on a rainy afternoon, sipping a glass of complimentary sherry before venturing out for dinner in the trendy West End. On a summer day, the front porch with its comfortable chairs makes for a great spot to read a book. All rooms are beautifully furnished in Victorian style, a number of the pieces are family heirlooms. The modern conveniences such as CD players, TV/VCRs, and luxurious bathrooms blend in perfectly. It is hard to pick a favorite room, but it would probably be the Penthouse suite with its skylights and claw-foot tub, or maybe the south room with a queen-size brass bed and an elegant sitting room overlooking the front of the house.

✪ **Blue Horizon.** 1225 Robson St., Vancouver, B.C. V6E 1C5. ☎ **800/ 663-1333** or 604/688-1411. Fax 604/688-4461. www.bluehorizon.com. E-mail: info@bluehorizon.com. 214 units. A/C MINIBAR TV TEL. C$159–C$199 (US$107–US$133) double; C$279 (US$187) suite. Children under 16 stay free in parents' room. Extra person C$15 (US$10). AE, DC, MC, V. Parking C$8 (US$5).

This unmistakable, blue-tiled, 1960s high-rise on Robson Street capitalizes on one of Vancouver's' best assets—the view. The small lobby, designed by artist Pam Pavelek, features her tall glass sculpture *Water and Air,* a theme she has carried throughout the restaurant and lounge on the ground floor. Upstairs, the rooms are spacious—every room is a corner room, which maximizes light and window space. The best views are on the 15th floor and higher. All feature safes, voice mail, data ports, coffee/tea makers, ironing boards, sitting areas, and, of course, balconies. There is no concierge or room service, but all rooms have either a refrigerator or a minibar. The next-door bar, Shenanigan's, features sidewalk seating, darts, big-screen sports, a good selection of ales and beers, and a reasonably priced pub and pasta menu. The exercise area includes a lap pool, Jacuzzi, sauna, and exercise equipment.

✪ **Coast Plaza Suite Hotel at Stanley Park.** 1763 Comox St., Vancouver, B.C. V6G 1P6. ☎ **800/663-1144** or 604/688-7711. Fax 604/688-5934. www.coasthotels.com. E-mail: info@coastplazasuitehotel.com. 267 units. A/C MINIBAR TV TEL. C$129–C$199 (US$86–US$133) double, C$155–C$290 (US$104–US$194) suite. AE, DC, DISC, MC, V. Parking C$8 (US$5).

This 35-story hotel above the Denman Place Mall attracts a wide variety of guests, from business travelers and bus tours to film and TV actors. The guest rooms are large, each with in-room coffeemaker and balcony; many have commanding views of English Bay—the best seats in the city for the Symphony of Fire fireworks display in late July and early August. Most of the units are suites with fully equipped kitchens.

The Comox Street Long Bar & Grill is open from lunch through late dinner, serving simple bar fare. The Brasserie specializes in lamb chops, steaks, and some seafood.

There's an indoor pool, an outstanding full-service health club with squash courts and saunas, and a gift shop. Denman Place Mall's 30 shops and restaurants are accessible via the lobby.

Parkhill Hotel. 1160 Davie St., Vancouver, B.C. V6E 1N1. ☎ **800/ 663-1525** or 604/685-1311. Fax 604/681-0208. www.parkhillhotel.com. E-mail: prkhillres.aol.com. 192 units. A/C TV TEL. Apr 16–Oct 15 C$185–C$200 (US$124–US$134) double; Oct 16–Apr 15 C$89–C$135 (US$60–US$90) double with continental breakfast. AE, DC, ER, JCB, MC, V. Parking C$7 (US$4.70).

This modern 24-story hotel is the only accommodation of merit on Davie Street, one of the West End's residential, shopping, and dining strips. The dark-marble lobby is welcoming and tastefully decorated. The guest rooms are large and decorated in tranquil, pale tones. The small, private balconies offer fabulous views of either False Creek and Granville Island or English Bay and the Gulf Islands. All rooms are equipped with coffeemakers and hair dryers. The deluxe rooms on the upper floors (comprising the upper end of the rate range above) have in-room safes, terry robes, and upgraded amenities. The hotel has an indoor pool, sundeck, sauna, and large gift shop.

Byron's restaurant provides standard continental fare; Taiko's Japanese Noodle restaurant is very casual. The Lounge serves snacks and drinks, and for your caffeine fix, the hotel has a cappuccino bar.

✪ Rosellen Suites. 102–2030 Barclay St., Vancouver, B.C. V6G 1L5. ☎ **888/317-6648** or 604/689-4807. Fax 604/684-3327. www.rosellensuites. com. E-mail: info@rosellensuites.com. 30 apts. A/C TV TEL. May–Aug C$175 (US$117) 1-bedroom apt, C$200–C$280 (US$134–US$188) 2-bedroom apt, C$375 (US$251) penthouse; Sept–Apr C$110 (US$74) 1-bedroom apt, C$140–C$200 (US$94–US$134) 2-bedroom apt, C$300 (US$201) penthouse. Minimum 3-night stay. Extra person C$15 (US$10). Cots and cribs free. AE, CB, DC, DISC, JCB, MC, V. Limited parking in the rear of the building C$5 (US$3.35).

On a quiet residential street, this unpretentious low-rise apartment building is just a few hundred yards from Stanley Park and 2 blocks from loads of restaurants. Converted into an apartment hotel in the 1960s, the Rosellen has no lobby, and the manager's office is open only from 9am to 5pm. Each guest receives a front door key and a personal phone number with voice mail. Modern and extremely comfortable, each suite features a spacious living room, separate dining area, and full-size kitchen with all necessary utensils. It's just like having an apartment in Vancouver. Autographed movie-star photos in the manager's office give you an idea of the luminaries who have stayed here. The penthouse is named after Katharine Hepburn, who has called this her favorite Vancouver hotel.

There's full maid service twice a week, coin laundry facilities, dry cleaning, free local calls, a business center, and access to the West End Community Centre's weight room.

Sunset Inn Travel Apartments. 1111 Burnaby St., Vancouver, B.C. V6E 1P4. ☎ **800/786-1997** or 604/688-2474. Fax 604/669-3340. www.sunsetinn. com. E-mail: sunsetinn@netcom.ca. 50 units. A/C TV TEL. C$88–C$158 (US$59–US$106) studio, C$98–C$168 (US$66–US$113) 1-bedroom suite. Weekly rates and other off-season discounts available. AE, DC, MC, V. Free parking.

Located on a quiet side street, this tall gray concrete structure looks like any other West End apartment building. It offers self-contained suites that are nicely furnished in strikingly contemporary if slightly mismatched colors. Each has a small private balcony. Kitchens are completely equipped with toaster, coffeemaker, can opener, and utensils. The living rooms are spacious, the beds comfortable, and the closets reasonably large. There are leather armchairs and settees as well as a dining table and chairs. There's also a small fitness room on the main floor.

✪ **West End Guest House.** 1362 Haro St., Vancouver, B.C. V6E 1G2. ☎ **604/681-2889.** Fax 604/688-8812. www.westendguesthouse.com. E-mail: wegh@idmail.net. 7 units. TV TEL. C$145–C$225 (US$97–US$151) double. Rates include full breakfast. AE, MC, V. Free valet parking.

Experience the West End the way it was. A beautiful heritage home built in 1906, the West End Guest House is a fine example of what the neighborhood looked like up until the early '50s, before the concrete towers and condos replaced the original Edwardian homes. Decorated with beautiful early century antiques and an amazing collection of old photographs of Vancouver, this is a wonderful respite from the hustle and bustle of the West End. The seven guest rooms are beautifully furnished with antiques, ensuite bathrooms, and the ultimate in bedtime luxury: feather mattresses, down duvets, and pillows, robes, and your very own resident stuffed animal. Particularly indulgent is the Grand Queen Suite, an attic-level bedroom with skylights, brass bed, fireplace, sitting area, and claw-foot bathtub. Owner Evan Penner pampers his guests with a scrumptious breakfast and serves iced tea and sherry in the afternoon. Throughout the day, guests have access to the parlor, sundeck, porch kitchen stocked with home-baked munchies and refreshments, and bikes. If you ask nicely, Penner will crank up the gramophone.

INEXPENSIVE

✪ **Buchan Hotel.** 1906 Haro St., Vancouver, B.C. V6G 1H7. ☎ **604/ 685-5354.** Fax 604/685-5367. www.3bc.sympatico.ca/buchan/. E-mail: buchanhotel@telus.net. 60 units, 30 with bathroom. TV. May–Sept C$75–C$95 (US$50–US$64) double, C$125–C$145 (US$84–US$97) executive room; Oct–Apr C$45–C$70 (US$30–US$47) double, C$100–C$140 (US$67–US$94) executive room. Children under 12 stay free in parents' room. Weekly rates and off-season discounts available. AE, DC, MC, V. Street parking available.

Built in the 1930s, this charming three-story building overlooks a small park on a quiet tree-lined residential street. It's less than 2 blocks from Stanley Park and Denman Street and 10 minutes by foot from the business district. The rooms are small and the bathrooms smaller, but the rates are low and the staff is friendly. Rooms overlooking the park are brighter; the four front-corner executive rooms are the largest. The hotel also offers in-house bike and ski storage and a coin laundry. There are no exercise facilities, but the nearby West End Community Centre has weights, aerobics, sauna, and a pool, and charges a nominal visitor's fee. Smoking isn't permitted in the rooms.

Hostelling International Vancouver Downtown Hostel. 1114 Burnaby St. (at Thurlow St.), Vancouver, B.C. V6E 1P1. ☎ **888/203-4302** or 604/ 684-4565. Fax 604/684-4540. www.hihostels.bc.ca. E-mail: van-downtown@ hihostels.bc.ca. 239 beds in 4-person units; some double and triple units. Beds C$20 (US$13) IYHA members, C$24 (US$16) nonmembers; doubles C$55 (US$37) members, C$64 (US$43) nonmembers; triples C$70 (US$47) members, C$86 (US$58) nonmembers. Annual adult membership C$27 (US$18). MC, V. Limited free parking.

Located in a converted nunnery, this new and modern hostel is an extremely convenient base of operations from which to explore downtown. The beach is a few blocks south; downtown is a 10-minute walk north. Most beds are in quad dorms, with a limited number of doubles and triples available. There are common cooking facilities, as well as a patio and game room. The hostel gets extremely busy in the summertime, so book ahead. Many organized activities and tours can be booked at the hostel. There's free shuttle service to the bus/train station and Jericho Beach. Open 24 hours.

✪ **Sylvia Hotel.** 1154 Gilford St., Vancouver, B.C. V6G 2P6. ☎ **604/ 681-9321.** Fax 604/682-3551. www.sylviahotel.com. 118 units. TV TEL. Apr–Sept C$75–C$125 (US$50–US$84) double; Oct–Mar C$75–C$100 (US$50–US$67) double. Children under 18 stay free in parents' room. AE, DC, MC, V. Parking C$7 (US$4.70).

Built in 1912, when the West End was relatively unpopulated, the Sylvia is on the shores of English Bay just a few blocks from Stanley Park. It's one of Vancouver's oldest hotels, and although it's only eight stories high, it was the tallest building in western Canada until World War II. In recent years, it has become deservedly trendy. The gray-stone, ivy-wreathed Sylvia resembles a mansion. The lobby sets the tone: It's small, restful, dark, and furnished with red carpets, ivory drapes, and overstuffed chairs. The same atmosphere prevails in the adjoining restaurant and crowded cocktail lounge (which was Vancouver's first when it opened in 1954). The restaurant emphasizes seafood and continental cuisine, and has the same fabulous view as the historic cocktail lounge.

In the guest rooms, furnishings from the 1950s through 1970s are appropriately mismatched. The views from the upper floors are unparalleled. The suites have fully equipped kitchens and are large enough for families. Sixteen rooms in the 12-year-old low-rise annex offer individual heating but have less atmosphere. Valet and room service are available in both sections. Make reservations a few months ahead for a summer stay.

3　The West Side

Right across False Creek from downtown and the West End is Vancouver's West Side. If your agenda includes a Granville Island shopping spree, exploration of the island's numerous artists' studios and galleries, or strolls through the sunken garden at Queen Elizabeth Park; or if you require close proximity to the airport without staying in an "airport hotel," you'll find both cozy B&Bs and hotels that'll meet your needs.

EXPENSIVE
✪ **Granville Island Hotel.** 1253 Johnston St., Vancouver, B.C. V6H 3R9. ☎ **800/663-1840** or 604/683-7373. Fax 604/683-3061. www. granvilleislandhotel.com. 54 units. A/C TV TEL. C$219 (US$147) double.

Off-season discounts available. AE, CB, DC, JCB, V. Parking C$6 (US$4). Pets welcome.

This small, modern hotel—with a unique waterfront location on the east end of Granville Island—is surrounded by artists' studios and galleries on one side and pleasure boats on the other. It has a cozy lobby, attractively decorated with dark wood paneling and stone floors. The guest rooms have skylights and bathrooms with marble floors and oversize tubs. Some accommodations also have balconies. Pets are welcome free of charge.

Dining/Diversions: The Creek microbrewery restaurant and bar has a harborside patio and a large humidor stocked with Cuban and Dominican cigars.

Amenities: Concierge, dry cleaning, laundry service, newspaper delivery, in-room massage, baby-sitting, secretarial services, express checkout, free coffee. The rooftop health club offers fitness equipment, a sauna, and a Jacuzzi. The hotel staff arranges boat charters at the marina. Downtown and English Bay are a 2-minute miniferry ride away.

MODERATE

The Cherub Inn. 2546 W. Sixth Ave., Vancouver, B.C. V6K 1W5. ☎ **604/ 733-3166.** Fax 604/733-3106. www.cherubinn.com. E-mail: unwind@ cherubinn.com. 5 units. May 1–Oct 15 C$139–C$180 (US$93–US$121); Oct 16–Apr 30 C$119–C$149 (US$80–US$100). MC, V. Free parking.

A beautifully restored and renovated character house from 1913, the Cherub Inn is a comfortable home away from home. In the heart of Kitsilano, you are only 2 blocks away from busy Fourth Avenue and Broadway, with great shopping and dining, and a 10-minute walk from the beach, the park, the outdoor swimming pool, museums, and Granville Island. All rooms are elegant and beautifully furnished with antiques and fine featherbeds and linen. For the romantically inclined, the Cherub room is a must: hand-carved walnut sleigh bed, cast-iron fireplace, skylight, and a large bathroom with an oversized bathtub and heated floors. On the ground floor, the Seraphim room is particularly attractive. Although smaller than some of the other rooms, its stained-glass bay windows, dark wood, and elegant furniture make it a little piece of paradise perfect for recovering from the stress of everyday life. For families or friends traveling together, the Amoretti suite on the ground floor provides you with a spacious one-bedroom suite with full kitchen, dining area, and a four-piece (separate shower and bath) bathroom, as well as a sizable toy chest and a VCR.

Kenya Court Guest House. 2230 Cornwall Ave., Vancouver, B.C. V6K 1B5. ☎ **604/738-7085.** E-mail: htdwilliams@telus.net. 4 units. TV TEL. C$135–C$165 (US$90–US$111) double. Rates include full breakfast. Extra person C$50 (US$34). No smoking. No credit cards. Garage or street parking.

Every room in this three-story apartment building at Kitsilano Beach has an unobstructed waterfront view of Vanier Park, English Bay, downtown Vancouver, and the Coast Mountains. This architectural landmark is an ideal launching pad for strolls around Granville Island, Vanier Park, the Maritime Museum, the Vancouver Museum, and other Kitsilano sights. An outdoor pool, tennis courts, and jogging trails are nearby. Run by a retired doctor and his wife (Dr. and Mrs. Williams), the Kenya Court has the feel of a bed-and-breakfast. Each guest suite—with a living room, bathroom, separate bedroom, and full kitchen—is a large converted apartment that has been tastefully furnished. A full breakfast (including eggs and bacon) is served in a glass solarium up on the rooftop, where there's a spectacular view of English Bay.

Pillow 'n Porridge Guest Suites. 2859 Manitoba St., Vancouver, B.C. V5Y 3B3. ☎ **604/879-8977.** Fax 604/879-8966. www.pillow.net. E-mail: suitespillow.net. 7 suites. TV TEL. May 15–Sept C$115–C$255 (US$77–US$171) suite; Oct to May 14 C$85–C$195 (US$57–US$131) suite. 5-night minimum. Monthly rates available. 1 suite wheelchair accessible. No credit cards. Free parking.

Pillow 'n Porridge's one-, two-, and three-bedroom suites are in three side-by-side heritage buildings. Each suite has a theme, from Mayan to West Coast to Corner Store. The antique-filled suites have working fireplaces and fully equipped kitchens stocked with the basics. All have dishwashers, and the two- and three-bedroom suites also have washers and dryers. Situated in the City Hall heritage district, the suites are within walking distance of fine dining, ethnic restaurants, retail shops, Granville Island, and Queen Elizabeth Park. The minimum stay varies depending upon availability.

INEXPENSIVE

Hostelling International Vancouver Jericho Beach Hostel. 1515 Discovery St., Vancouver, B.C. V6R 4K5. ☎ **888/203-4303** or 604/224-3208. Fax 604/224-4852. www.hihostels.bc.ca. E-mail: van-jericho@hihostels.bc.ca. 286 beds in 14 dorms; 10 private family rooms. C$18 (US$12) IYHA members, C$22 (US$15) nonmembers dorm rooms; C$47–C$53 (US$31–US$36) members, C\$56–C\$62 (US\$38–US\$42) nonmembers family rooms. Annual adult membership C\$27 (US\$18). MC, V. Not wheelchair accessible. Parking C\$3 (US\$2).

Located in an old military barracks, this hostel is surrounded by an expansive lawn right next to Jericho Beach. Individuals, families, and groups are welcome, but there are no facilities for children under 5 or pets. The 10 private rooms can accommodate up to six people. These particular accommodations go fast, so if you want one, call far in advance. The dormitory-style arrangements are well maintained and supervised. Linens are provided. Basic, inexpensive food is served in the cafe from April through October. During the rest of the year, food is available at the front desk. You have the option of cooking for yourself year-round in the hostel's kitchen. If you're looking for adventures, an on-premises program director operates tours and activities outside of the hostel.

Johnson Heritage House Bed & Breakfast. 2278 W. 34th Ave., Vancouver, B.C. V6M 1G6. ☎ **604/266-4175.** Fax 604/266-4175. www.johnsons-inn-vancouver.com. E-mail: fun@johnsons-inn-vancouver.com. 4 units. C\$115–C\$180 (US\$77–US\$121) double. Rates include full breakfast. No credit cards. Free parking.

This charming white-shingled home, in Vancouver's quiet residential district of Kerrisdale, is within a 15-minute drive of the Vancouver airport and about a 10-minute drive from the University of British Columbia campus. Outside the house, the rock garden and sculpture catch your eye; inside, there are wooden carousel animals and other antiques. The cozy guest rooms are outfitted with an eclectic array of antique trunks, biplane propellers, and gramophones, and feature queen-size brass beds. A full breakfast is served in the spacious dining room that looks out onto the tree-shaded garden.

Maple House Bed and Breakfast. 1533 Maple St., Vancouver, B.C. V6J 3S2. ☎ **604/739-5833.** Fax 604/739-5877. www.maplehouse.com. E-mail: info@maplehouse.com. 5 units. June–Sept C\$95–C\$130 (US\$64–US\$87) double; Oct–May C\$75–C\$105 (US\$50–US\$70) double. No credit cards. Free parking.

This conveniently located Kitsilano B&B is 2 blocks from the beach, half a block from the buses to downtown, and 6 blocks from the trendy shopping and restaurant area on Fourth Avenue. Maple House is a simple and elegant home that dates back to the turn of the nineteenth century. The breakfast parlor overlooks the street and is decorated with a mix of antique and Japanese furniture, reflecting the tastes of hosts Brian and

Fumi, the Canadian and Japanese owners. The house has a total of five rooms. Of the three on the second floor, one has a queen-size bed with private ensuite bathroom, while the other two have double beds and share a bathroom. On the third floor, the attic has two cozy twin rooms with a separate, shared bathroom one floor down. A full breakfast is included with your stay.

✪ **Penny Farthing Inn.** 2855 W. Sixth Ave., Vancouver, B.C. V6K 1X2. ☎ **604/739-9002.** Fax 604/739-9004. www.pennyfarthinginn.com. E-mail: farthing@uniserve.com. 4 units. May–Oct C$115 (US$77) double, C$170 (US$114) suite; Nov–Apr C$95 (US$64) double, C$145 (US$97) suite. Rates include full breakfast. No credit cards. Street parking.

Built in 1912, this landmark house on a quiet residential street is filled with antiques and stained glass. The guest rooms are decorated with pine furniture and distinctive touches like four-poster beds. "Abigail's Suite" is a favorite with honeymooners; it's bright and self-contained, featuring a terrific view, a sitting room with a TV/VCR and CD player, and a private bathroom with a skylight. Breakfast is served on the brick patio of an English-country–style garden filled with trees and fragrant flowers. You can watch the resident cats at play while you relax. Bikes are available for guest use, as are free videos. Smoking isn't permitted inside.

✪ **The University of British Columbia Conference Centre.** 5961 Student Union Blvd., Vancouver, B.C. V6T 2C9. ☎ **604/822-1000.** Fax 604/822-1001. www.conferences.ubc.ca. E-mail: reservation@housing.ubc.ca. About 1,900 units. Walter Gage Residence units available only May 10–Aug 26: C$34–C$52 (US$23–U$35) standard or premium single with shared bathroom; C$69–C$172 (US$46–US$115) studio, 1-, or 6-bedroom suites. Vanier Hostel: C$24 (US$16) single, C$48 (US$32) double, C$59 (US$40) studio suite with private bathroom. Located adjacent to the Gage Residence, the 47 Gage Court Suites are available year-round: May–Sept C$99–C$124 (US$66–US$83) suite; Oct–Apr C$81–C$91 (US$54–US$61) suite. AE, MC, V. Free parking May 4–Aug 26 at Walter Gage Residence, other areas C$5 (US$3.35) per day. Bus: 4, 10, or 99.

The University of British Columbia is in a gorgeous forested setting on the tip of Point Grey—a convenient location if you plan to spend a lot of time either in Kitsilano or at the university itself. It's also not bad if you have a car, but otherwise it's a good half-hour bus ride from downtown. With two residences and nearly 2,000 rooms, there's also plenty of variety. The 17-story Walter Gage Residence has new, comfortable studio, one-bedroom, and six-bedroom suites, as well as single rooms with shared bathrooms. Many are located on the upper floors with sweeping views of the city and ocean. All rooms are furnished with extra-long twin beds. All suites in the Gage Residence come equipped with private bathrooms, kitchenettes, TVs, and phones. Each studio suite has a twin bed; each one-bedroom suite features a queen bed; the six-bedroom Tower suites—a particularly good deal for families—each feature one double bed and five twin beds. Located next door, the year-round Gage Court suites have two twin beds in one bedroom and a queen-size Murphy bed in the sitting room. Housekeeping is provided daily in the Gage Residence, but only weekly in the more Spartan Vanier residence. Breakfast can be purchased in the campus cafeteria. There are plenty of on-campus facilities and services, including restaurants, a pub, tennis courts, and banking. Athletic facilities, including the campus gym and pool, are open to guests for about C$5 (US$3.35) per use per person. Nearby attractions include Spanish Banks, Wreck Beach, Pacific Spirit Park, Nitobe Memorial Gardens, the Museum of Anthropology, and the University Golf Course.

4 The North Shore (North Vancouver & West Vancouver)

The North Shore cities of North and West Vancouver are pleasant and lush and much less hurried than Vancouver. Staying here also offers easy access to the North Shore mountains and its attractions, including hiking trails, the Capilano Suspension Bridge, and the ski slopes on Mount Seymour, Grouse Mountain, and Cypress Bowl. Staying here is also often cheaper than in Vancouver. The disadvantage is that if you want to take your car into Vancouver, there are only two bridges, and during rush hours they're painfully slow. The SeaBus, however, is not only quick, but kind of scenic.

EXPENSIVE

Lonsdale Quay Hotel. 123 Carrie Cates Ct., North Vancouver, B.C. V6M 3K7. ☎ **800/836-6111** or 604/986-6111. Fax 604/986-8782. www. lonsdalequayhotel.bc.ca. E-mail: sales@lonsdalequayhotel.bc.ca. 83 units. A/C MINIBAR TV TEL. High season C$150–C$225 (US$101–US$151) double or twin, C$350 (US$235) suite; low season C$140–C$165 (US$94–US$111) double or twin, C$250 (US$168) suite. Extra person C$25 (US$17). Senior discount available. AE, CB, DC, DISC, ER, MC, V. Parking C$7 (US$4.70), free on weekends and holidays. No smoking. SeaBus: Lonsdale Quay.

Directly across the Burrard Inlet from the Canada Place Pier, the Lonsdale Quay Hotel is at the water's edge above the Lonsdale Quay Market at the SeaBus terminal. An escalator rises from the midst of the market's food, crafts, and souvenir stalls to the front desk on the third floor. The rooms are simply furnished and tastefully decorated, without the grandeur or luxurious touches of comparably priced downtown hotels. Nevertheless, the hotel has unique and fabulous harbor and city views, and is only 15 minutes by bus or car from Grouse Mountain Ski Resort and Capilano Regional Park.

Dining: The Waterfront Bistro serves lunch, cocktails, and dinner. The relaxed Q Café serves three meals daily.

Amenities: Whirlpool, weight and exercise room, in-room coffeemakers and water coolers.

Park Royal Hotel. 540 Clyde Ave., West Vancouver, B.C. V7T 2J7. ☎ **877/ 926-5511** or 604/926-5511. Fax 604/926-6082. www.parkroyalhotel.com. 30 units. TV TEL. May–Sept C$159–C$189 (US$107–US$127) double, C$229 (US$153) suite; Oct–Apr C$99–C$129 (US$66–US$86) double, C$169 (US$113) suite. AE, DC, MC, V. Free parking. Cross the Lions Gate Bridge into West Vancouver, and take the first right onto Taylor Way. Turn right immediately at Clyde Ave. Bus: 250, 251, 252, 253.

Make reservations months in advance for this Tudor-style country inn with exposed beams, a stone fireplace, and a pub. The hotel sits on the bank of the Capilano River—a great place for salmon and steelhead fly-fishing. The comfortably sized rooms, furnished in the same Tudor decor, have nice touches like brass beds. The only tricky part of this hideaway is finding it. Once you do, it's a 1-minute drive to the Park Royal Mall, one of North America's largest shopping centers.

Dining/Diversions: The Tudor Room Restaurant offers three meals daily plus Sunday brunch; the Pub is a popular gathering spot for more genteel locals.

Amenities: Complimentary coffee or tea and a morning newspaper.

MODERATE

✪ **Beachside Bed & Breakfast.** 4208 Evergreen Ave., West Vancouver, B.C. V7V 1H1. ☎ **800/563-3311** or 604/922-7773. www.beach.bc.ca. E-mail: info@beach.bc.ca. 3 units. C$150–C$250 (US$101–US$168) double. Extra person C$30 (US$20). Rates include full breakfast. MC, V. Free parking. Bus: 250, 251, 252, 253.

Bouquets of fresh flowers in every room are a signature touch at this beautiful, modern waterfront home located at the end of a quiet cul-de-sac. The all-glass southern exposure of this Spanish-style house affords a panoramic view of Vancouver. The private beach is just steps from the door. You can watch the waves from the patio or outdoor Jacuzzi, or just spend the afternoon fishing and sailing. Hosts Gordon and Joan Gibb know the area and will direct you to Stanley Park, hiking, skiing, and other highlights. (Gordon is a registered tour guide.)

INEXPENSIVE

Deep Cove Bed & Breakfast. 2590 Shelley Rd., North Vancouver, B.C. V7H 1V9. ☎ **604/929-3932.** Fax 604/929-9330. E-mail: deepcove@istar.ca. 2 units. TV. C$90 (US$60) double. Rates include breakfast. MC, V. Free parking. Bus: 210 from Vancouver to Phibbs Exchange in North Vancouver, transfer to bus 214. Driving: Hwy. 1, Exit 22 (Mt. Seymour Pkwy.), east on Mt. Seymour to Berkley, left on Berkley for a few blocks, right on Shelley Rd.

Only 20 minutes from downtown Vancouver, Diane and Wayne Moore's B&B provides the privacy of a large, secluded property and easy access to city attractions. The rooms—one with twin beds, one with a queen-size bed—are in a separate guest cottage, with private entrances. There's a red-cedar hot tub on the outside terrace between the cottage and the house; the cottage's guest lounge has a billiard table, wood-burning fireplace, TV, and VCR. Hearty breakfasts of French toast, omelets, freshly baked breads, and muffins topped with homemade jams and jellies or Quebec maple syrup are served in the morning room or on the patio. The Moores also accommodate special diets, and request that guests refrain from smoking in the rooms.

Mountainside Manor. 5909 Nancy Greene Way, North Vancouver, B.C. V7R 4W6. ☎ **604/990-9772.** Fax 604/985-8484. E-mail: mtnside@attglobal.net. 4 units. TV. May–Oct C$95–C$155 (US$64–US$104) double; Nov–Apr C$85–C$135 (US$57–US$90) double. Rates include breakfast. Off-season discounts available. DC, MC, V. Free parking.

This is the closest house to both the ski slopes on Grouse Mountain and the 42-kilometer-long (26 miles) Baden-Powell hiking trail. It's a spectacular, modern home nestled in a peaceful alpine setting. High above the city on a tree-covered ridge, the Mountainside Manor has a magnificent view of the Coast Mountains and the Burrard Inlet from the rooms and the outdoor hot tub. The Panorama Room—the largest of the rooms—has a queen-size bed, rosewood furniture, a Jacuzzi with a separate shower, and views of the mountains and the city. All rooms are stocked with fresh flowers and lots of amenities.

4

Dining

*T*wo thousand restaurants? Five thousand? Hard to say really, but Vancouverites do dine out more than residents of any other Canadian city. Outstanding meals are available in all price ranges and in many different cuisines—Caribbean, Chinese, Japanese, Greek, French, Italian, Spanish, Mongolian, Ethiopian, Vietnamese. Even better, over the past few years Vancouverites have come to expect top quality, and yet they absolutely refuse to pay the kind of top dollar restaurant goers pay in New York or San Francisco. Somehow, restaurateurs have managed to square this circle. For discerning diners from elsewhere, Vancouver is a steal.

The cuisine buzzwords here are tapas and West Coast. Justifiable pride in local produce, game, and seafood is combined with innovation and creativity. More and more restaurants are shifting to seasonal, even monthly, menus, giving their chefs greater freedom. As for tapas, it seems that diners in Vancouver have grown more sociable, ordering two or three small tapas plates and sharing them with their friends.

Once less than palatable, British Columbian wines have improved to the point that local vintners are now winning international acclaim. The big wine-producing areas are in the Okanagan Valley (in southern British Columbia's dry interior) or else on southern Vancouver Island. In the hills surrounding Lake Okanagan and the Okanagan River, there are more than 30 wineries, including Mission Hill, Grey Monk, Summerhill, Quail's Gate, Cedar Creek, and Sumac Ridge. On the Island, Burrowing Owl and Venturi-Shultz are the vintners to watch. Fortunately, these wines have received far less publicity than they deserve, so some great bargains can still be had.

Because they're so numerous, Vancouver restaurants aren't hard to find. If you're staying in downtown Vancouver, you can walk to the West End and English Bay (west of downtown from Thurlow Street to Stanley Park), Gastown, or Chinatown. If you're willing to travel farther, you can venture to the

West Side. Or if you'd like to head in the opposite direction, cross the Lions Gate Bridge and turn left, and you'll be in West Vancouver. For something fun and casual, head east to a bistro on Main Street or Commercial Drive.

There's no provincial tax on restaurant meals in British Columbia, but venues add the 7% federal goods and services tax (GST). Restaurant hours vary. Lunch is typically served from noon to 1 or 2pm; Vancouverites begin dining around 6:30pm, later in summer. Reservations are recommended at most restaurants and are essential at popular places. Reservations may not be accepted at some inexpensive and moderately priced restaurants.

1 Downtown & Yaletown

VERY EXPENSIVE

✪ **C.** 1600 Howe St. ☎ **604/681-1164.** Fax 604/605-8263. www. crestaurant.com. E-mail: info@crestaurant.com. Reservations recommended. Main courses C$21–C$32 (US$14–US$21). AE, DC, MC, V. Daily 11:30am–2:30pm and 5:30–11pm; Sun brunch 11am–2pm. Valet parking C$6 (US$4). Bus: 1, 2. SEAFOOD.

It's become almost habit to quietly backhand the conspicuous consumption of the '80s generation—what's forgotten is just how well they consumed. C brings it all back, in a room done up in brilliant shades of Miami white, with the food itself providing a little postindustrial commentary. Look for pale-green bread baskets made from cut sheets of heavy-gauge rubber, footrests upholstered with truck-tire retreads, and faux vinyl siding in the washrooms. Beyond the decor, however, C re-creates the '80s through the sheer indulgent quality with which they serve fish. C's taster box—a kind of small wooden high-rise of appetizers—includes salmon gravlax cured in Saskatoonberry tea, artichoke carpaccio, abalone tempura, and grilled garlic squid. A variety of seafood main courses are available, but for the ultimate dining experience, let chef Robert Clark show off (he's dying to), and order the seven-course sampling menu. First up is a Maui ahi tuna sashimi, lightly dabbed with 50-year balsamic vinegar and presented on a piece of rough-cut marble. Artichoke carpaccio, pan-seared Dover sole, and spotted prawns with kumquat follow, as does a Nova Scotia lobster. Then comes the Alaskan scallop wrapped in octopus bacon. Wine pairings throughout are brought to you by Peter, a sommelier of exceptional

Downtown Vancouver Dining

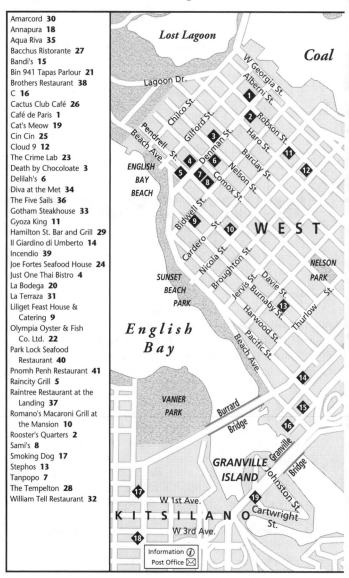

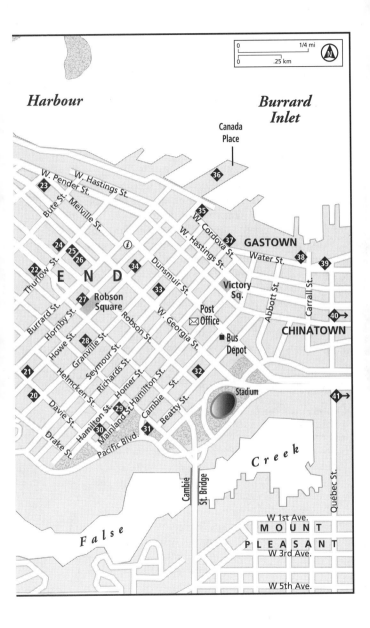

knowledge. Savor the exquisite cuisine as you watch the sun go down over the marina.

✪ **Cloud 9.** 1400 Robson St. ☎ **604/662-8328.** Reservations recommended. Lunch main courses C$8–C$12 (US$5–US$8), dinner main courses C$20–C$40 (US$13–US$27), brunch C$22 (US$15). AE, DC, ER, MC, V. Daily 6:30–11am, 11:30am–2pm, and 5–10pm; Sun brunch 11:30am–2pm. Bus: 5. PACIFIC NORTHWEST.

Want the city laid out at your feet and delivered to your table? Take the elevator to the Landmark Hotel's 42nd floor. The view may be of English Bay, Stanley Park with the North Shore Mountains, or the towers of downtown. Yes, it's a revolving restaurant, but hang on just a minute before you think "tourist trap" and dive for the escape hatch. Things at Cloud 9 have been . . . ahem . . . evolving. The restaurant has been working hard on improving the menu, and the new chef is able to offer cuisine that almost equals the superlative views. Appetizers feature mostly seafood—the platter allows you to sample the smoked salmon, oysters, sushi, and pâté. For main courses, seafood plays an important role, but other high points include steak, lamb, chicken, and a few Asian dishes. The prices are slightly higher than in comparable restaurants, but consider that a fair premium for the million-dollar view.

If you decide not to stay for supper, the lounge has excellent—and reasonably priced—martinis. On weekends there's a small cover.

✪ **Diva at the Met.** 645 Howe St. ☎ **604/602-7788.** www.metropolitan. com. E-mail: reservations@divamet.com. Reservations recommended. Dinner main courses C$26–C$38 (US$17–US$25), lunch C$12–C$23 (US$8–US$15). AE, DC, DISC, JCB, MC, V. Daily 6:30am–11pm. Bus: 4, 7. WEST COAST.

Since opening a few years ago next to the newly revamped Metropolitan Hotel, Diva at the Met and its chef Michael Noble have made walking off with city restaurant awards a bit of a habit. Noble himself has represented Canada at the Bocuse d'Or competition in France. His dishes extol the virtues of fresh seasonal ingredients and a light approach to spices and seasonings. Starters include house-smoked salmon with Québec foie gras. For the main course, try halibut cheeks with black-olive tapenade. Diva's tasting menu is also very popular, and its weekend brunch is among the best in town.

✪ **The Five Sails.** 999 Canada Place Way, in the Pan-Pacific Hotel. ☎ **604/891-2892.** Reservations recommended. Main courses C$23–C$38

(US$15–US$25), tasting menu C$34–C$45 (US$23–US$30). AE, DC, ER, JCB, MC, V. Daily 6–10pm. SkyTrain: Waterfront. WEST COAST.

The Five Sails' view of Coal Harbour, the Lions Gate Bridge, and the Coast Mountains is as spectacular as the food. Where other city restaurants have scrambled over each other trying to bring ingredients and seasonings from the four corners of the world together on a single plate, the Five Sails has taken a steadier, more cautious approach. That's not to say they don't create winning combinations—witness the pan-seared halibut cheeks with cardamom-scented tomato fondue on a bed of saffroned potatoes, or the poached oyster glazed with a hollandaise sauce just lightly infused with chili. But equally indicative of the Five Sails approach are top-quality ingredients given just enough preparation to bring out their finest flavors. Think dry-aged Angus beef done to perfection, or fresh-caught Pacific salmon. The Five Sails' wine selection leans slightly towards hard-to-find Cascadian bottles. The decor is elegant, refined, and very simple, and the view is among the best in town.

✪ **Gotham Steakhouse and Cocktail Bar.** 615 Seymour St. ☎ **604/ 605-8282.** Fax 604/605-8285. www.gothamsteakhouse.com. Reservations recommended. Main courses C$27–C$42 (US$18–US$28). AE, MC, V. Mon–Fri 11:30am–2:30pm; daily 5–11pm (cocktail bar somewhat later). Bus: 4, 7. STEAK.

Vegetarians beware: Gotham means meat. Okay, potatoes and a bit of seafood, but that's it. The room is of ambitious proportions—a 40-foot high timber ceiling divided down the middle with a cocktail bar on one side, a dining room on the other, and a patio with fireplace balancing things out. Furnishings are aggressively masculine—thick leather, dark wood, plush velvet, acrylic paintings of women in half-laced corsets. The wine list is encyclopedic. And then there's the food. The deep-fried calamari appetizer was a light and tasty revelation. Jumbo shrimp were sumo-sized. And the steaks, these were incredible: a porterhouse cut the size of a catcher's mitt; a petit filet mignon as tall as half a bread loaf. The meat just melts away on your tongue. Veggie side dishes are eminently forgettable. Better to pass on them entirely and spend the money on another glass of French merlot. The service is impeccable.

William Tell Restaurant. 765 Beatty St., in the Georgian Court Hotel.
☎ **604/688-3504.** Reservations recommended at dinner. Lunch main courses
C$8–C$15 (US$5–US$10), dinner main courses C$20–C$30 (US$13–US$20).
AE, DC, ER, JCB, MC, V. Daily 7–11am; Mon–Fri 11:30am–2pm; Mon–Sat
5:30–9:30pm; Sun buffet 5:30–8pm. SkyTrain: Stadium. CONTINENTAL.

One of Vancouver's foremost restaurateurs, Erwin Doebeli,
has maintained the William Tell as one of the city's premier
places for 30 years. His traditional Swiss cuisine is a sharp con-
trast to the trendy dishes you'll find elsewhere downtown. The
decor is refined and up-to-date. The breaded veal Schnitzel
Holstein is crisp and tender; the cheese fondue is superb. A
few lighter alternatives have crept onto the menu, but most
dishes are loaded with cream and butter. And that's exactly
what keeps people coming back. This is the place for a
business lunch.

EXPENSIVE

Amarcord. 104–1168 Hamilton St. ☎ **604/681-6500.** Reservations recommended. Main courses C$13–C$19 (US$9–US$13). AE, DC, MC, V. Mon–Fri
11:30am–2pm; daily 5:30–10pm. Bus: 2. ITALIAN.

Traditional Italian cuisine doesn't get much respect these days,
but that's just what Amarcord does, and so well that it's worth
swearing off mango-corn chutney sauté and rediscovering the
joys of freshly made pasta or risotto teamed with a lovingly prepared sauce. Think gnocchi with Italian sausage, fresh tomato
and basil, or linguini with mussels, scallops, and tiger prawns.
Wines hail from Tuscany and California. The atmosphere is
formal without being fussy—a place you could bring your
nine-year-old. Service is knowledgeable and very friendly.

Aqua Riva. 30–200 Granville St. ☎ **604/683-5599.** www.aquariva.com.
Reservations recommended. Main courses C$19–C$24 (US$13–US$16).
AE, MC, V. Daily 11:30am–10pm. Bus: 4, 7. SEAFOOD/PACIFIC NORTHWEST.

It's rare to find a place with both stunning views and top-
quality cuisine, but Aqua Riva has both. Located at the foot of
Granville Street, the restaurant commands stunning views of
the North Shore Mountains and Burrard Inlet, allowing you
to watch the tugs, freighters, and cruise ships while biting into
wood-roasted ahi tuna steaks, pan-seared salmon, or spit-
roasted chicken with lemon-herb seasonings. The lunchtime
crowd buzzes with media people (the city's two major newspapers are located in the same building).

Bacchus Ristorante. 845 Hornby St., in the Wedgewood Hotel. ☎ **604/608-5319.** www.wedgewoodhotel.com. Reservations required for dinner. Breakfast main courses C$6–C$16 (US$4–US$11), lunch main courses C$13–C$16 (US$9–US$11), dinner main courses C$18–C$35 (US$12–US$23). AE, DC, MC, V. Daily 6:30am–2:30pm and 6–10pm; lounge menu until 11pm, Sat lounge menu until midnight. Weekend tea 2–4pm, weekend brunch 11am–2pm. Live entertainment daily. MEDITERRANEAN.

Bacchus is the centerpiece of Eleni Skalbania's Wedgewood Hotel. With cherry-wood paneling, a carved limestone fireplace, white linens, and comfortable chairs, the decor is wonderfully romantic. Award-winning chef Robert Sulatycky has created an eclectic menu that includes such diverse dishes as Brill sole and spot prawns and saddle of spring rabbit with sage jus and pâté de truffle. For dessert, the apricot soufflé Rothschild and caramelized apple tart with cardamom ice cream are luscious.

Bandi's. 1427 Howe St. ☎ **604/685-3391.** Reservations recommended. Main courses C$17–C$23 (US$11–US$15). AE, MC, V. Tues–Fri 11:30am–2pm; Tues–Sun 5:30–11pm. Bus: 1, 2. HUNGARIAN.

Owner, proprietor, chef, and occasional maître d' Bandi Rinkhy serves up big, garlicky, paprika-laden country specialties in this pretty yellow dollhouse of a restaurant. The formula's been the same for years, but with a romantic house for a setting and old-world panache in the service, who needs innovation? Savor the sour cherry soup before moving on to the signature crispy duck with red cabbage. Other options include pan-fried trout, stuffed herring fillets, breaded mushrooms, and the inevitable goulash. Servings are very generous, so if you're headed here for dinner, skip lunch.

✪ Il Giardino di Umberto. 1382 Hornby St. ☎ **604/669-2422.** Fax 604/669-9723. www.umberto.com. E-mail: umberto@intergate.ca. Reservations required. Main courses C$14–C$33 (US$9–US$22). AE, DC, MC, V. Mon–Fri noon–2:30pm; daily 5:30–11pm. Bus: 1, 22. ITALIAN.

Restaurant magnate Umberto Menghi's empire includes Umberto al Porto Borgo Antico on Water Street and two locations in Whistler. Il Giardino has created its own niche. Decorated in tones of burnt sienna with exposed wood beams, this restaurant re-creates the ambience of an Italian seaside villa, down to the enclosed garden terrace and a Tuscan menu emphasizing pasta and game. Entrees include osso bucco Milanese with saffron risotto, tortellini with portobello mushrooms in truffle oil, roasted reindeer loin with port peppercorn sauce, and pheasant breast stuffed with wild mushrooms. After sampling the cuisine, more than a few devoted foodies have run off to enroll in Umberto's Tuscan cooking school, set in one of the hill towns of Tuscany.

✪ **Joe Fortes Seafood House.** 777 Thurlow St. (at Robson). ☎ **604/ 669-1940.** www.joefortesseafoodrest.com. Reservations recommended. Main courses C$17–C$37 (US$11–US$25). AE, DC, DISC, ER, MC, V. Mon–Fri 11:30am–10:30pm, Sat–Sun 11am–10:30pm. Bus: 5. SEAFOOD.

Named after the burly Caribbean seaman and popular local hero who became English Bay's first lifeguard, Joe Fortes has been known for years as the place where the young and tanned would meet for mutual schmoozing and raw oysters.

Joe's staff still all look like extras on a "90210" episode, but lately, under the direction of chef Brian Faulk, Joe's has been making a serious play as a top spot on the city's list of best seafood fusion. And the oyster bar is still among the city's best. Joe's rooftop patio—equipped with its own bar and kitchen— makes an extremely pleasant retreat on sunny days, particularly if you've just come from the Robson Street shopping bustle.

La Terrazza. 1088 Cambie St. ☎ **604/899-4449.** Reservations recommended. Main courses C$16–C$30 (US$11–US$20). AE, DC, ER, MC, V. Mon–Thurs 5–11pm, Fri–Sat 5pm–midnight, Sun 5–10pm. Bus: 2. ITALIAN.

Located on the edge of Yaletown, La Terrazza's sleek, modern exterior contrasts sharply with the warm bustling dining room inside. Two of the three owners hail from Italy and the kitchen is in the capable hands of chef Gennaro Iorio, originally from Naples. You will not find fusion or complicated culinary acrobatics on his menu. On the contrary, many of his dishes stand out for their simplicity. The menu changes with the seasons, and a tasting menu with matching wines highlights a different culinary region of Italy every month. One of the more intriguing appetizers is the bocconcini cheese, wrapped in prosciutto and raddicchio, grilled and drizzled with strawberry vinaigrette. Main courses include various pasta dishes, but following the chef's recommendation, we tried the roasted guinea hen and duck breast with frangelico brandy. Fresh vegetables and risotto or polenta accompany the dishes. The wine list offers bottles from most continents. A number of these are available by the glass. Save room for dessert, particularly the white cheesecake baked in phyllo pastry topped with sour cherries and fruit coulis.

MODERATE

Bin 941 Tapas Parlour. 941 Davie St. ☎ **604/683-1246.** Reservations not accepted. Tapas C$3–C$10 (US$2–US$7). MC, V. Mon–Sat 5pm–2am, Sun 5pm–midnight. Bus: 4, 5, 8. TAPAS.

Still booming two years on, Bin 941 is the latest in trendy tapas dining. True, the music's too loud and the room's too small, but the food that alights on the bar or ever so tiny tables is quite delicious, and, like all tapas, a lot of fun to eat. Look especially for local seafood offerings like scallops and tiger prawns in bonito butter sauce. Sharing is unavoidable in this sliver of a bistro, so come prepared for socializing. So successful was the original model that a second Bin, dubbed Bin 942, has opened up at 1521 West Broadway.

The Crime Lab. 1280 W. Pender St. ☎ **604/732-7463.** Reservations accepted. Main courses C$15–C$16 (US$10–US$11). AE, DC, MC, V. Sun–Thurs 5:30pm–midnight, Fri–Sat 5:30pm–2am. Bus: 135. WEST COAST/ FUSION.

Illuminated by the cheap glow of neon and with menus covered by lurid jacket drawings of 1930s pulp fiction, the Crime Lab is an eternity of fun. The martini list is inspired by figures from Vancouver's underworld. Tables are tight in this stiletto-thin establishment, but for a group of 8 to 12, it's tough to beat the triangular table set at the point of the Lab's long blade. And then, of course, there's the food. Like most Vancouver restaurants, the menu covers all possibilities, but seafood is the specialty. Appetizers are superb—crab cakes with mango ginger aioli; mussels steamed with a salsa of scallions, cilantro, and vinegar; or Earl Bay oysters with a vinaigrette of sake ginger and cucumber. And when it comes to main courses, the seafood paella provides proof of the kitchen's abilities. The wine list sticks close to home, and service is both friendly and knowledgeable.

Hamilton Street Bar and Grill. 1009 Hamilton St. ☎ **604/331-1511.** Reservations recommended. Main courses C$12–C$34 (US$8–US$23) AE, DC, JCB, MC, V. Mon–Thurs 5pm–midnight, Fri–Sat 5pm–1am, Sun 5–11pm. Bus: 2. PACIFIC NORTHWEST.

This fun and funky eatery in the heart of Vancouver's dot-com district offers a superior brand of comfort food. Grab a seat at the long bar or sink into a plush booth and try one of the many warm tapas dishes, like tiger prawns in garlic or chicken sate in peanut sauce, or one of the well-prepared burgers or steaks. Together with a craft-brewed beer and a warm and buzzing atmosphere, it's the perfect way to cap off a hectic day of seeing the sights or launching a Web startup.

✪ **La Bodega.** 1277 Howe St. ☎ **604/684-8814.** Reservations accepted. Main courses C$10–C$16 (US$7–US$11). AE, DC, JCB, MC, V. Mon–Fri 11:30am–midnight, Sat 5pm–midnight, Sun 5–11pm. Bus: 4, 7. TAPAS/SPANISH.

This warm, dark Spanish bar has a dozen or so tables and some great little romantic corners. Expect authentic Spanish tapas—garlic prawns, ceviche, marinated mushrooms, pan-fried squid, and good black olives. Specials on the blackboard regularly include *conejo* (rabbit with tomatoes and peppers), quail, and B.C. scallops. All of it comes with lots of crusty bread for soaking up the wonderful garlicky goo. La Bodega has a good selection of Portuguese and Spanish wines and the best sangria in town.

INEXPENSIVE

✪ **Olympia Oyster & Fish Co. Ltd.** 820 Thurlow St. ☎ **604/685-0716.** Main courses C$6–C$10 (US$4–US$7). AE, MC, V. Mon–Thurs 10am–8pm, Fri 8:30am–8pm, Sat 10am–7pm, Sun 11am–7pm. Bus: 5. FISH & CHIPS.

In a brand-new spot just around the corner from its old Rob-son Street location, this tiny fish store and restaurant is still a neighborhood favorite. And it still produces Vancouver's best fish-and-chips. There are only a few tables and a window-seat counter, plus three sidewalk tables, weather permitting, but the fish is always fresh and flaky and can be grilled if you prefer. The seafood platter is enough for two. If the place is packed, ask for a takeout order and head 2 blocks east down Robson Street to Robson Square for a picnic. Or you can shop for smoked salmon or caviar which can be shipped home. Sip a ginger beer while you wait.

The Tempelton. 1087 Granville St. ☎ **604/685-4612.** Main courses C$3.50–C$9 (US$2.35–US$6). V. Sun–Mon 10am–10pm, Tues 10am–midnight, Wed–Thurs 10am–11pm, Fri–Sat 10am–1am. Bus: 4, 7, 8, 10. AMERICAN.

A diner, but not really a diner. More like a trendy retro commentary on the diner, except that this place has been in continuous operation since 1934. True, back then the green Hamilton Beach milkshake makers were the height of modern and the serving staff likely didn't go in for nose and belly-button rings and tattoos. Don't show up with a hangover and expect greasy eggs and bacon. Instead, think jambalaya, chili, blackened chicken breast, or a portobello-mushroom vegetarian burger. (Okay, there are eggs and burgers too, but they almost always have little fusion-y touches.) Saturday brunch is 10% off if you arrive in your pajamas. Staff already have them on.

2 Gastown & Chinatown

EXPENSIVE

The Cannery. 2205 Commissioner St., near Victoria Dr. ☎ **604/254-9606.** www.canneryseafood.com. E-mail: info@canneryseafood.com. Reservations recommended. Main courses C$17–C$27 (US$11–US$18). AE, DC, DISC, JCB, MC, V. Daily 11:30am–2:30pm; Sun–Fri 5:30–9:30pm, Sat 5:30–10pm. Closed Dec 24–26. Bus: 7 to Victoria Dr. From downtown, head east on Hastings St., turn left on Victoria Dr. (2 blocks past Commercial Dr.), then right on Commissioner St. SEAFOOD.

At least some of the pleasure of eating at The Cannery comes from simply finding the place. Hop over the railway tracks and thread your way past container terminals and fish packing plants until you're sure you're lost and then with a last turn the road opens onto a brightly lit parking lot and there it is—a great ex-warehouse of a building hanging out over the waters of Burrard Inlet. The building itself—its beam-laded warehouse interior, loaded with old nets and seafaring memorabilia—is another hefty portion of The Cannery's charm. As for the view, it's simply stunning, one of the best in Vancouver. So how about the food? Good, solid, traditional seafood, often alder-grilled, with ever-changing specials to complement the salmon and halibut basics. Chefs Frederic Couton and Jacques Wan have been getting more inventive of late, but when an institution's 27 years old and still going strong, no one's ever *too* keen to rock the boat. The wine list is stellar and the desserts are both wonderful and wonderfully inventive.

Raintree Restaurant at the Landing. 375 Water St. ☎ **604/688-5570.** Reservations recommended. Main courses C$16–C$27 (US$11–US$18). AE, DC, JCB, MC, V. Daily 11:30am–2:30pm and 5:30–10pm. Skytrain: Waterfront. WEST COAST.

Once the darling of food critics and fusion aficionados, the Raintree fell on (comparatively) hard times for a few years. But it's back with a new chef and a new focus on West Coast cuisine, local ingredients (including wild salmon), and vegetarian and vegan dishes. Located in a beautiful heritage building in Gastown, the dining room's exposed brick walls frame a fabulous panoramic harborside view of the North Shore. The service is attentive and professional, and the menu is filled with the creativity that made Raintree the city's first and best spot for West Coast cuisine. Try the kelp-crusted sea scallops, the broiled Pacific snapper, or the seared Washington duck breast with grilled pear and gooseberry compote.

MODERATE

Park Lock Seafood Restaurant. 544 Main St. (at E. Pender St.). ☎ **604/ 688-1581.** Reservations recommended. Main courses C$10–C$35 (US$7– US$23); dim sum dishes C$2.50–C$3.25 (US$1.65–US$2.15). AE, MC, V. Daily 8am–3pm; Tues–Sun 5–9:30pm. Bus: 19, 22. CHINESE/DIM SUM.

If you've never done dim sum, this traditional dining room in the very heart of Chinatown is the place to give it a try. From 10am to 3pm daily, waitresses wheel little carts loaded with Chinese delicacies past white-linen–covered tables. When you see something you like, you grab it. The final bill is based upon how many little dishes are left on your table. Dishes include spring rolls, *hargow* and *shumai* (steamed shrimp, beef, or pork dumplings), prawns wrapped in fresh white noodles, small steamed buns, sticky rice cooked in banana leaves, curried squid, and lots more. Parties of four or more are best—that way you get to try each other's food.

✪ **Pink Pearl.** 1132 E. Hastings St. ☎ **604/253-4316.** www.pinkpearl. com. Main courses C$12–C$35 (US$8–US$23); dim sum C$2.95–C$6 (US$1.95–US$4). AE, DC, MC, V. Daily 9am–10pm. CHINESE/DIM SUM.

This is the city's best spot for dim sum. The sheer volume and bustle are astonishing. Dozens of waiters parade a cavalcade of little trolleys stacked high with baskets and steamers and bowls filled with dumplings, spring rolls, shrimp balls, chicken feet, and even more obscure and delightful offerings. At the tables, extended families of Chinese banter, joke, and feast. Towers of empty plates and bowls pile up in the middle, a tribute to the appetites of hungry brunchers, as well as the growing bill; fortunately, dim sum is still a steal, perhaps the best and most fun way to sample Cantonese cooking.

INEXPENSIVE

✪ **Brothers Restaurant.** 1 Water St. ☎ **604/683-9124.** Fax 604/ 683-9124. Reservations recommended. Main courses C$8–C$25 (US$5– US$17); children's courses C$2.95–C$4.95 (US$1.95–US$3.30). AE, DC, MC, V. Daily 11:30am–10pm. Bus: 1, 50. AMERICAN.

Dinner on the *Starlight Express*

BC Rail's Pacific Starlight Dinner Train departs from the North Vancouver train terminal, transporting passengers past West Vancouver's waterfront mansions, along Howe Sound's scenic shoreline, past Porteau Cove, and back. The elegant restored coaches recall a time when rail travel was as much about going as it was about getting somewhere. The cars are appointed with inlaid wood, brass, and all the other touches you'd expect in a first-class dining car from rail travel's golden age. Seating in the salon (C$84/US$56 per person, excluding taxes, tips, and alcohol) is slightly less expensive than seating in the glass-domed observation car (C$100/US$67 per person), but the spectacular 360° view of the sun setting over Howe Sound and the surrounding mountains is worth every cent. Bring your camera. But even more than the views, the fine service and outstanding West Coast cuisine make either choice worthwhile. Recent entree selections have included roasted British Columbia salmon, stuffed breast of guinea fowl, filet of beef tenderloin, beef Wellington, and vegetable rotolo (a medley of roasted vegetables and pasta topped with sage-and-tomato sauce and ricotta cheese). For dessert, the white-chocolate soup is fast becoming the signature dish.

The train operates every Wednesday to Sunday evening from May 1 to November 1, departing from the BC Rail Station, 1311 W. First St., North Vancouver, at 6:15pm and returning at 9:45pm. The dress code stipulates "fine dining attire" but recommends that women shouldn't wear high heels. For information or reservations, call BC Rail Passenger Services (☎ **800/363-3733** or 604/984-5246).

Decorated like a Franciscan monastery, complete with staff in friars' robes, Brothers has a warm ambiance especially appealing to families. Main dishes include chowder, pastas, burgers, and serious prime rib. Children get balloons and their own menu. A bistro lounge featuring sushi and an oyster bar caters primarily to a younger crowd.

✪ **Incendio.** 103 Columbia St. ☎ **604/688-8694.** E-mail: incendio@imag.net. Main courses C$7–C$12 (US$4.70–US$8). AE, MC, V. Mon–Fri 11:30am–3pm and 5–10pm; Sat–Sun 5–11pm. Bus: 1, 8. PIZZA.

If you're looking for something casual and local that won't be full of other people reading downtown maps, this little Gastown hideaway is sublime. The 22 pizza combinations are served on fresh, crispy crusts baked in an old wood-fired oven. Pastas are homemade, and you're encouraged to mix and match—try the mussels with spinach fettuccine, capers, and tomatoes in lime butter. The wine list is decent; the beer list is inspired. And now, there's a patio. Sunday night features all-you-can-eat pizza for C$8 (US$5).

Phnom Penh Restaurant. 244 E. Georgia St., near Main St. ☎ **604/682-5777.** Dishes C$4.50–C$11 (US$3–US$7). DC, MC. Wed–Mon 10am–9:30pm. Bus: 8, 19. CAMBODIAN/VIETNAMESE.

This family-run restaurant serves a mixture of Vietnamese and slightly spicier Cambodian cuisine. Phnom Penh is a perennial contender for, and occasional winner of, *Vancouver Magazine*'s award for the city's best Asian restaurant. The walls are adorned with artistic renderings of ancient Cambodia's capital, Angkor. Khmer dolls are suspended in glass cases, and the subdued lighting is a welcome departure from the harsh glare often found in inexpensive Chinatown restaurants. Try the outstanding hot-and-sour soup, loaded with prawns and lemongrass. The deep-fried garlic squid served with rice is also delicious. For dessert, the fruit-and-rice pudding is an exotic treat. There's a second location at 955 Broadway at Oak Street (☎ **604/734-8898**), open during the same hours.

3 The West End

EXPENSIVE

Café de Paris. 751 Denman St. (at Robson). ☎ **604/687-1418.** Reservations recommended. Main courses C$18–C$26 (US$12–US$17), fixed-price menu C$23 (US$15). AE, MC, V. Mon–Fri 11:30am–2pm, Sun 11am–2:30pm and 5–9pm; Mon–Sat 5:30–10pm. Bus: 5. FRENCH.

The bike-and-blade rental zone on lower Denman would seem an unlikely place to seek out Paris, but enter and there you are on the Left Bank. Edith Piaf's voice fills a cozy room of wood and brass, decorated with Rabelaisian oil paintings and a map of Haussmann's Paris. A big wood bar is stocked with an empire of fine French liquors and cognacs. The wine list never leaves the Fifth Republic (you expected otherwise?) and ranges from a C$24 house red to a C$1,500 (US$16 to US$1,000) bottle of Chateau Haut-Brion Bordeaux, 1985.

Cuisine is ever so French (though the friendly service is anything but). Appetizers include Burgundy snails in garlic butter, braised rabbit in Dijon mustard sauce, and, of course, onion soup. The menu also includes classics such as tournedos, pepper steak, and roasted chicken. Whatever you do, make sure you save some room for dessert. Selections include frangelico-poached pears, fresh raspberry custard tart, and maraschino chocolate cake. Odds are, after a meal at Café de Paris, you'll leave a little heavier. I did. Do I care? *"Non, je ne regrette rien."*

Cin Cin. 1154 Robson St. ☎ **604/688-7338.** www.cincin.net. Reservations recommended. Main courses C$16–C$40 (US$11–US$27). AE, DC, MC, V. Mon–Fri 11:30am–2:30pm; daily 5–11pm. Bus: 5, 22. MEDITERRANEAN.

Cin Cin is known almost as well for who eats here as for what's eaten here. Celebrities, models, politicians, and tourists all frequent this second-story, villa-style bistro. The dining room is built around the open kitchen, which is built around a huge alderwood-fired oven. The heated terrace overlooking Robson Street is an equally nice dining and people-watching spot. Food? Dishes range from elegant pastas and pizzas— capellini alla pomodoro, penne puttanesca, and pizza Margherita—to more substantial dishes such as rosemary-marinated rack of lamb, sea bass crusted with porcini mushrooms, and smoked chicken breast. The wine list is extensive, as is the selection of wines by the glass.

✪ **Delilah's.** 1789 Comox St. ☎ **604/687-3424.** Reservations accepted for parties of 6 or more. Fixed-price menu C$21–C$34 (US$14–US$23). AE, DC, ER, MC, V. Daily 5:30pm–midnight. Bus: 5 to Denman St. CONTINENTAL.

Walk down the steps from the Denman Place Mall and you've entered Delilah's French bordello of a room—red velvet chaise lounges, little private corner rooms, cherubim cavorting on the ceiling, and wall-mounted lamps with glass shades blown to look like orchids at their most outrageously sensuous. First order of business is a martini—Delilah's forte, and the fuel firing the laughter and conversation all around. The two-page martini list comes with everything from the basic Boston Tea Partini (Citron vodka and iced tea in a glass with sugared rim and lemon wedge) to the ultimate in Southern excess, the Miranda (pineapple, vodka, and fresh floating fruit). The staff are brisk and helpful and run to the Miranda side—flamboyant, friendly, and over the top. The menu is seafood heavy, which Delilah's does well, sticking to freshness and simple sauces such as the seared jumbo scallops with saffron risotto or grilled swordfish with a sun-dried cherry-cranberry compote. The chef gets a bit over his head with land-based fare, so go with the flow and order something from the sea.

The Fish House in Stanley Park. 8901 Stanley Park Dr. ☎ **604/ 681-7275.** www.fishhousestanleypark.com. Email: info@fishhousestanleypark. com. Reservations recommended. Main courses C$17–C$30 (US$11–US$20). AE, DC, DISC, JCB, MC, V. Mon–Sat 11:30am–10pm, Sun 11am–10pm. Bus: 1, 35, 135. SEAFOOD.

Reminiscent of a more genteel era, this white-clapboard clubhouse is surrounded by public tennis courts, bowling greens, and ancient cedar trees. Three rooms decorated in hunter green with dark wood and whitewashed accents complete the clubhouse atmosphere. The menu includes some innovative dishes, such as tender pan-seared Alaskan scallops with sweet chili glaze, lemongrass crusted prawn satay, and a smoked-salmon sampler. The oyster bar has at least a half dozen fresh varieties daily. The desserts are sumptuous. The restaurant and the bar draw a mix of golfers, strollers, and local execs.

Liliget Feast House & Catering. 1724 Davie St. ☎ **604/681-7044.** Reservations recommended. Main courses C$16–C$30 (US$11–US$20). Daily 5–10pm. AE, DC, ER, MC, V. Bus: 5. WEST COAST/FIRST NATIONS.

The nondescript entrance gives no hint of the unique restaurant located downstairs from an East Indian restaurant. The dining room is filled with natural cedar columns rising from the water-worn stone floor; the tables are sunken into stone platforms around a central cedar-and-stone walkway. Recorded song-stories about potlatch ceremonies play in the background. The food is traditional West Coast First Nations fare. Appetizers include grilled oysters, clam fritters, grilled prawns, breaded and fried smelt, salmon or venison soup, and bannock (delicious fried bread). Entrees like sweet alder-smoked salmon, lightly smoked duck breast, and grilled marinated venison steak are sumptuous. Local side dishes include fiddleheads, sea asparagus, and wild rice. Available in various sizes, the "Potlatch Platters" are an ideal way to sample a bit of everything. For people curious about modern First Nations culture, this is one experience that shouldn't be missed.

✪ **Raincity Grill.** 1193 Denman St. ☎ **604/685-7337.** www.raincitygrill. com. Reservations recommended. Main courses C$18–C$34 (US$12–US$23).

AE, DC, ER, MC, V. Mon–Fri 11:30am–2:30pm, Sat–Sun 10:30am–2:30pm; daily 5–10:30pm. Bus: 1, 5. WEST COAST.

Raincity's room is long and low and hugs the shoreline, the better to let the evening sun pour in. With the location—by English Bay Beach—and the spacious patio, you wonder if the owner didn't have to kill for the spot. Then you realize he's paying off the view with volume—they do pack 'em in at Raincity, making dinner more of a social occasion than you may have wished. Ah, but the view. And the food. Raincity's forte is local ingredients, West Coast style. That means appetizers of barbecued quail with a sage and goat-cheese polenta, crispy jumbo spot prawns, or a salad of smoked steelhead. Entrees include grilled Fraser Valley free-range chicken and fresh-caught spring salmon. And then there's the award-winning wine list. It's huge and, in keeping with the restaurant's theme, it sticks pretty close to home. Better yet, most varieties are available by the glass.

◎ The Teahouse Restaurant. Ferguson Point, Stanley Park. ☎ **604/ 669-3281.** www.sequoiarestaurants.com. Reservations required. Lunch main courses C$11–C$17 (US$7–US$11), dinner main courses C$17–C$28 (US$11–US$19). AE, MC, V. Mon–Sat 11:30am–2:30pm, Sun brunch 10:30am–2:30pm; daily 5:30–10pm. Bus: 135 or 1. CONTINENTAL.

Nestled into secluded Ferguson Point on the far side of Stanley Park are the low main building and greenhouse that make up The Teahouse Restaurant. The original structure was built in 1928 as a troop barracks, but time and careful decorating have transformed it into something resembling an English hunter's cottage. Soft light and muted florals create what would be one of Vancouver's most romantic locations—if it weren't for the busloads of big-eyed tourists. Still, even with lots of company, the Teahouse is a special spot. Book a table on the terrace—at least a day in advance, longer on weekend evenings—and arrive in time to dine while the sun slowly sets behind Vancouver Island far across the Strait of Georgia. And surprisingly enough, the food is consistently high caliber. The menu covers all the bases—a tender, delicious roasted rack of lamb is the signature dish, though the breast of Barbary duck with squash cappelletti and tarragon jus is a strong contender—yet still manages to do some innovative West Coast dishes, especially with fresh-caught salmon. Desserts include baked Alaska for two and orange Grand Marnier crème brûlée. Monday to Saturday between 2:30 and 5pm, the tearoom and (weather permitting) the patio serve light snacks and refreshments.

MODERATE

✪ **Cactus Club Café.** 1136 Robson St. ☎ **604/687-3278.** (Also 1508 Broadway at Granville, and 15 other locations.) Main courses C$6–C$19 (US$4–US$13). AE, MC, V. Daily 11am–midnight (later in the summer). SOUTHWESTERN.

So it's not fine dining. That's not why you come. The crowd is young, the room is fun, the beer is cold, and the waitresses invariably beautiful. Dinner almost always starts at the bar, 'cause there's always a line and they don't take reservations. Hang out, have a beer and some calamari, hot wings, or potato skins. When you finally reach your table, the food is consistently good—sizzling fajitas, six variations of Caesar salad, slow-cooked Jamaican-style jerk chicken, and succulent barbecued ribs.

✪ **Romano's Macaroni Grill at the Mansion.** 1523 Davie St. ☎ **604/689-4334.** Reservations recommended. Main courses C$8–C$16 (US$5–US$11), children's courses C$3.95–C$6 (US$2.65–US$4). AE, DC, MC, V. Sun–Thurs 4–10pm, Fri–Sat 4–11pm. Bus: 5. FAMILY-STYLE ITALIAN.

Housed in a huge stone mansion built in the early 20th century by sugar baron B. T. Rogers, Romano's is fun and casual. Wood paneling, stained-glass windows, and chandeliers surround tables covered with red-and-white checked tablecloths. The menu is Southern Italian, and the pastas are definitely favorites. This isn't high-concept Italian; the food is simple, understandable, and consistently good. You're charged for the house wine based on how much you pour from the bottle. Your kids will love the children's menu, which features lasagna and meat loaf as well as tasty pizzas, and the permissive staff that bursts into opera at the slightest provocation.

✪ **Sami's.** 1795 Pendrell St. ☎ **604/915-7264.** Bus: 5. Also at 986 W. Broadway. ☎ 604/736-8330. Bus: 10. Reservations not accepted. Main courses C$12 (US$8). DC, MC, V. Daily May–Oct 11:30am–2pm and 4–11pm, Nov–Apr 4–11pm. INDIAN.

Who says things don't get better with time? A year ago anyone wanting to try Sami Lalji's fabulous East-meets-West South Asian cooking had to make the trip out to a strip mall off West Broadway. True, the food was worth the journey, but so successful was this formula that Lalji decided to open a second Sami's downtown, just off Denman Street and a stroll-and-a-half from English Bay. Like the original, Sami's on Denman offers inventive and delicious dishes—try the Mumbai-blackened New York steak set atop spiked mashers with blueberry coriander jus—that won't put a large hole in your wallet. Service is efficient, if a tad too friendly.

Tanpopo. 1122 Denman St. ☎ **604/681-7777.** Reservations recommended. Main courses C$7–C$19 (US$4.70–US$13). AE, DC, MC, V. Daily 11:30am–10:30pm. Bus: 5. JAPANESE.

Occupying the second floor of a corner building on Denman Street, Tanpopo has a partial view of English Bay, a large patio, and a huge menu of hot and cold Japanese dishes. But the lines of people waiting 30 minutes or more for a table every night are here for the all-you-can-eat sushi. The unlimited fare includes the standards—makis, tuna and salmon sashimi, California and B.C. rolls—as well as cooked items such as tonkatsu, tempura, chicken kara-age, and broiled oysters. There are a couple of secrets to getting seated. Call ahead, but they take only an arbitrary percentage of reservations for dinner each day, or ask to sit at the sushi bar.

INEXPENSIVE

Gyoza King. 1508 Robson St. ☎ **604/669-8278.** Main courses C$6–C$13 (US$4–US$9). MC, V. Sat–Sun 11:30am–3pm; Mon–Sat 5:30pm–2am, Sun 5:30pm–midnight. Bus: 5. JAPANESE.

Gyoza King features an entire menu of *gyoza*—succulent Japanese dumplings filled with prawns, pork, vegetables, and other combinations—as well as Japanese noodles and staples like *katsu-don* (pork cutlet over rice) and *o-den* (a rich, hearty soup). This is the gathering spot for hordes of young Japanese visitors looking for cheap eats that still taste close to home cooking. Seating is divided among Western-style tables, the bar (where you can watch the chef in action), and the Japanese-style front table, which is reserved for larger groups if the restaurant is busy. The staff is very courteous and happy to explain the dishes if you're not familiar with Japanese cuisine.

Just One Thai Bistro. 1103 Denman St. ☎ **604/685-8989.** www.thaihouse.com. Main courses C$10–C$15 (US$7–US$10). AE, MC, V. Daily 11am–11pm. Bus: 5. THAI.

The rare four-headed golden Buddha at the entrance and the collection of smaller Buddhas set into wall recesses, combined with stone floors, palm trees, and fresh flowers, give this place the serenity of a temple and the exotic elegance of a Thai palace garden. The house specialty is Thai barbecue, the beef satay is outstanding, and the curries and stir-fries are equally good. If you have a cold, there's no better cure than a steaming bowl of *tom yum goong,* a hot-and-sour soup heaping with prawns, mushrooms, and lemongrass.

Rooster's Quarters. 836 Denman St. ☎ **604/689-8023.** Dishes C$8–C$14 (US$5–US$9). AE, MC, V. Daily 11am–11pm. Bus: 5. CANADIAN.

Rooster's Quarters offers the antidote to diet food. Succulent baby back ribs are served in a sweet-and-tangy, maple barbecue sauce, and the Québec-style barbecued chicken is crispy on the outside, tender and juicy on the inside. If those don't hit the spot, try the *poutine,* a Quebec dish of french fries covered with melted curd cheese and brown gravy. The decor is as casual as the menu and the atmosphere, with wallpaper images of garden scenes, potted plants, and shelves with over 300 rooster and chicken knickknacks. It can get a little crowded, but just pick out a table and seat yourself if there is no line. That's what the regulars do.

✪ **Stephos.** 1124 Davie St. ☎ **604/683-2555.** Reservations accepted for parties of 5 or more. Main courses C$4.25–C$10 (US$2.85–US$7). AE, MC, V. Daily 11:30am–11:30pm. Bus: 5. GREEK.

There's a reason Stephos is packed every day for lunch and dinner: The cuisine is simple Greek fare at its finest and cheapest. Customers line up outside to wait up to 30 minutes for a seat amid Greek travel posters, potted ivy, and whitewashed walls. (The average wait is about 10 to 15 minutes.) But once you're inside, the staff will never rush you out the door. Generous portions of delicious marinated lamb, chicken, pork, or beef over rice pilaf; *tzatziki* (a garlicky yogurt dip); and heaping platters of calamari are just a few of the offerings. While success is too often the downfall of a neighborhood restaurant, Stephos recently doubled in size and completely renovated, without raising its prices or compromising its quality.

4 The West Side

VERY EXPENSIVE

✪ **Bishop's.** 2183 W. Fourth Ave. ☎ **604/738-2025.** www.bishops.net. Reservations required. Main courses C$27–C$34 (US$18–US$23). AE, MC, V. Mon–Sat 5:30–11pm, Sun 5:30–10pm. Closed Jan 1–15. Bus: 4, 7. FRENCH.

🕐 Family-Friendly Restaurants

Romano's Macaroni Grill at the Mansion (*see p. 90*) The huge children's menu offers numerous dinner choices, and the friendly staff will even let kids wander up the inviting mansion staircase to explore the upper rooms.

Brothers Restaurant (*see p. 84*) Kids get balloons along with a special menu at this Gastown establishment.

Mark's Fiasco (*see p. 97*) Crayons on every paper-covered table and a friendly staff are coupled with excellent burgers and fries, pizzas, and pasta.

The Naam Restaurant (*see p. 98*) The Naam offers highchairs, very easy going service, a big patio for kids to run around on, and lots of good finger food.

Sophie's Cosmic Café (*see p. 99*) Great finger food, crayons and coloring paper, and lots and lots of eye-candy to keep kids occupied.

Any Chinese Restaurant Chinese families almost always dine en masse, so Chinese restaurants are used to accommodating children. And given the size of most menus, there's guaranteed to be something they'll like.

John Bishop doesn't behave like someone who owns what has been one of Vancouver's finest restaurants for the past decade. He personally greets you, escorts you to your table, and introduces you to an extensive list of fine wines and a menu he describes as "contemporary home cooking." The atmosphere is set by candlelight, white linen, and soft jazz playing in the background. The service is impeccable, and the food is even better. The menu changes three or four times a year. Recent dishes have included roast duck breast with sun-dried Okanagan Valley fruits and candied ginger glacé; steamed smoked black cod with new potatoes and horseradish sabayon; and marinated lamb with garlic mashed potatoes and a fresh mint, tomato, and balsamic vinegar reduction. If you plan on splurging one night, this is one of the best places to do it.

✪ **Lumière.** 2551 W. Broadway. ☎ **604/739-8185.** Reservations recommended. Tasting menu (8 courses) C$60–C$100 (US$40–US$67). AE, DC, MC, V. Tues–Sun 5:30–9:30pm. Bus: 9, 10. FRENCH/WEST COAST.

The success of this French-fusion dining experiment in the heart of Kitsilano has turned chef Rob Feenie into a very hot commodity. He now regularly jets off to New York to teach folks back east how to do it right. And how is that? Preparation and presentation are immaculately French, while ingredients are resolutely local, which makes for interesting surprises like fresh local ginger with the veal, or raspberries in the foie gras. Lumière's tasting menus are a series of 8 or 10 delightful plates that change with the season, perfectly matched to a local wine vintage (not included in the fixed price) and gorgeously presented. Diners simply choose one of the four tasting menus (including one vegetarian menu) and then sit back and let the pilots in Lumière's kitchen take them on a culinary journey they won't soon forget. If you can afford it, it's a voyage you shouldn't miss.

✪ **Tojo's Restaurant.** 777 W. Broadway. ☎ **604/872-8050.** Reservations required for sushi bar. Full dinners C$23–C$100 (US$15–US$67). AE, DC, MC, V. Mon–Sat 5–11pm. Closed Christmas week. Bus: 9. JAPANESE.

I had never met Hideki Tojo, or even tried his cooking, until one afternoon at Vancouver's first-ever sumo wrestling demonstration, when a diminutive man on the tatami mat next to me lifted up a bento box and proffered a tray of delicate sushi rolls. As two thunderous giants eyed each other in the ring, I picked out a piece with fresh salmon and popped it in my mouth. Incredible. A thousand pounds of screaming human flesh were smashing each other in the ring, but my attention was entirely captured by the exquisite flavors exploding in my mouth. Back in Tojo's modest sushi bar, the ever-changing menu offers such specialties as sea urchin on the half shell, herring roe, lobster claws, tuna, crab, and asparagus. I'd like to say I've since become a regular, but at the prices Tojo charges for his creations, regulars are either film stars or fully mortgaged for the next seven generations. Still, if you don't mind splurging and you want the very best, Tojo is your man.

EXPENSIVE

Pastis. 2153 W. Fourth Ave. ☎ **604/731-5020.** Reservations recommended. Main courses C$16–C$26 (US$11–US$17). AE, DC, MC, V. Mon–Sat 5:30–10:30pm, Sun 5:30–10pm. Bus: 4, 7. FRENCH.

For those seeking an elegant refuge on the city's west side there's Pastis, a candlelit French outpost in the heart of Kitsilano. Appetizers include escargot with portobello mushrooms and goat cheese with oven-dried tomatoes, while mains include such delectables as sweetbreads and morels cooked *en cocotte* (in a puff pastry), roasted duck with field rhubarb, and pan-seared ahi tuna on celery hearts. The accompanying wine list is excellent, as is the service.

The Smoking Dog. 1889 W. First Ave. ☎ **604/732-8811.** Reservations accepted. Main courses C$22–C$30 (US$15–US$20). AE, ER, MC, V. Mon–Fri 11:30am–2:30pm; Mon–Sat 5:30–10:30pm. Bus: 2, 22. FRENCH.

To date, the little Kitsilano neighborhood of Yorkville Mews has remained a local secret, perhaps because those few tourists who do venture into this delightful 1-block stretch are immediately confronted with a confusing variety of choices. Should one stop at one of the three cafes, the tapas bar, the sushi spot, the vegan cafe, or this traditional Parisian bistro, complete with patio umbrellas, obsequious waiters dressed in black, and a friendly bear of an owner who greets everyone at the door? Food-wise, the Dog is undoubtedly the best (and priciest) of the lot, featuring New York pepper steak, grilled halibut with Pernod sauce, and scallops with beurre blanc. If the weather allows, grab a spot on the heated patio and enjoy the bustling street life.

Star Anise. 1485 W. 12th Ave. ☎ **604/737-1485.** Reservations recommended. Main courses C$16–C$29 (US$11–US$19). AE, DC, ER, MC, V. Daily 11am–2pm and 5:30–midnight. Bus: 8, 10. PACIFIC NORTHWEST.

When the Star first opened back in 1993, Vancouver foodies were wowed by the kitchen's innovative combinations of Indian and Chinese flavors with traditional West Coast ingredients such as salmon and scallops. Since then, however, the fusion boundaries have been pushed even farther elsewhere, so the fickle foodie crowd has largely moved on. Too bad. Quality at this intimate eatery on the edge of South Granville's gallery row has never faltered. Ingredients are fresh, presentation scrumptious, and the service welcoming and knowledgeable. The wine list leans heavily on French and Californian vintages, and the small number available by the glass are well chosen. The room is warm to the point of being cozy, and owners Justin Cote and Ellen Lalji recently brought in Toronto chef Robert Fortin to rekindle some of that early excitement. Look for new dishes like chilled curry-mango soup with mint yogurt; roast rabbit-leg confit with sweet-potato galette, mizuna leaves, and Saskatoonberry chutney; or marinated ahi tuna with baby bok choy and cilantro pomme purée. As for dessert, however, tradition reigns: Cardamom crème brûlée is fine, but the real treat is chocolate tarte cooled with crème anglaise.

MODERATE

Andales. 3211 W. Broadway. ☎ **604/738-9782.** Reservations accepted. Main courses C$10–C$18 (US$7–US$12). AE, MC, V. Daily 11am–midnight. Bus: 9. MEXICAN/SPANISH.

Mexican food has had a hard time. In this part of the world it's gone from nonexistent to suddenly trendy to the equivalent of the '50s burger and fries. Nobody takes it seriously, not even the folks at Andales—they just do it well. The menu borrows a lot from Spain, so look for (and order) the sautéed squid with garlic and tortillas, chorizo con queso, or the 10-layer dip. All make a good beginning for fajitas, chimichangas, or paella. Better yet, order the Puntas a las Mexicanas, a kind of spicy beef stew. Your taste buds will thank you, even if your waistline won't. The decor leans toward bullfight posters and silly Mexican hats, but don't let that scare you off. Also at 1175 Davie St. (☎ **604/ 682-8820**).

Avenue One Bistro. 2209 W. First Ave. ☎ **604/734-1113.** Fax 604/ 421-0788. Main courses C$13–C$32 (US$9–US$21). MC, V. Daily 5:30– 11:30pm; Sat–Sun 9:30am–3:30pm. Bus 2 or 22. BISTRO/WEST COAST FUSION.

If you're ever in the neighborhood of Kits Beach and find yourself hankering after something more than nachos and home brew, walk two blocks uphill on Yew Street and sit yourself down at this little gem of a bistro. In the summer, the small patio provides a quiet refuge from the traffic and crowds. The tapas menu has plenty of nibbling options. The seared ahi tuna with lime and ginger or the mango salad masala prawns don't skimp on flavor or spices and are perfect for sharing. The main menu offers a range of seafood choices (as well as a few non-seafood options), but the real stars here are the lobsters. A steaming lobster pot set up outside the main entrance will cook them just right. Real seafood gluttons shouldn't miss the seafood platter (C$32/US$21) of lobster, crab, scallops, and mussels. Wines are mostly British Columbian, Italian, or French with a decent selection by the glass. As a juiced-up alternative, the bar offers 24 different martinis.

The Cat's Meow. 1540 Old Bridge St. (Granville Island). ☎ **604/647-2287.** Main courses C$8–C$19 (US$5–US$13). AE, MC, V. Mon–Fri 11am–midnight, Sat 9am–1am, Sun 9am–10am. Bus: 50. CASUAL.

Locals may be unfamiliar with the Cat's Meow, but if you tell them it's where Isadora's used to be, their eyes will light up. The long-running cooperative restaurant was sadly missed when it finally closed its doors. Fortunately, the Cat's Meow has done a good job filling the delightful room and patio by providing tasty and affordable sandwiches, burgers, pizzas, and pastas. Appetizers such as crab cakes and salmon canapés perfectly match a beer on a sunny day. The back patio overlooks the kids' water-play area, where they can frolic in the sprinklers and fountains. Later on in the evening kids and parents give way to a younger crowd.

Mark's Fiasco. 2468 Bayswater St. (at W. Broadway). ☎ **604/734-1325.** Reservations recommended. Main courses C$7–C$19 (US$4.70–US$13). AE, MC, V. Daily 11:45am–11pm (bar stays open later). Bus 9. STEAK.

Mark's is the casual pub of choice for the Kitsilano jock-boy crowd, with a brass bar, 15 microbrews on tap, and at least four channels of sports on strategically placed boob tubes. On the restaurant side, Mark's offers a well-rounded menu of pastas, pizzas, seafood, and meat dishes. Appetizers include steamed mussels, fried calamari, and a delicious baked spinach dip. With a burger and fries starting at C$7 (US$4.70), crayons on every paper-covered table, and a congenial staff, Mark's is also kid-friendly.

✪ **Vij's.** 1480 W. 11th Ave. ☎ **604/736-6664.** Fax 604/736-3701. Reservations not accepted. Main courses C$14–C$19 (US$9–US$13). AE, MC, V. Daily 5:30–10pm, later if busy. Bus: 8, 10. INDIAN.

Vij doesn't take reservations, but then he really doesn't have to: There's a line outside his door every single night. Patrons huddled under Vij's violet neon sign are treated to complimentary tea and *papadums*. For a few dollars more, an Indian Pale Ale (IPA) can be rustled up to help soothe the wait. Inside, the decor is as warm and subtle as the seasonings, which are all roasted and ground by hand, then used with studied delicacy. The menu changes monthly, though some of the more popular entrees remain constants. Recent offerings included coconut curried chicken and saffron rice, and marinated pork medallions with garlic-yogurt curry and *naan* (flat bread). Vegetarian selections abound, including curried vegetable rice pilaf with cilantro cream sauce, and Indian lentils with naan and *raita* (yogurt-mint sauce). The wine and beer list is short but carefully selected. And for teetotalers, Vij has developed a souped-up version of the traditional Indian chai, the chaiuccino.

INEXPENSIVE

✪ **Annapurna.** 1812 W. Fourth Ave. ☎ **604/736-5959.** Main courses C$10–C$11 (US$7). AE, MC, V. Daily 11:30am–10pm. Bus: 4, 7. INDIAN/ VEGETARIAN.

Annapurna gets my vote as Vancouver's best vegetarian restaurant, and it's up there in the running for best Indian as well. A Kitsilano favorite, the restaurant's small dining room is hung with dozens of rice-paper lamps in whites, yellows, oranges, and reds that, when combined with the mirrors, bask the room in a soft, warm glow. The menu is all vegetarian, but with the amazing combinations of Indian spices, herbs, and local vegetables, the dishes are rich and satisfying. Appetizers include samosas, pakoras, and lentil dumplings soaked in tangy yogurt with chutney. A variety of breads, such as paratha, naans, and chapatis, are served piping hot. Entrees such as *aloo-ghobi* (potato curry with cauliflower, onions, and cilantro) or *navrattan korma* (seasonal vegetables simmered in poppy-seed paste, flavored with saffron, aniseed, and sliced almonds) can be prepared from mild to screaming hot. The wine list is small but very reasonably priced. With food, wine, and atmosphere this good, Annapurna lets you feel like you're splurging when you're not.

The Naam Restaurant. 2724 W. Fourth Ave. ☎ **604/738-7151.** www. thenaam.com. Reservations accepted on weekdays only. Main courses C$4.95–C$10 (US$3.30–US$7). AE, ER, MC, V. Daily 24 hours. Live music every night 7–10pm. Bus: 4, 22. VEGETARIAN.

Back in the sixties, when Kitsilano was Canada's hippie haven, the Naam was tie-dye central. Things have changed a tad since then, but Vancouver's oldest vegetarian and natural-food restaurant retains a pleasant granola feel. The decor is simple, earnest, and welcoming: well-worn wooden tables and chairs, plants, and an assortment of local art. The brazenly healthy fare ranges from open-face tofu melts, enchiladas, and burritos to tofu teriyaki, Thai noodles, and a variety of pita pizzas. The sesame spice fries are a Vancouver institution. And though the Naam is not yet vegan, they do cater to the anti-egg-and-cheese crowd with specialties like the macrobiotic Dragon Bowl of brown rice, tofu, peanut sauce, sprouts, and steamed vegetables. As with all Naam dishes, quality is excellent. The only real trick is to arrive well before you're actually hungry. Serving staff will invariably disappear on an extended search for personal fulfillment at some point during your meal.

Shao Lin Noodle Restaurant. 548 W. Broadway. ☎ **604/873-1816.** Main courses C$5–C$10 (US$3.35–US$7). Daily 24 hours. No credit cards. Mon–Fri 11am–3pm, Sat–Sun 11:30am–3:30pm; daily 5–9:30pm. Bus: 9. CHINESE.

Why play with your food when you can eat here and watch the professionals do it? Traditional Chinese noodle shops are a rarity in North America, which is a shame because the experience is so much fun. Enclosed by glass, the noodle makers toss the pasta, stretch it over their heads, spin it around, and dramatically transform it into fine strands. All noodles are handmade and contain no MSG. (Unfortunately, the classic trick of cutting the noodle dough on top of their heads with a cleaver is banned in Canada. However, there is a picture of it on the wall.) Bowls of noodles are served with a vast selection of meat and vegetable combinations. Tea is poured from a 3-foot-long pot originally designed to allow male servants to maintain a polite distance from an 18th-century Chinese empress.

Sophie's Cosmic Café. 2095 W. Fourth Ave. ☎ **604/732-6810.** Main courses C$4.85–C$16 (US$3.25–US$11). MC, V. Daily 8am–9:30pm. Bus: 4, 7. FAMILY-STYLE AMERICAN.

Sophie's is readily identifiable by the giant silver knife and fork bolted to the outside front walls. Inside, every available space has been crammed with toys and knickknacks from the 1950s and 1960s, creating an experience much akin to having lunch inside a McDonald's Happy Meal. For that very reason, children are inordinately fond of Sophie's. Crayons and coloring paper are always on-hand. The menu is simple: pastas, burgers and fries, great milkshakes, and a few classic Mexican dishes. The slightly spicy breakfast menu is hugely popular with Kitsilano locals. Lines can stretch to half an hour on post-hangover Sunday mornings, but the staff eases the wait with outdoor coffee.

5   The East Side

Many of these "east side" restaurants are on Main Street, which is on the borderlands between upscale west and working-class east. Main thus has some funky urban authenticity to go with its ever-increasing trendiness.

EXPENSIVE

Sun Sui Wah. 3888 Main St. ☎ **604/872-8822.** Also in Richmond: 102 Alderbridge Place, 4940 No. 3 Rd. ☎ 604/273-8208. Reservations accepted. Main courses C$11–C$50 (US$7–US$34). AE, MC, V. Daily 10:30am–3pm and 5–10:30pm. Bus: 3. CHINESE/SEAFOOD.

One of the most elegant and sophisticated Chinese restaurants in town, the award-winning Sun Sui Wah is well known for its seafood. Fresh and varied, the catch of the day can include fresh crab, rock cod, geoduck, scallops, abalone, oyster, prawns, and more. Pick your own from the tank or order from the menu if you don't like to meet your food eye-to-eye before it's cooked. The staff is quite helpful for those unfamiliar with the cuisine. Dim sum is a treat, with the emphasis on seafood. Just point and choose. For land lovers and vegetarians there are plenty of other choices, though they are missing out on one of the best seafood feasts in town.

MODERATE

✪ **The Brickhouse Bistro.** 730 Main St. ☎ **604/689-8645.** Reservations accepted. Main courses C$10–C$16 (US$7–US$11). MC, V. Tues–Thurs 5:30pm–1am, Fri–Sat 5:30pm–2:30am. Bus: 3. BISTRO.

There were once two partners who opened a bar in a slightly seedy section of town. It ought to do well, they reasoned, for there are many with money who have recently bought condos, and right now they have nowhere to drink. And do well it did. Encouraged, the partners refurbished the room right above their very successful bar, and opened up a bistro—a casual funky kind of place, all bricks and wood beams. They hired a chef capable of cooking up simple but superior food, dishes like New Zealand rib eye in Madeira jus and roast potatoes or specials of fresh fish. To lure customers, the partners kept their prices very low. A selection of B.C. wines was also available, at two-thirds the price charged by other bistros. Word of the cuisine and ambiance has spread far and wide enough to make dinner on a weekend a pleasant social affair, but the Brickhouse is still a tasty steal.

✪ **Bukowski's.** 1447 Commercial Dr. ☎ **604/253-4770.** Reservations accepted. Main courses C$8–C$15 (US$5–US$10). MC, V. Mon–Thurs 5pm–1am, Fri–Sat noon–1am, Sun noon–midnight. Live Jazz Mon–Tues. Bus: 20. BISTRO/WEST COAST FUSION.

The last and booziest of the American Beat poets gets what he always wanted, a bistro named in his honor. So what if he never made it to Vancouver, much less the Bohemian-and-becoming-more-so strip on Commercial Drive. The cuisine is not Polish, but instead a fusion-y kind of comfort food perfectly suited to casual dining. Think beef satay, charbroiled chicken on focaccia bread, catfish with black-bean salsa, or steak with peppercorn garlic jus. And beer. Or any one of several wines featured on a daily blackboard. Even more attractive than the food is the friendly, buzzing atmosphere, and a clientele slightly too rich to really be artists, but hip enough to dress the part. Service is wonderfully unhurried. Dawdle for hours if you will, reading the snippets of Sylvia Plath inscribed on your table.

The Locus Café. 4121 Main St. ☎ **604/708-4121.** Reservations not accepted. Main courses C$9–C$14 (US$6–US$9). AE, MC, V. Mon–Fri 11:30am–1am, Sat 11am–1am, Sun 11am–midnight. Bus: 3. SOUTHWEST/FUSION.

Even if you arrive on your lonesome, you'll have plenty of friends soon enough—the Locus is a cheek-by-jowl kind of place, filled to bursting with a friendly, funky crowd of arty Mount Pleasant types. A big bar dominates the center of the room, overhung with "swamp-gothic" lacquer trees and surrounded by a tier of stools with booths and tiny tables farther out. Cuisine originated in the American Southwest but picked up an edge somewhere along the way—think roasted half-chicken with a cumin-coriander crust and sambuca citrus demi-glace. Keep an eye out for fish specials, such as grilled tomba tuna with a grapefruit and mango glaze. The pan-seared calamari makes a perfect appetizer. Bowen Island brewery provides the beer, so quality's high. You're only real problem is catching the eye of the hyper-busy bartender.

✪ **The Reef.** 4172 Main St. ☎ **604/874-JERK.** www.thereefrestaurant. com. Reservations accepted. Main courses C$9–C$15 (US$6–US$10). AE, MC, V. Sun–Wed 11am–midnight, Thurs–Sat 11am–1am. Bus: 3. CARRIBEAN.

The JERK in the phone number refers neither to a Steve Martin film nor to the guy two cubicles down from you at the office, but rather to a spicy marinade: bay leaves, scotch bonnets, allspice, garlic, soya, green onions, vinegar, and cloves. The result is piquant, scrumptious chicken. The Reef serves up a number of jerk dishes, including their signature quarter jerk chicken breast. Other dishes are equally delightful, including a tropical salad of fresh mango, red onions, and tomatoes; shrimp with coconut milk and lime juice; grilled blue marlin; and Trenton spiced ribs. Choose a glass of wine from the thoughtfully selected list and you've got gourmet dining in a great room—cleverly decorated with chicken wire, bamboo, and original mixed media artwork—at a bargain price. Afternoons, the tiny patio is drenched in sunlight, while in the evenings a DJ spins the sounds of the Islands.

Sun Wong Kee. 4136 Main St. ☎ **604/879-7231.** Reservations accepted. Main courses C$9–C$15 (US$6–US$10). AE, MC, V. Wed–Mon 11am–3pm and 5pm–midnight. Bus: 3. CHINESE.

This is a great little place for tasty everyday Chinese cooking. The thick menu has all the usual suspects, but the real fun is the specials board above the door to the kitchen. It's there you'll find fresh delectables such as live crab, lobster, and rock cod. As always with Chinese food, it's best to bring lots of folks so you can share many plates, but if you go for the spicy salt spareribs, make sure you get yours first. The spicy crab—said to be the best in the city—is another dish tough to share with competitive eaters. The room is a crab's leg up from the basic Chinese eatery—tablecloths are linen and some thought has gone into the decor. Not that any of Sun Wong Kee's many Chinese patrons seem to notice. Whole families, from Grandma down through four generations, sit around tables set for 14, intent on nothing but the food.

6 The North Shore

EXPENSIVE

✪ **The Beach House at Dundarave Pier.** 150 25th St., West Vancouver. ☎ **604/922-1414.** www.beachhousewestvan.com. Reservations recommended. Lunch main courses C$12–C$16 (US$8–US$11), dinner main courses C$19–C$35 (US$13–US$23). AE, DC, ER, MC, V. Mon–Fri 11:30am–3pm; Sat–Sun brunch 11am–3pm; Sun–Thurs 5–10pm, Fri–Sat 5–11pm. Light appetizers served 3–5pm. Bus: 255 to Ambleside Pier. WEST COAST.

Set on a dramatic waterfront location, the House offers a panoramic view of English Bay. Those on the heated patio also get sunshine, but they miss out on the rich interior of this restored 1912 teahouse. The food is consistently good—innovative, but not so experimental that it leaves the staid West Van burghers gasping for breath. Appetizers include soft-shell crab with salt-and-fire jelly; grilled scallops with baby spinach, crispy onions, and red-pepper cream; and grilled portobello mushroom with Okanagan Valley goat cheese. Entrees have included garlic-crusted rack of lamb with honey balsamic glaze and baked striped sea bass with basil mousse and rock prawns. The wine list is award-winning.

✪ **The Salmon House on the Hill.** 2229 Folkstone Way, West Vancouver. ☎ **604/926-3212.** www.salmonhouse.com. Reservations recommended for dinner. Lunch main courses C$6–C$15 (US$4–US$10), dinner main courses C$16–C$30 (US$11–US$20). AE, DC, ER, MC, V. Mon–Sat 11:30am–2:30pm, Sun brunch 11am–2:30pm; Sun–Thurs 5–10pm, Fri–Sat 5–10:30pm. Bus: 251 to Queens St. WEST COAST/SEAFOOD.

High above West Vancouver, The Salmon House offers a spectacular view of the city and Burrard Inlet. The rough-hewn cedar walls are adorned with a growing collection of indigenous West Coast art; the colorful masks and figurative works by modern First Nations craftspeople relate the traditional myths and legends of the ancient culture. Chef Dan Atkinson's menu reflects his extensive research into local ingredients and First Nations cuisine. An alderwood-fired grill dominates the kitchen, lending a delicious flavor to many of the dishes. To start, we recommend the Salmon House Sampler, featuring salmon, fresh salsas, chutneys, and relishes. Entrees include grilled British Columbia salmon with local prawns, fiddlehead ferns, and Fraser Valley blueberry salsa; Fraser Valley free-range chicken with roasted onion jus; and smoked West Coast black cod with wasabi cream and balsamic mustard-seed vinaigrette. Desserts bear little resemblance to early First Nations cuisine: mocha torte with pecan-toffee crust, turtle pie, blueberry tiramisu. The wine list earned an award of excellence from *Wine Spectator.*

INEXPENSIVE

The Tomahawk Restaurant. 1550 Philip Ave., North Vancouver. ☎ **604/988-2612.** Reservations not accepted. Main courses C$4.25–C$17 (US$2.85–US$11). MC, V. Sun–Thurs 8am–9pm, Fri–Sat 8am–10pm. Bus: 239 to Philip Ave. FAMILY-STYLE AMERICAN.

Just a typical American-style diner, but with one critical difference that makes it worth a visit. It's not that a teenaged

Brian Adams used to work here. Nor is it simply longevity—the restaurant's been around since 1926. The Tomahawk's worth a visit 'cause it's wall-to-wall and roof-beam tall with Native knickknacks and gewgaws and some truly first-class First Nations art. It all started back in the 1930s when proprietor Chick Chamberlain began taking carvings from Burrard Band Natives in lieu of payment. Over the years the collection just kept growing. So how's the food? Good, in a burgers-and-fries kind of way. Portions are large, burgers are tasty, and milkshakes come so thick the spoon stands up straight like a totem pole. If you're on the North Shore and wracked by hunger, the Tomahawk's worth a chop.

7 Coffee & Sweets

Death by Chocolate. Various locations, including 1001 Denman St., ☎ **604/899-CHOC,** and 1598 W. Broadway, ☎ 604/730-CHOC. www. deathbychocolate.com. C$4.95–C$10 (US$3.30–US$7). AE, MC, V. Generally open until midnight; hours vary at each location.

If your idea of heaven includes rich desserts, then Death by Chocolate is the place to get dispatched. The large menu comes with photographs, but beware—objects on the page may appear smaller than they are; sharing is encouraged. Some of the tested favorites include: Simply Irresistible—a chocolate pudding with fudge center, covered in chocolate sauce; and Devil in Disguise—mocha fudge ice cream in Kahlúa chocolate sauce. Guilt-prone types can salve their consciences with a more wholesome, fruitier dessert like Sticky Bits—strawberries with chocolate sauce and whipped cream for dipping. Hell-bent ultra-chocoholics, on the other hand, should order up a Multitude of Sins—chocolate cake, chocolate mousse, chocolate crepes stuffed with fruit, chocolate sauce, and, well, you get the idea. To wash it all down, the restaurant serves a variety of coffees, teas, and hot chocolates, as well as alcoholic beverages.

Exploring Vancouver

A city perched on the edge of a great wilderness, Vancouver offers unmatched opportunities for exploring the outdoors. Paradoxically, within the city limits, Vancouver is intensely urban. There are sidewalk cafes to match those in Paris, and shopping streets that rival London's. The forest of downtown residential high-rises looks somewhat like New York, while the buzz and movement of Chinatown reminds you of San Francisco or Canton. Comparisons with other places soon begin to pall, however, as you come to realize that Vancouver is entirely its own creation: a self-confident, sparklingly beautiful city, like no place else on earth.

1 The Top Attractions

DOWNTOWN & THE WEST END

B.C. Sports Hall of Fame and Museum. 777 Pacific Blvd. S. (B.C. Place Stadium, Gate A, Beatty and Robson sts.). ☎ **604/687-5520.** Admission C$6 (US$4) adults, C$4 (US$2.70) seniors and students, free for children under 5. MC, V. Daily 10am–5pm. SkyTrain: Stadium. Bus: 15.

A great destination for sports-minded, active kids with endless energy, the museum's Participation Gallery features interactive running, climbing, throwing, riding, rowing, and racing competitions where they can pit themselves against video-simulated competitors. You'll also find a climbing wall, pitching cages, and stationary bikes. For parents, the Hall of Champions and Builders Hall document the achievements of British Columbia's most lauded athletes, including runners Terry Fox and Rick Hansen and the Vancouver Canucks hockey team, in both video and photographic displays.

The Canadian Craft Museum. 639 Hornby St. ☎ **604/687-8266.** E-mail: craftmus@direct.ca. Admission C$5 (US$3.35) adults, C$3 (US$2) seniors and students, free for children under 12. Thurs evening 5–9pm admission is by donation. Mon–Wed and Fri–Sat 10am–5pm, Thurs 10am–9pm, Sun and holidays noon–5pm. Closed Tues Sept–May. SkyTrain: Granville. Bus: 3.

Hidden behind the Cathedral Place building at the edge of a beautiful outdoor courtyard, the Canadian Craft Museum presents a vast collection of Canadian and international crafts in glass, wood, metal, clay, and fiber. A top-quality small museum, it will appeal to anyone who devours interior design and architectural magazines. Recent shows have included an impressive display of carved Chinese signature seals and calligraphy, British Columbian artist Bill Reid's gold and silver jewelry, and furniture created by Canada's best industrial designers. You can also purchase some of the unique ceramics, sculptures, and crafts in the museum's gift store.

✪ **Vancouver Aquarium Marine Science Centre.** Stanley Park. ☎ **604/ 659-FISH.** www.vanaqua.org. Admission C$13 (US$9) adults, C$11 (US$7) seniors/students/youths 13–18, C$9 (US$6) children 4–12, free for children under 4, C$43 (US$29) family. June 23–Sept 4 daily 9:30am–7pm; Sept 5– June 22 daily 10am–5:30pm. Parking C$5 (US$3.35) summer, C$3 (US$2) winter. Bus: 135; "Around the Park" shuttle bus June–Sept only.

One of North America's largest and best, the Vancouver Aquarium houses more than 8,000 marine species, most in meticulously re-created environments.

In the icy-blue Arctic Canada exhibit, you can see beluga whales whistling and blowing water at unwary onlookers. Human-sized freshwater fish inhabit the Amazon Rain Forest gallery, while overhead an hourly rainstorm is unleashed in an atrium and exhibit that houses three-toed sloths, brilliant blue and green poison tree frogs, and piranhas. Regal angelfish glide through a re-creation of Indonesia's Bunaken National Park coral reef, and blacktip reef sharks menacingly scour the Tropical Gallery's waters. (Call for the shark and sea otter feeding times.) The Pacific Canada exhibit is dedicated to sea life indigenous to B.C. waters, including the Pacific salmon and the giant Pacific octopus.

On the Marine Mammal Deck, there are sea otters, Steller sea lions, beluga whales, and a Pacific white-sided dolphin. During regularly scheduled shows, the aquarium staff explain marine mammal behavior while working with these impressive creatures.

In addition to tours, the aquarium has a regular program of special events, including behind-the-scenes tours, sleepover programs for children and youths, and evening barbecues.

The **Clamshell Gift Shop** (☎ **604/659-3413**) sells a great collection of marine-oriented mementos, crafts, souvenirs, and books. The aquarium's Upstream Café is open daily for lunch, snacks, and coffee.

Vancouver Art Gallery. 750 Hornby St. ☎ **604/662-4719** or 604/662-4700. www.vanartgallery.bc.ca. Admission C$10 (US$7) adults and seniors, C$6 (US$4) students and youths, free for children 12 and under, C$30 (US$20) family. Thurs 6–9pm by donation. Mon–Wed and Fri–Sun 10am–5:30pm, Thurs 10am–9pm. SkyTrain: Granville. Bus: 3.

Designed as a courthouse by British Columbia's leading early 20th-century architect Francis Rattenbury (the architect of Victoria's Empress Hotel and the Parliament buildings), and renovated into an art gallery by British Columbia's leading late 20th-century architect Arthur Erickson (see the special feature in this chapter), the VAG is an excellent stop for anyone who wants to see what sets Canadian and West Coast art apart from the rest of the world. There is an impressive collection of paintings by B.C. Native Emily Carr, as well as examples of a unique Canadian art style created during the 1920s by members of the "Group of Seven," who included Vancouver painter Fred Varley. The first Canadian artists to break free from the then-dominant European schools of painting, their bold and dramatic style was strongly influenced by the dramatic Canadian landscape. On the contemporary side, the VAG hosts rotating exhibits of sculpture, graphics, photography, and video art, some from B.C. artists, many from around the world. Geared to younger audiences, the Annex Gallery offers rotating presentations of visually exciting educational exhibits. Thanks to its selection of art books, crafts, multiples (original prints, jewelry, and objects produced and signed by artists), and toys (lots of toys), the Gift Shop is a favorite destination. The Gallery Café, overlooking the Sculpture Garden, is a great place to snack.

THE WEST SIDE

✪ **Museum of Anthropology.** 6393 NW Marine Dr. ☎ **604/822-3825.** www.moa.ubc.ca. Admission C$7 (US$4.70) adults, C$5 (US$3.35) seniors, C$4 (US$2.70) students and children 6–18, free for children under 6, C$20 (US$13) family. Free Tues after 5pm. May 20–Sept 30 Wed–Mon 10am–5pm, Tues 10am–9pm; Oct 1–May 19 Wed–Sun 11am–5pm, Tues 11am–9pm. Closed Dec 25–26. Bus: 4 or 10.

This isn't just any old museum. In 1976, architect Arthur Erickson (see the special feature in this chapter) re-created a classic Native post-and-beam structure out of modern

Downtown Vancouver Attractions

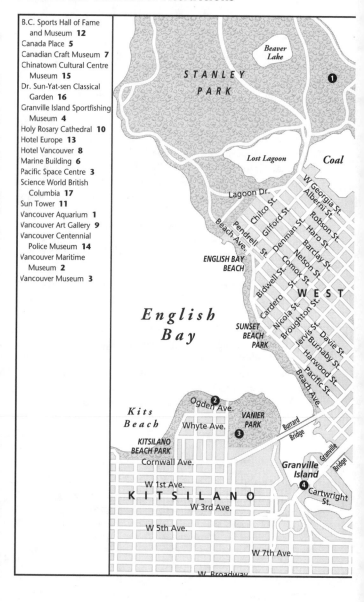

Burrard

Inlet

Harbour

Canada
Place
5

Canadian
National
S.S. Pier

Centennial
Pier

W. Hastings St.
W. Pender St. **6**

E N D

Melville St.

Bute St.
Thurlow St.

i Dunsmuir St.
7
8

NELSON
PARK

Burrard St.

9

Robson
Sq.

Hornby St.

Granville St.

Seymour St.

Robson St.

W. Georgia St.
10

Post
11 Office

W. Cordova St.

GASTOWN

Water St.

Victory
Sq.

Abbott St.

Carrall St.
13

Railway St.

Powell St. JAPAN
E. Cordova St. TOWN
14

E. Hastings St.

CHINATOWN

Gore Ave.

15

Dunlevy Ave.

16

Howe St.

Helmcken St.

Richards St.

Homer St.

Hamilton St.

Cambie St.

Beatty St.

Bus
Depot

12

Stadium

Main St.

17

VIA/Amtrak Station

Terminal Ave.

Davie St.

Drake St.

Pacific Blvd.

Cambie
St Bridge

Creek

Québec St.

Great Northern

False

W 1st Ave.

W 3rd Ave.

M O U N T

P L E A S A N T

Way

W 5th Ave.

F A I R V I E W

W 7th Ave.

Information *i*
Post Office ✉

0   1/2 mi
0   .5 km

concrete and glass to house one of the world's finest collections of West Coast Native art.

You enter through doors that resemble a huge, carved bent-cedar box. Artifacts from potlatch ceremonies flank the ramp leading to the Great Hall's collection of totem poles. Haida artist Bill Reid's touchable cedar bear and sea-wolf sculptures sit at the Cross Roads, where source books rest on a reading-height display wall. Reid's masterpiece, *The Raven and the First Men,* is worth the price of admission all by itself. The huge carving in glowing yellow cedar depicts a Haida creation myth, in which Raven—the trickster—coaxes humanity out into the world from its birthplace in a clamshell. Some of Reid's fabulous creations in gold and silver are also on display. Intriguingly, curators have recently begun salting contemporary Native artworks in among the old masterpieces—a sign that West Coast artistic traditions are alive and well.

The Koerner Ceramics Gallery's European collection is unique to North America. The Masterpiece Gallery's argillite sculptures, beaded jewelry, and hand-carved ceremonial masks lead the way to the Visible Storage Galleries, where more than 15,000 artifacts are arranged by culture. You can open the glass-topped drawers to view small treasures and stroll past larger pieces housed in tall glass cases. (You can also read more detailed information about the items in conveniently placed reference catalogues.)

The gift shop sells contemporary Native artwork as well as books and publications. Don't forget to take a walk around the grounds behind the museum. Overlooking Point Grey are two longhouses built according to the Haida tribal style, resting on the traditional north-south axis. Ten hand-carved totem poles stand in attendance along with contemporary carvings on the longhouse facades.

Pacific Space Centre. 1100 Chestnut St., in Vanier Park. ☎ **604/738-STAR.** www.hrmacmillanspacecentre.com. Admission C$13 (US$9) adults, C$10 (US$7) seniors and youths 11–18, C$9 (US$6) children 5–10, C$5 (US$3.35) children under 5, C$40 (US$27) family (up to 5, maximum 2 adults). Additional family members C$8 (US$5) each. Additional Virtual Voyages experiences C$5 (US$3.35) each. Tues–Sun 10am–5pm, daily in July and Aug. Closed Dec 25. Bus: 22.

Housed in the same building as the Vancouver Museum, the space center and observatory has hands-on displays and exhibits that will delight both kids and astronomy, space, science, and computer buffs. In the Virtual Voyages Simulator you can go on a voyage to Mars, or collide with an oncoming comet. In the interactive Cosmic Courtyard, you can look at an Apollo 17 manned-satellite engine, try your hand at designing a spacecraft, or maneuver a lunar robot. In the GroundStation Canada Theatre there are video presentations about Canada's contributions to the space program, and about space in general. The StarTheatre shows movies—many of them for children—on an overhead dome. And on selected nights, you can shoot the moon through a half-meter telescope for C$10 (US$7) per camera (☎ **604/736-2655**).

✪ **Science World British Columbia.** 1455 Quebec St. ☎ **604/443-7443**. www.scienceworld.bc.ca. Admission C$12 (US$8) adults; C$8 (US$5) seniors, students, and children; free for children under 4. Combination tickets available for OMNIMAX film. Mon–Fri 10am–5pm, Sat–Sun and holidays 10am–6pm. SkyTrain: Main Street–Science World.

Science World is impossible to miss. It's in the big blinking geodesic dome on the eastern end of False Creek. Inside, it's a hands-on scientific discovery center where you and your kids can light up a plasma ball, walk through a 1,700-square-foot maze, lose your shadow, walk through the interior of a camera, create a cyclone, blow square bubbles, watch a zucchini explode as it's charged with 80,000 volts, stand inside a beaver lodge, play in wrist-deep magnetic liquids, create music with a giant synthesizer, and watch mind-blowing three-dimensional slide and laser shows as well as other optical effects. In the OMNIMAX Theatre—a huge projecting screen equipped with Surround-Sound—you can take a death-defying flight through the Grand Canyon and perform other spine-tingling feats. Science World also hosts many spectacular traveling exhibitions, such as "Backyard Monsters," which features giant robotic bugs. Call for presentation times and current productions. When it's time for a break, the cafeteria and a science-oriented gift shop offer refreshments and shopping.

✪ **Vancouver Maritime Museum.** 1905 Ogden Ave., in Vanier Park. ☎ **604/257-8300**. www.vmm.bc.ca. Admission C$7 (US$4.70) adults, C$4 (US$2.70) seniors and students, free for children under 6, C$16 (US$11) family. Daily 10am–5pm; closed Mon from Labour Day to Victoria Day (early Oct to late May). Bus: 22, then walk 4 blocks north on Cypress St. Boat: False Creek Ferries dock at Heritage Harbour.

This museum houses the 1920s RCMP Arctic patrol vessel *St. Roch.* That may not sound like much, but from the time Chris Columbus proved that the continent directly west of Europe was not Cathay, every European explorer's overriding quest was to find the Northwest Passage, the seagoing short-cut to the riches of the east. This little ship is the one that finally did it. The boat has been preserved in a large atrium, with most of its original stores and equipment still onboard. Tours of the *St. Roch* are particularly popular with children—they get to clamber around the boat poking and prodding stuff.

The other half of the museum holds intricate ship models (a few too many of these, unless you're a serious model buff), antique wood and brass fittings, maps, prints, and a number of permanent exhibits including "Pirates!," a treasure chest of an exhibit filled with pirate lore, artifacts, and a miniature ship where kids can dress up and play pirate for the day. The aft cabin of a schooner and the bridge of a modern tugboat lead the way to the Children's Maritime Discovery Centre, which houses computers, a wall of drawers filled with ship models and artifacts, and observation telescopes aimed at the ships moored in English Bay. You can maneuver an underwater robot in a large water tank. And kids can dress up in more naval costumes.

If the weather is pleasant, be sure to walk across the expansive front lawn at the edge of False Creek to Heritage Harbour, where the museum keeps a collection of beautiful vintage boats. It's also where you can catch the miniferry to Granville Island or the West End.

Vancouver Museum. 1100 Chestnut St. ☎ **604/736-4431.** www.vanmuseum.bc.ca. Admission C$8 (US$5) adults, C$6 (US$4) youths. Group rates available. Fri–Wed 10am–5pm, Thurs 10am–9pm. Closed Mon Sept–June. Bus: 22, then walk 3 blocks south on Cornwall Ave. Boat: Granville Island Ferry to Heritage Harbour.

Established in 1894, the Vancouver Museum is dedicated to amassing evidence of the city's history, from its days as a Native settlement and European outpost to the city's early 20th-century maturation into a modern urban center. The exhibits allow visitors to walk through the steerage deck of a 19th-century passenger ship, peek into a Hudson's Bay Company frontier trading post, or take a seat in an 1880s Canadian-Pacific Railway passenger car. Re-creations of Victorian and Edwardian rooms show how early Vancouverites decorated their homes. Rotating exhibits include a display of the museum's collection of neon signage from Vancouver's former glory days as the West Coast's glitziest neon-sign–filled metropolis during the 1940s and 1950s.

The museum's self-service vending-machine lunch area offers simple sandwiches and refreshments. The gift shop sells contemporary Native jewelry and crafts as well as publications and souvenirs.

GASTOWN & CHINATOWN

Chinese Cultural Centre Museum Archives. 555 Columbia St. ☎ **604/ 687-0729.** Free admission. Mon–Sat 11am–5pm. Bus: 4 or 7.

Recently opened, this small museum has rotating exhibits of photographs, documents, and other artifacts depicting the Chinese experience in Canada. Many of the exhibits are designed to help promote cultural understanding.

✪ **The Dr. Sun-Yat-sen Classical Garden.** 578 Carrall St. ☎ **604/ 689-7133.** www.discovervancouver.com/sun. E-mail: sunyatsen@telus.net. C$8 (US$5) adults, C$6 (US$4) seniors, C$5 (US$3.35) children and students. Daily May 1–June 14 10am–6pm, June 15–Sept 30 9:30am–7pm, Oct 1–Apr 30 10am–4:30pm. Bus: 4, 7.

This small, tranquil oasis is concealed behind high, white-washed walls. Gnarled limestone scholar rocks jut skyward amid clusters of pine, bamboo, and winter-blooming plum; dark reflecting pools are filled with turtles and *koi* (decorative carp); and a meandering tiled path connects the various spaces. The Classical Garden was built in the Suzhou province of northern China around 1492 and relocated to Vancouver just in time for Expo '86. It was packed in 950 crates, and 52 artisans took nearly 10 years to completely reassemble it, replant it, and stock it with turtles and ornamental carp. This serenely beautiful garden is the only one of its kind in the western hemisphere.

✪ **Vancouver Centennial Police Museum.** 240 E. Cordova St. ☎ **604/665-3346.** www.city.vancouver.bc.ca/police/museum. Admission C$5 (US$3.35) adults, C$3 (US$2) students and seniors, children under 6 free. Year-round Mon–Fri 9am–3pm; May 1–Aug 31 Sat 10am–3pm. Bus: 4 or 7.

A bizarre, macabre, and utterly delightful little museum, dedicated to memorializing some of the best crimes and crime-stoppers in the city's short but colorful history. Housed in the old Vancouver Coroner's Court—where actor Errol Flynn was autopsied after dropping dead in the arms of a

Arthur Erickson

Vancouver's greatest architect, Arthur Erickson, is a puzzling contradiction. Avowedly modernist in principle, he nonetheless never hesitates to put form over function in order to satisfy his unique aesthetic sense. A firm believer in listening to what the landscape has to say, Erickson often turns a deaf ear to the needs of those who inhabit his buildings. Combine these features with exceptional eloquence, a driven personality, and flamboyant charm, and you get a lot of buildings, all of which look good on paper—and some that also work in real life. As this is his native town, Vancouver is blessed with a great deal of Erickson's work. Those with an interest can check out the **Museum of Anthropology** (1973), 6993 NW Marine Dr., UBC; the **Provincial Law Courts** (1973), 800 Smithe St.; **Simon Fraser University** (1963), Burnaby Mountain, Burnaby; the **MacMillan Bloedel Building** (1969), 1075 W. Georgia St; and the **Khalsa Diwan Society Sikh Temple** (1970), 8000 Ross St.

17-year-old girl—the museum features photos, text, and vintage equipment from files and evidence rooms of Vancouver's finest. The confiscated illegal-weapons display looks like the props department for the film *Road Warrior.* There's also a morgue with bits and pieces of damaged body parts on the wall, a simulated autopsy room, a forensics lab, and a police radio room. One display shows how the police solved the case of the milkshake poisoner, involving a local radio celebrity who was feeding his wife milkshakes made from arsenic. On the lighter side, the museum also houses an immense collection of matchbox-sized toy police cars from around the world. And the Cop Shoppe carries caps, pins, T-shirts, and books.

NORTH VANCOUVER & WEST VANCOUVER

Capilano Suspension Bridge & Park. 3735 Capilano Rd., North Vancouver. ☎ **604/985-7474.** www.capbridge.com. Admission C$11 (US$7) adults, C$9 (US$6) seniors, C$7 (US$4.70) students, C$3.25 (US$2.15) children 6–12, free for children under 6. Winter discounts available. May–Sept daily 8:30am–dusk, Oct–Apr daily 9am–5pm. Closed Dec 25. Bus: 246 from downtown Vancouver, 236 from Lonsdale Quay SeaBus terminal.

Vancouver's first and oldest tourist trap (built in 1889), this attraction still works—mostly because there's still something inherently thrilling about standing on a narrow, shaky walkway,

69 meters (230 ft.) above the canyon floor, held up by nothing but a pair of miserable cables. Set in an 8-hectare (20-acre) park about 15 minutes from the city, the suspension bridge itself is a 135-meter-long (450-ft.) cedar-plank and steel-cable footbridge, which sways gently above the Capilano River. You can nervously cross above kayakers and salmon shooting the rapids far below, shrouded by mist from a 60-meter (200-ft.) waterfall.

In addition to the bridge, there's a **carving centre** where Native carvers show their skill, an exhibit explaining the region's natural history, a pair of restaurants, and—surprise—a gift shop. For those who want a less commercial experience, the nearby Lynn Canyon Suspension Bridge stands 3 meters (10 ft.) higher and is free of charge, but has no gift shops.

Grouse Mountain Resort. 6400 Nancy Greene Way, North Vancouver. ☎ 604/984-0661. www.grousemountain.com. SkyRide C$18 (US$12) adults, C$16 (US$11) seniors, C$12 (US$8) youths, C$7 (US$4.70) children 6–12, free for children under 6. SkyRide free with advance Grouse Nest restaurant reservation. Daily 10am–10pm. SeaBus: Lonsdale Quay, then transfer to bus no. 236.

Once a small local ski hill, Grouse has been slowly developing itself into a year-round mountain recreation park, offering impressive views and instantaneous access to the North Shore mountains. Located only a 20-minute drive from downtown, the SkyRide gondola transports you to the mountain's 1,110-meter (3,700-ft.) summit in about 10 minutes. (Hikers and cardio-fitness fiends can take a near vertical trail called the Grouse Grind. The best of them can do it in 28 minutes.) At the top, there's a bar, restaurant, large-screen theatre, ski and snowboard area, hiking and snowshoeing trails, skating pond, children's snow park, interpretive forest trails, logger sports show, helicopter tours, mountain bike trails, and Native feast house. Some of these are free with your SkyRide ticket—most aren't—and the view is one of the best around: the city and the entire lower mainland, from far up the Fraser Valley east across the Gulf of Georgia to Vancouver Island. The Himwus Feast House has gotten good reviews for its Native food and dance.

2 Vancouver's Plazas & Parks

OUTDOOR PLAZAS

A waterfall serves as the centerpiece of the **Burrard Street Plaza,** between Alberni and Dunsmuir Streets in the heart of downtown Vancouver. You can rest here for a moment and ponder the Hotel Vancouver and Christ Church Cathedral or the bustle of nearby business traffic.

Designed by architect Arthur Erickson to be Vancouver's central plaza, **Robson Square**—between Hornby and Howe Streets from Robson to Smithe Streets—has never really worked. Though beautifully executed with shrubbery, cherry trees, sculptures, and a triple-tiered waterfall, the square suffers from a basic design flaw: It's sunk one story below street grade. Even though there are cafes and an outdoor skating rink, people just don't seem to like going down.

At the opposite end of things, **Library Square**—at the corner of Robson and Homer Streets—is immensely popular with locals, and has been since it was built just 4 years back. People sit on the Coliseum-like steps, bask in the sunshine, read, harangue passersby with half thought-out political ideas, and generally seem to enjoy themselves.

PARKS & GARDENS

The city's parks and gardens are filled with life and amusements. Scattered throughout Vancouver are publicly and privately maintained areas appealing to anyone seeking an hour or two of escape from urban life. You can encounter raccoon families in the West End, go downhill or cross-country skiing in West Vancouver, spot bald eagles and peregrine falcons in Richmond, or observe tai chi masters in Chinatown. For general information about Vancouver's parks, call ☎ **604/257-8400.**

✪ **Stanley Park** is a 400-hectare (1,000-acre) rain forest near the busy West End. It is named after the same Lord Stanley whose name is synonymous with professional hockey success—the Stanley Cup. The park is filled with towering western red cedar trees, placid lagoons, walking trails, manicured lawns, and flower gardens. It's surrounded by water except for a small portion of its eastern edge that connects it to the West End. Stanley Park houses the Vancouver Aquarium, a petting zoo, three restaurants and a handful of snack bars, cricket greens, a swimming pool, a miniature railway, and a water park. It also boasts abundant wildlife, including beavers, coyotes, bald eagles, raccoons, trumpeter swans, brant geese, ducks, and skunks, as well as pristine natural settings and amazing marine views. This is where Vancouverites go to run, skate, bike, walk, or just sit. As North America's largest urban park, it is 20% larger than New York's Central Park (which is only 354 hectares/886 acres) and considerably safer. Take bus no. 23, 35, or 135 to the Stanley Park loop at the base of West Georgia Street.

In Chinatown, the **Dr. Sun-Yat-sen Classical Garden** (see "The Top Attractions," above) is a small, tranquil oasis in the heart of the city. On the West Side, **Queen Elizabeth Park**—at Cambie Street and West 33rd Avenue—sits atop a 150-meter-high (500-ft.) extinct volcano and is the highest urban vantage point south of downtown, offering panoramic views in all directions. It's Vancouver's most popular location for wedding-photo sessions, with well-manicured gardens and a profusion of colorful flora. There are areas for lawn bowling, tennis, pitch-and-putt golf, and picnicking. The **Bloedel Conservatory** (☎ **604/257-8570**) stands next to the park's huge sunken garden, an amazing reclamation of an abandoned rock quarry. A 42-meter-high (140-ft.) domed structure with a commanding 360° view, the conservatory houses a tropical rain forest with more than 100 plant species as well as free-flying tropical birds. Admission for the conservatory is C$3.50 (US$2.35) for adults and C$2 (US$1.35) for seniors and children. Take bus no. 15 to reach the park.

VanDusen Botanical Garden, 5251 Oak St. at 37th Avenue (☎ **604/878-9274**), is nearby. Formerly the Shaughnessy Golf Course, the 22-hectare (55-acre) formal garden features rolling lawns, lakes, Elizabethan hedge mazes, and marble sculptures. The **Sino-Himalayan Garden** is just one of its international displays. Admission is C$6 (US$3.75) for adults; C$2.75 (US$1.85) for seniors, students, and children; and C$11 (US$7) for families. Off-season admission is usually less expensive. The garden opens at 10am, and closing hours vary between 6 and 9pm, depending on the time of year. Take bus no. 17.

The University of British Columbia campus incorporates a number of parks and gardens. Established nearly a century ago, the **UBC Botanical Garden,** 6250 Stadium Rd., Gate 8 (☎ **604/822-9666**), has 28 hectares (70 acres) of formal alpine, herb, and exotic plantings. Nearby is the **Nitobe Memorial Garden,** 6565 NW Marine Dr., Gate 4 (☎ **604/ 822-6038**), a traditional Japanese garden. From early March to mid-October, both gardens are open daily from 10am to

6pm. Admission to the Botanical Garden is C$4.50 (US$3) for adults, C$1.75 (US$1.15) for seniors, C$2.25 (US$1.50) for students, C$1.75 (US$1.15) for children 6 to 12, and children under 6 are free. Admission for Nitobe Memorial Garden is C$2.50 (US$1.65) for adults and C$1.75 (US$1.15) for seniors, students, and children 7 to 18 years old. A dual pass for both gardens is C$6 (US$4), for adults only. From October 5 to March 6, the Botanical Garden is open daily during daylight hours, while the Nitobe Memorial Garden is open Monday to Friday from approximately 10am to 2:30pm.

Out near UBC, **Pacific Spirit Park** (usually called the **Endowment Lands**) comprises 754 hectares (1,885 acres) of temperate rain forest, marshes, and beaches and includes nearly 35 kilometers (22 miles) of trails suitable for hiking, riding, mountain biking, and beachcombing.

Across the Lions Gate Bridge, there are six provincial parks that delight outdoor enthusiasts year-round. The publicly maintained **Capilano River Regional Park,** 4500 Capilano Rd. (☎ **604/666-1790**), surrounds the Capilano Suspension Bridge & Park (see "The Top Attractions," above). Hikers can follow the river for 7 kilometers (4½ miles) down the well-maintained **Capilano trails** to the Burrard Inlet and the Lions Gate Bridge, or about a mile upstream to **Cleveland Dam,** which serves as the launching point for white-water kayakers and canoeists.

The **Capilano Salmon Hatchery,** on Capilano Road (☎ **604/666-1790**), is on the river's east bank about a half a kilometer (quarter mile) below the Cleveland Dam. Approximately two million Coho and Chinook salmon are hatched annually in glass-fronted tanks connected to the river by a series of channels. You can observe the hatching fry (baby fish) before they depart for open waters, as well as the mature salmon that return to the Capilano River to spawn. Admission is free, and the hatchery is open daily from 8am to 7pm (until 4pm in the winter). Drive across the Lions Gate Bridge and follow the signs to North Vancouver and the Capilano Suspension Bridge. Or take the SeaBus to Lonsdale Quay and transfer to bus no. 236; the trip takes less than 45 minutes.

Eight kilometers (5 miles) west of the Lions Gate Bridge on Marine Drive West, West Vancouver, is **Lighthouse Park.** This 74-hectare (185-acre) rugged-terrain forest has 13 kilometers

(8 miles) of groomed trails and—because it has never been clear-cut—some of the largest and oldest trees in the Vancouver area. One of the paths leads to the 18-meter (60-ft.) **Point Atkinson Lighthouse,** on a rocky bluff overlooking the Strait of Georgia and a panoramic view of Vancouver. It's an easy trip on bus no. 250. For information about other West Vancouver parks, call ☎ **604/925-7200** weekdays.

Driving up-up-up the mountain from **Lighthouse Park** will eventually get you to the top of **Cypress Provincial Park.** Stop halfway at the scenic viewpoint for a sweeping vista of the Vancouver skyline, the harbor, the Gulf Islands, and Washington State's Mount Baker, which looms above the eastern horizon. The park is 12 kilometers (7½ miles) north of Cypress Bowl Road and the Highway 99 junction in West Vancouver. Cypress Provincial Park has an intricate network of trails maintained for hiking during the summer and autumn, and for downhill and cross-country skiing during the winter.

Rising 1,430 meters (4,767 ft.) above Indian Arm, **Mount Seymour Provincial Park,** 1700 Mt. Seymour Rd., North Vancouver (☎ **604/986-2261** or 604/872-6616), offers another view of the area's Coast Mountains range. The road to this park roams through stands of Douglas fir, red cedar, and hemlock. Higher than Grouse Mountain, Mount Seymour has a spectacular view of Washington State's Mount Baker on clear days. It has challenging hiking trails that go straight to the summit, where you can see Indian Arm, Vancouver's bustling commercial port, the city skyline, the Strait of Georgia, and Vancouver Island. The trails are open all summer for hiking; during the winter, the paths are maintained for skiing, snow-boarding, and snowshoeing. A cafeteria and gift shop are open year-round. Mount Seymour is open daily from 7am to 10pm.

The Fraser River delta is south of Vancouver. Thousands of migratory birds following the Pacific flyway rest and feed in this area, especially at the 340-hectare (850-acre) **George C. Reifel Bird Sanctuary,** 5191 Robertson Rd., Westham Island (☎ **604/946-6980**), which was created by a former bootlegger and wetland-bird lover. Many other waterfowl species have made this a permanent habitat. More than 263 species have been spotted, including a Temminck's stint, a spotted redshank, bald eagles, Siberian (trumpeter) swans, peregrine falcons, blue herons, owls, and coots. The **Snow Goose Festival,** celebrating the annual arrival of the huge, snowy white flocks, is held here during the first weekend of November. The snow geese stay in the area until mid-December. (High tide, when the birds are less concealed by the marsh grasses, is the best time to visit.) An observation tower, 3 kilometers (2 miles) of paths, free birdseed, and picnic tables make this wetland reserve an ideal outing spot from October through April, when the birds are wintering in abundance. The sanctuary is wheelchair accessible and open daily from 9am to 4pm. Admission is C$4 (US$2.70) for adults and C$2 (US$1.35) for seniors and children.

The **Richmond Nature Park,** 1185 Westminster Hwy. (☎ 604/273-7015), was established to preserve the Lulu Island wetlands bog. It features a Nature House with educational displays and a boardwalk-encircled duck pond. On Sunday afternoons, knowledgeable guides give free tours and acquaint visitors with this unique environment. Admission is by donation.

3 Especially for Kids

Pick up copies of the free monthly newspapers *BC Parent,* 4479 W. 10th Ave., Vancouver, B.C. V6R 4P2 (☎ **604/ 221-0366**); and *West Coast Families,* 8–1551 Johnston St., Vancouver, B.C. V6H 3R9 (☎ **604/689-1331**). *West Coast Families'* centerfold "Fun in the City" and event calendar list everything currently going on, including **CN IMAX** (see chapter 7) shows at Canada Place Pier, **OMNIMAX** (☎ **604/ 443-7443**) shows at Science World British Columbia, and free children's programs. Both publications are available at Granville Island's Kids Only Market and at neighborhood community centers throughout the city.

Stanley Park offers a number of attractions for children. Stanley Park's Children's Farm (☎ **604/257-8530**) has peacocks, rabbits, calves, donkeys, and Shetland ponies (see "Parks & Gardens," above). Next to the petting zoo is Stanley Park's Miniature Railway (☎ **604/257-8531**). The diminutive steam locomotive with passenger cars runs on a circuit through the woods, carrying nearly as many passengers annually as all of the Alaska-bound cruise ships combined. During the holidays, the railway is strung with festive lights. The zoo and railway are open daily from April through September, plus Christmas week and on weekends from October through March. Admission for the petting zoo is C$2.50 (US$1.65) for anyone over 12 and C$1.75 (US$1.15) for kids 6 to 12 (admission is free for kids under 6 accompanied by a paying adult). Admission for the railway is C$6 (US$4) for anyone over 12 and C$3.95 (US$2.65) for kids 6 to 12 (admission is free for kids under 6 accompanied by a paying adult).

Also in Stanley Park, the ✪ **Vancouver Aquarium** has sea otters, sea lions, whales, and numerous other marine creatures, as well as many exhibits geared towards children (see "The Top Attractions," above). Across Burrard Inlet on the North Shore, **Maplewood Farm,** 405 Seymour River Place, North Vancouver (☎ **604/929-5610**), has more than 200 barnyard animals (cows, horses, ponies, pigs, sheep, donkeys, ducks, chickens, and more) living on its 2-hectare (5-acre) farm, which is open daily year-round. A few working farms once operated in the area but were put out of business by competition from the huge agricultural concerns in Fraser River valley. The parks department rescued this one and converted it into an attraction. The ticket booth (a former breeding kennel) sells birdseed for feeding the ducks and other fowl, as well as guidebooks. The farm also offers pony rides. Special events include the summertime Sheep Fair, the mid-September Farm Fair, 101 Pumpkins Day in late October, and the Country Christmas weekend. The farm is open Tuesday to Sunday from 10am to 4pm, and on designated holiday Mondays during the same hours. Admission is C$1.75 (US$1.15) for adults, C$1.25 (US85¢) for seniors and children, and C$6 (US$4) for families. Take bus no. 210 and transfer to the no. 211 or 212.

Three-quarters of an hour east of the city, the **Greater Vancouver Zoological Centre,** 5048–264th St., Aldergrove (☎ **604/856-6825**), is a lush 48-hectare (120-acre) farm filled with lions, tigers, jaguars, ostriches, elephants, buffalo, elk, antelope, zebras, giraffes, a rhino, hippos, and camels. In all, 124 species roam free or in spacious paddocks on the grounds. Located 48 kilometers (30 miles) from Vancouver, the wildlife reserve also has food service and a playground. It's open daily from 9am until dusk. Admission is C$11 (US$7) for adults, C$8 (US$5) for seniors and children 3 to 15, and free for children under 3 with an adult.

Right in town, **Science World** is a hands-on kids' museum where budding scientists can get their hands into everything (see "The Top Attractions," above). At the **Vancouver Maritime Museum,** kids can dress up like a pirate or a naval captain for a day, or board the RCMP ice-breaker *St. Roch* (see "The Top Attractions," above).

The **Burnaby Village Museum,** 6501 Deer Lake Ave., Burnaby (☎ **604/293-6501**), is a 3.5-hectare (9-acre) re-creation of the Victorian era. You can walk along boardwalk streets among costumed townspeople, watch a blacksmith pound horseshoes, shop in a general store, ride a vintage carousel, peek into an authentic one-room schoolhouse, and visit a vintage ice-cream parlor that's been at the same location since the turn of the 20th century. At Christmastime, the whole village is aglow in Christmas lights and Victorian decorations. Admission is C$7 (US$4.70) for adults; C$4.35 (US$2.90) for seniors, travelers with disabilities, and students; C$4.55 (US$3.05) for youths 13 to 18; C$3.75 (US$2.50) for children 6 to 12; and free for children under 6. It's open daily from 11am to 4:30pm. From the Metrotown Skystation, take bus no. 110 to Deer Lake.

The **Fort Langley National Historic Site,** 23433 Mavis Ave., Fort Langley (☎ **604/513-4777**), is the birthplace of British Columbia. In 1827, the Hudson's Bay Company established this settlement to supply its provincial posts. Costumed craftspeople demonstrate blacksmithing, coppering, and woodworking skills, bringing this landmark back to life. It's open daily from 10am to 5pm, March 1 to October 31. From November 1 to February 28, pre-booked groups only; please call ahead. Admission is C$4 (US$2.70) for adults, C$3 (US$2) for seniors, C$2 (US$1.35) for children 6 to 16, and free for children under 6. Take the SkyTrain to Surrey Central Station; transfer to bus no. 501.

Athletic kids can work up a sweat at the Participation Gallery in the **B.C. Sports Hall of Fame and Museum** (see "The Top Attractions," above). They can run, jump, climb, race, throw fastballs, and attempt to beat world records. At **Granville Island's Water Park and Adventure Playground,** 1496 Cartwright St., kids can really let loose with movable water guns and sprinklers. They can also have fun on the water slides or in the wading pool. The facilities are open during the summer daily (weather permitting) from 10am to

6pm. Admission is free; changing facilities are nearby at the False Creek Community Centre (☎ **604/257-8195**).

Granville Island's **Kids Only Market,** 1496 Cartwright St. (☎ **604/689-8447**), is open daily from 10am to 6pm. Playrooms and 21 shops filled with toys, books, records, clothes, and food are all child-oriented. Kids will also love taking the Aquabus or Granville Island Ferry (see "By Ferry," in chapter 2) to get there.

4 Organized Tours

If you don't have the time to arrange your own sightseeing tour, let the experts take you around Vancouver. They will escort you in a bus, trolley, double-decker bus, seaplane, helicopter, boat, ferry, taxi, vintage car, or horse-driven carriage.

BUS TOURS

Gray Line of Vancouver, 255 E. First Ave. (☎ **604/ 879-3363**), offers a wide array of tour options. The "Deluxe Grand City Tour" is a 3½-hour excursion through Stanley Park, Gastown, Chinatown, Canada Place, Queen Elizabeth Park, Robson Street, Shaughnessy, and English Bay Beach. Offered year-round, it costs C$44 (US$29) for adults, C$42 (US$28) for seniors, and C$31 (US$21) for children. Departing at 9:15am and 2pm, the bus picks you up from downtown hotels approximately 30 minutes before departure. The "Mountains and Sea Tour" takes you up to Grouse Mountain and the Capilano Suspension Bridge. Departing daily at 2pm, it costs C$71 (US$48) for adults, C$65 (US$44) for seniors, and C$46 (US$31) for children, including admission and the skytram. Other offerings include day, overnight, and multinight package tours of Vancouver, Victoria, and Whistler, plus helicopter tours and dinner cruises.

Vancouver Trolley Company, 4012 Myrtle St., Burnaby (☎ **604/451-5581;** www.vancouvertrolley.com), operates gas-powered trolleys along a route through downtown, Chinatown, the West End, and Stanley Park. Between 9am and 6pm in summer (4:30pm in winter), passengers can get on and off at any of the 16 stops, explore, and catch another scheduled trolley. Onboard, drivers provide detailed tour commentary. Tickets are C$22 (US$15) for adults and C$10 (US$7) for children 4 to 12.

West Coast City and Nature Sightseeing, 4012 Myrtle St., Burnaby (☎ **604/451-1600**), offers seven different mini-coach tours, including a Native Culture Tour for C$45 (US$30) for adults and C$27 (US$18) for children, which includes a stop at the Stanley Park totem poles and a visit to the Museum of Anthropology at UBC; Grouse Mountain/ Capilano Suspension Bridge for C$65 (US$44) for adults and C$42 (US$28) for children; and Whistler/Shannon Falls for C$62 (US$42) for adults and C$38 (US$25) for children; as well as Vancouver City/Capilano Suspension Bridge with a new price: C$48 (US$32) for adults, C$45 (US$30) for seniors, students and youth (13 to 18), C$29 (US$19.50) children 4 to 12. Children under 4 are free. Minicoaches pick up passengers from downtown hotels, cruise ships, the airport, and the bus/railway station; phone for departure times. Charters and private tours are also available.

RAIL TOURS

On the **Pacific Starlight Dinner Train** (☎ 800/363-3733), a gourmet meal is served in the dome or salon car onboard a vintage locomotive as it travels from North Vancouver to Porteau Cove along the edge of Howe Sound. It costs C$84 (US$56) for adults and C$64 (US$43) per child for the salon car. For the dome car the cost is C$100 (US$67), with no discount for children. The dinner train runs from May to late September, Wednesday to Sunday; in October, weekends only. Call ahead for days of operation.

A 1939 Hudson steam engine chugs up through Howe Sound from North Vancouver to Squamish. The **Royal Hudson Steam Train** (☎ 604/984-5246) departs North Vancouver at 10am daily, returning at 4pm, and costs C$48 (US$32) for adults, C$41 (US$27) for seniors and youths, and C$13 (US$9) for children.

BOAT TOURS

Harbour Cruises, Harbour Ferries, no. 1, north foot of Denman Street (☎ **604/688-7246;** www.boatcruises.com), will take you on a 3-hour Sunset Dinner Cruise, including a catered gourmet meal and onboard entertainment; cost for adults/seniors/youths is C$60 (US$40); for children 2 to 11, C$50 (US$34). The cruise leaves at 7pm, May through October. The 4-hour Indian Arm Luncheon Cruise includes a salmon lunch, with departure at 11am. Cost for adults and seniors is C$45 (US$30), C$40 (US$27) for children. A senior special of C$40 (US$27) applies on Monday and Tuesday.

The company also conducts a 75-minute narrated Harbour Tour aboard the **MPV** *Constitution,* an authentic 19th-century stern-wheeler with a smokestack. Tours depart at 11:30am, 1pm, and 2:30pm daily from mid-May to mid-September, once a day at 2pm in April and October. Fares are C$18 (US$12) for adults, C$15 (US$10) for seniors and youths (12 to 17), C$6 (US$4) for children 5 to 11, and free for children under 5. Boat/train day trips depart Wednesday to Sunday and holiday Mondays from May through September at 9am aboard the **MV** *Britannia,* with a run up Howe Sound, and passengers return on the **Royal Hudson Steam Train** at about 4:40pm. Prices, including lunch, are C$75 (US$50) for adults, C$70 (US$47) for seniors and youths 12 to 17, and C$30 (US$20) for 5- to 11-year-olds.

From June through September, **Paddlewheeler River Adventures,** New Westminster Quay, New Westminster (☎ **604/525-4465**), operates Fraser River tours from New Westminster aboard the 19th-century vessel SS *Native.* The company offers a 3-hour lunch cruise on Tuesday, Wednesday, and Friday. Ticket prices, which include a luncheon buffet, are C$36 (US$24) for adults, C$32 (US$21) for seniors and students, C$12 (US$8) for children 6 to 12, and children under 6 are free. On Thursday and Saturday at 9:30am, there's a 7-hour Show Boat river cruise to historic Fort Langley (see "Especially for Kids," above) along the Fraser River. The fare is C$90 (US$60) for adults, C$80 (US$54) for seniors and students, and C$40 (US$27) for children 6 to 12, including breakfast, lunch, live entertainment, and a visit to Fort Langley. Ask about one-way cruises to Fort Langley. English High Tea is served Tuesday and Friday, with staff dressed the part. Tea cruises depart at 3pm. Adult fare is C$36 (US$24), seniors and students C$32 (US$21). You can also book sunset dinner cruises, theme cruises, and event cruises year-round, including Christmas Carol and Santa cruises in December.

Experience one of the world's largest commercial ports on **Burrard Water Taxi,** 2255 Commissioner St. (☎ **604/ 293-1160**). There are no scheduled tour times, so call ahead to book. The guides offer a fascinating insider's view of the busy harbor. The water taxis are available for tours at a rate of C$145 (US$97) per hour for 12 people. When the boats aren't escorting visitors around the harbor, they're shuttling the captains and crews of the freighters anchored in the Burrard Inlet to and from their vessels.

AIR TOURS

Baxter Aviation, Barbary Coast Marina, P.O. Box 1110, Nanaimo, B.C. V9R 6E7 (☎ **800/661-5599** or 604/683-6525; www.baxterair.com), operates 11 daily floatplane flights from downtown Vancouver. The 30-minute "Vancouver Scenic" tour flies over Stanley Park and the Coast Mountains; the 5-hour "Whistler Mountain Resort" tour includes a 3-hour stopover. Fares range from C$76 (US$51) per person for 30 minutes to C$359 (US$241) per person for 5 hours, with a variety of midrange tours in between. Other packages offer flights to Victoria, Johnstone Strait, glacial lakes, and prime fly-in fishing and whale-watching spots.

　Harbour Air (☎ **604/688-1277;** www.harbour-air.com) is on Coal Harbour just steps west of the Canada Place Pier. Look for the seaplanes arriving and departing. Thirty-minute seaplane flights over downtown Vancouver, Stanley Park, and the North Shore are C$76 (US$51) for adults, C$38 (US$25) for children under 12, and free for infants under 2. Many longer tours to alpine lakes and glaciers and nearby islands, as well as regularly scheduled flights to Victoria and Prince Rupert, are also available.

　Helijet Charters, 5911 D Airport Rd. S., Richmond (☎ **800/987-4354** or 604/270-1484; www.helijet.com), offers a variety of daily tours that depart from the Vancouver Harbour Heliport near Canada Place Pier. The "West Coast Spectacular" is a 20-minute tour of the city, Stanley Park, and North Shore mountains for C$110 (US$74) per person. For a bird's-eye view of the city, the 30-minute "Greater Vancouver Scenic Tour" costs C$155 (US$104) per person; and the "North Shore Discovery" tour lasts 45 minutes and costs C$215 (US$144) per person. Tours that depart from the Grouse Mountain summit take 10 to 15 minutes and cost C$50 to C$90 (US$34 to US$60) per person. The "Fly, Dine, and Drive" package takes you by helicopter from downtown Vancouver to the top of Grouse Mountain for dinner, returning to the city by limousine; it costs C$250 (US$168) per person for a party of two. Custom mountaintop heli-picnics, heli-golfing packages, and special trips can also be arranged.

SPECIALTY TOURS

Early Motion Tours, 1–1380 Thurlow St. (☎ **604/ 687-5088**), offers private sightseeing tours around Vancouver aboard a restored 1930 Model A Ford Phaeton convertible that holds up to four passengers plus the driver. Reservations are required. Limousine rates apply, C$100 (US$67) per hour for up to four people, and include a souvenir Polaroid of you in the car. There is a 1-hour minimum. The office is open daily from 7:30am to 8pm.

AAA Horse & Carriage Ltd., Stanley Park (☎ **604/ 681-5115**), carries on a century-old tradition of horse-drawn carriage rides through Stanley Park. Tours depart every 30 minutes between May and October from the lower aquarium parking lot on Park Drive across from the Vancouver Rowing Club near the park entrance. Tours last an hour and cover portions of the park that even most locals have never seen. Rates are C$17 (US$11) for adults, C$16 (US$11) for seniors and students, C$11 (US$7) for children 6 to 12, and children under 6 are free.

X Tour (☎ **604/609-2770**) offers guided tours of *X-Files* shooting locations around Vancouver, along with other sights guaranteed to delight an *X-Files* fan. Costs are from C$59 (US$40).

WALKING TOURS

Walkabout Historic Vancouver (☎ **604/720-0006**) offers 2-hour walking tours through Vancouver historic sites, complete with guide dressed as a 19th-century schoolmarm. Tours depart daily at 9am, noon, and 3pm June through September, by request during other months. The cost is C$18 (US$12) per person. Walking tours of Chinatown are available from the **Chinese Cultural Centre** (☎ **604/687-7993**) for C$5 (US$3.35) adults, C$4 (US$2.70) seniors, and C$3 (US$2) students and children. July through September, tours depart daily at 11am and 1:30pm; during other times, please phone ahead to book a tour. The Vancouver Tourism Info Centre at 200 Burrard St. (see chapter 2) has a number of brochures on self-guided tours throughout the city.

5 Outdoor Activities

Just about every imaginable sport has a world-class outlet within the Vancouver city limits. Downhill and cross-country skiing, snowshoeing, sea kayaking, fly-fishing, diving, hiking, paragliding, and mountain biking are just a few of the options.

Pick up a copy of ***Coast: The Outdoor Recreation Magazine*** (☎ 604/876-4980), which is published every other month. Available at many outfitters and recreational-equipment outlets, it lists snow conditions, bike trails, climbing spots, competitions, and organized events, as well as where to get bike tune-ups, where to find equipment rentals, and what to look for when purchasing sports equipment.

An excellent resource for outdoor enthusiasts is **Mountain Equipment Co-op,** 130 W. Broadway (☎ 604/872-7858). The MEC's retail store has a knowledgeable staff, and the Co-op also publishes an annual mail-order catalogue.

Spectators will also find plenty of activities in Vancouver. You can get schedule information on all major events at Tourism Vancouver's **Travel Info Centre,** 200 Burrard St. (☎ 604/683-2000). You can also get information and purchase tickets from Ticketmaster at the **Vancouver Ticket Centre,** 1304 Hornby St. (☎ 604/280-3311), which has 40 outlets in the greater Vancouver area. (Like every other Ticketmaster, they do charge a fee.) Popular events like Grizzlies and Canucks games and the Vancouver Indy can sell out weeks or months in advance, so it's a good idea to book ahead.

BEACHES   A great place for viewing sunsets is **English Bay Beach,** at the end of Davie Street off Denman Street and Beach Avenue. South of English Bay Beach, near the Burrard Street Bridge and the Vancouver Aquatic Centre, is **Sunset Beach.** Running along False Creek, it's actually a picturesque strip of sandy beaches filled with hulking sections of driftwood that serve as windbreaks and provide a little privacy for sunbathers and picnickers. There's a snack bar, a soccer field, and a long, gently sloping grassy hill for people who prefer lawn to sand.

On **Stanley Park's** western rim, **Second Beach** is a quick stroll north from English Bay Beach. A playground, a snack bar, and an immense heated freshwater pool—C$3.80 (US$2.55) for adults, C$2 (US$1.35) for seniors, C$2.55 (US$1.70) for youths 13 to 18, and C$8 (US$5) for families—make this a convenient spot for families. Farther along the seawall lies secluded **Third Beach,** which is due north of Stanley Park Drive. Locals tote along grills and coolers to this spot, a popular place for summer-evening barbecues and sunset watching. The hollow tree, Geographic Tree, and Siwash Rock are neighboring points of interest.

Kitsilano Beach, along Arbutus Drive near Ogden Street, is affectionately called Kits Beach. It's an easy walk from the Maritime Museum and the False Creek ferry dock. A heated saltwater swimming pool is open throughout the summer. Admission is the same as for Second Beach Pool, above. The summertime amateur theater, **Kitsilano Showboat,** attracts a local crowd looking for evening fun.

Farther west on the other side of Pioneer Park is **Jericho Beach** (Alma Street off Point Grey Road). This is another local after-work and weekend social spot. **Locarno Beach,** off Discovery Street and NW Marine Drive, and **Spanish Banks,** NW Marine Drive, wrap around the northern point of the UBC campus and University Hill. (Be forewarned that beach-side rest rooms and concessions on the promontory end abruptly at Locarno Beach.) Below UBC's Museum of Anthropology is **Point Grey Beach,** a restored harbor defense site. The next beach is **Wreck Beach**—Canada's largest nude beach. You get down to Wreck Beach by taking the very steep Trail 6 on the UBC campus near Gate 6 down to the water's edge. Extremely popular with locals, Wreck Beach is also the city's most pristine and least-developed sandy stretch. The Wreck Beach Preservation Society maintains it. It's bordered on three sides by towering trees.

At the northern foot of the Lions Gate Bridge, **Ambleside Park** is a popular North Shore spot. The quarter-mile beach faces the Burrard Inlet.

BICYCLING & MOUNTAIN BIKING   The most popular cycling path in the city runs along the Seawall around the perimeter of Stanley Park. Offering stunning views of the city, the Burrard Inlet, and English Bay, this pathway is extremely popular with cyclists, in-line skaters, and pedestrians alike. Other marked cycle lanes traverse the rest of the city, among them the cross-town Off-Broadway route, the Adanac route, and the Ontario route. Runners and cyclists have separate lanes on developed park and beach paths. Some West End hotels offer guests bike storage and rentals. One of the city's most scenic cycle paths has been extended and now runs all the way from Canada Place Pier to Pacific Spirit Park. It connects Canada Place, Stanley Park and the Seawall Promenade, English Bay and Sunset beaches, Granville Island to Vanier Park, Kitsilano and Jericho beaches, and Pacific Spirit Park. Cycling maps are available at most bicycle retailers and rental outlets.

Local mountain bikers love the cross-country ski trails on **Hollyburn Mountain** in Cypress Provincial Park. The Secret Trail Society started building trails 4 years ago along **Grouse Mountain's** backside, and they are now considered some of the lower mainland's best. Mount Seymour's very steep **Good Samaritan Trail** connects to the Baden-Powell Trail and the Bridle Path near Mount Seymour Road. The route is recommended only for world-class mountain bikers—the types who pour Gatorade on their Wheaties. Closer to downtown, both **Pacific Spirit Park** and **Burnaby Mountain** offer excellent beginner and intermediate off-road trails.

Hourly rentals run around C$3.75 (US$2.50) for a one-speed "Cruiser" to C$10 (US$7) for a top-of-the-line mountain bike, C$15 to C$40 (US$10 to US$27) for a day, helmets and locks included. Bikes and child trailers are available by the hour or day at **Spokes Bicycle Rentals & Espresso Bar,** 1798 W. Georgia St. (☎ **604/688-5141**). **Alley Cat Rentals,** 1779 Robson St., in the alley (☎ **604/684-5117**), is a popular shop that rents city or mountain bikes, child trailers, child seats, locks, helmets, and in-line skates (protective gear included). **Bayshore Bicycle and Rollerblade Rentals,** 745 Denman St. (☎ **604/688-2453**), rents 21-speed mountain bikes, bike carriers, tandems, city bikes, in-line skates and kids' bikes. **Cycling B.C.,** 1367 W. Broadway (☎ **604/ 737-3034;** www.cycling.bc.ca), is a nonprofit bicycling advocacy group.

BOATING   You can rent 15- to 17-foot power boats for as little as a few hours or up to several weeks at **Stanley Park Boat Rentals Ltd.,** Coal Harbour Marina (☎ **604/682-6257**). **Granville Island Boat Rentals, Ltd.,** 1696 Duranleau St., Granville Island (☎ **604/682-6287**), offers hourly, daily, and weekly rentals of 15- to 19-foot speedboats and also offers sportfishing, cruising, and sightseeing charters. **Jerry's Boat Rentals,** Granville Island (☎ **604/644-3256**), is just steps away and offers similar deals. Rates on all the above begin at around C$30 (US$20) per hour and C$135 (US$90) per day for a sport boat that holds four. **Delta Charters,** 3500 Cessna Dr., Richmond (☎ **800/661-7762** or 604/273-4211), has weekly and monthly rates for 32- to 58-foot powered boat craft. Prices begin around C$1,400 (US$938) per week for a boat that sleeps four (which isn't a bad deal when you consider that you won't need a hotel room).

CANOEING & KAYAKING   Both placid, urban False Creek and the incredibly beautiful 30-kilometer (19-mile) North Vancouver fjord known as Indian Arm have launching points that can be reached by car or bus. Rentals range from C$10 (US$7) per hour to C$40 (US$27) per day for single kayaks and about C$50 (US$34) per day for canoe rentals. Customized tours range from C$70 to C$110 (US$47 to US$74) per person.

Adventure Fitness, 1510 Duranleau St., Granville Island (☎ **604/687-1528**), rents canoes and kayaks, offers lessons, and has a cool showroom filled with outdoor gear. **Ecomarine Ocean Kayak Centre,** 1668 Duranleau St., Granville Island (☎ **604/689-7575**), has 2-hour, daily, and weekly kayak rentals. The company also has an office at the **Jericho Sailing Centre,** 1300 Discovery St., at Jericho Beach (☎ **604/ 222-3565**). In North Vancouver, **Deep Cove Canoe and Kayak Rentals** (at the foot of Gallant Street), Deep Cove (☎ **604/929-2268**), is an easy starting point for anyone planning an Indian Arm run. It offers hourly and daily rentals of canoes and kayaks as well as lessons and customized tours.

Lotus Land Tours, 2005–1251 Cardero St. (☎ **800/ 528-3531** or 604/684-4922), runs guided kayak tours on Indian Arm. Tours come complete with transportation to and from Vancouver, a barbecue salmon lunch, and incredible scenery. Operator Peter Loppe uses very wide stable kayaks, perfect for first-time paddlers. One-day tours cost C$135 (US$90).

ECOTOURS   **Lotus Land Tours,** 2005–1251 Cardero St. (☎ **800/528-3531** or 604/684-4922), runs guided kayak tours on Indian Arm (see "Canoeing & Kayaking," above). **Rockwood Adventures,** 1330 Fulton Ave. (☎ **604/926-7705**), has guided walks of the North Shore rain forest, complete with a trained naturalist and a gourmet lunch. Tours cover Capilano Canyon, Bowen Island, or Lighthouse Park, and cost C$49 (US$33) for a half day, including snack and drink, or C$105 (US$70) for a full day, including transportation, guide, and lunch.

FISHING   Five species of salmon, rainbow and Dolly Varden trout, steelhead, and even sturgeon abound in the local waters. To fish, you need a nonresident saltwater or freshwater license. Tackle shops sell licenses, have information on current restrictions, and often carry the BC Tidal Waters Sport Fishing Guide and BC Sport Fishing Regulations Synopsis for Non-tidal Waters. Independent anglers should also pick up a copy of the BC Fishing Directory and Atlas. **Hanson's Fishing Outfitters,** 102–580 Hornby St. (☎ **604/ 684-8988** or 604/684-8998), and **Granville Island Boat Rentals,** 1696 Duranleau St. (☎ **604/682-6287**), are outstanding outfitters. Licenses for freshwater fishing are C$16 (US$11) for 1 day or C$32 (US$21) for 8 days. Saltwater fishing licenses cost C$8 (US$5) for 1 day, C$20 (US$13) for 3 days, and C$39 (US$26) for 5 days.

   Bonnie Lee Fishing Charters Ltd., on the dock at the entrance to Granville Island (mailing address: 744 W. King Edward Ave., Vancouver, B.C. V5Z 2C8; ☎ **604/290-7447**), is another reputable outfitter. **Corcovado Yacht Charters Ltd.,** 1696 Duranleau St., Granville Island (☎ **604/ 669-7907**), has competitive rates.

   The *Vancouver Sun* prints a daily **fishing report** in the B section that details which fish are in season and where they can be found. You can pick up equipment at **Corcovado Saltwater Tackle Shop** (see Corcovado Yacht Charters Ltd., above) or **Ruddick's Fly Shop,** 1654 Duranleau St. (☎ **604/ 681-3747**). If you go to Granville Island, be sure to stop by the **Granville Island Sport Fishing Museum,** 1502 Duranleau (☎ **604/683-1939**).

   Fly-fishing in national and provincial parks requires special permits, which you can get at any park site for a nominal fee. Permits are valid at all Canadian parks.

GOLF   This is a year-round Vancouver sport. With five public 18-hole courses and half a dozen pitch-and-putt courses in the city and dozens more nearby, no golfer is far from his or her love. The public **University Golf Club,** 5185 University Blvd. (☎ **604/224-1818**), is a great 6,560-yard, par-71 course with a clubhouse, pro shop, locker rooms, bar and grill, and sports lounge. Or call **A-1 Last Minute Golf Hotline** (☎ **800/684-6344** or 604/878-1833) for substantial discounts and short-notice tee times at more than 30 Vancouver-area courses. There's no membership fee.

Leading private clubs are situated on the North Shore and in Vancouver. Check with your club at home to see if you have reciprocal visiting memberships with one of the following: **Capilano Golf and Country Club,** 420 Southborough Dr., West Vancouver (☎ **604/922-9331**); **Marine Drive Golf Club,** W. 57th Avenue and S.W. Marine Drive (☎ **604/ 261-8111**); **Seymour Golf and Country Club,** 3723 Mt. Seymour Pkwy., North Vancouver (☎ **604/929-2611**); **Point Grey Golf and Country Club,** 3350 SW Marine Dr. (☎ **604/266-7171**); and **Shaughnessy Golf and Country Club,** 4300 SW Marine Dr. (☎ **604/266-4141**). Greens fees range from C$42 to C$72 (US$28 to US$48).

HIKING   Great trails for hikers of all levels run through Vancouver's dramatic environs. Good trail maps are available from the **Greater Vancouver Regional Parks District** (☎ **604/432-6350**) and from **International Travel Maps and Books,** 552 Seymour St. (☎ **604/687-3320**), which also stocks guidebooks and topographical maps. Or pick up a local trail guide at any bookstore.

Just a few yards from the entrance to Grouse Mountain Resort is one entry to the world-famous **Baden-Powell Trail,** a 42-kilometer (26-mile) span of thick forest, rocky bluffs, and snow-fed streams racing through ravines. It starts at Cates Park on the Dollarton Highway and stretches west to Horseshoe Bay. Even if you only want to cover the stretch from Grouse Mountain to Mount Seymour, start early and be ready for some steep ascents. The timer guide at the trailhead marker has been annotated by hikers who've found it takes longer to do the loop than is indicated. Give yourself a full day for this hike.

Lynn Canyon Park, Lynn Headwaters Regional Park, Capilano River Regional Park, Mount Seymour Provincial Park, Pacific Spirit Park, and **Cypress Provincial Park** (see "Parks & Gardens," above) have good, easy to challenging trails that wind up through stands of Douglas fir and cedar and contain a few serious switchbacks. Pay attention to the trail warnings posted at the parks; some have bear habitats. And always remember to sign in with the park service at the start of your chosen trail. Golden Ears in Golden Ears Provincial Park, and The Lions, in West Vancouver, are for seriously fit hikers.

ICE-SKATING   Robson Square has free skating on a covered ice rink directly under Robson Street between Howe and Hornby Streets. It's open from November to early April. Rentals are available in the adjacent concourse. The **West End Community Centre,** 870 Denman St. (☎ **604/257-8333**), also rents skates at its enclosed rink, which is open from October through March. The enormous Burnaby 8 Rinks **Ice Sports Centre,** 6501 Sprott, Burnaby (☎ **604/291-0626**), is the Vancouver Canucks' official practice facility. It has eight rinks, is open year-round, and offers lessons and rentals.

IN-LINE SKATING   You'll find locals rolling along beach paths, streets, park paths, and promenades. If you didn't bring a pair of blades, go to **Alley Cat Rentals** (see "Bicycling & Mountain Biking," above), the preferred local outfitter because it has earlier and later shop hours than its competitors. Or try **Bayshore Bicycle and Rollerblade Rentals,** 745 Denman St. (☎ **604/688-2453**). Rentals generally run C$5 (US$3.35) per hour, or C$19 (US$13) for 8 hours.

JOGGING   You'll find fellow runners traversing the **Stanley Park Seawall, Lost Lagoon,** and **Beaver Lake.** If you're a dawn or dusk runner, take note that this is one of the world's safer city parks. However, if you're alone, don't tempt fate— stick to open and lighted areas. If you feel like doing a little racing, competitions take place throughout the year; ask at any runners' outfitters, such as **Forerunners,** 3504 W. Fourth Ave. (☎ **604/732-4535**), or **Running Room,** 679 Denman St. (corner of Georgia; ☎ **604/684-9771**).

SKIING & SNOWBOARDING   Top-notch skiing lies outside the city at the Whistler and Blackcomb Resorts, 112 kilometers (70 miles) north of Vancouver. However, if you have only a day or two in Vancouver, you don't even have to leave the city to get in a few runs. It seldom snows in the city's downtown and central areas, but Vancouverites can ski before work and after dinner at the three ski resorts in the North Shore mountains.

Grouse Mountain Resort, 6400 Nancy Greene Way, North Vancouver (☎ **604/984-0661;** snow report 604/ 986-6262; www.grousemountain.com), is about 3 kilometers (2 miles) from the Lions Gate Bridge, overlooking the Burrard Inlet and Vancouver's skyline (see "The Top Attractions," above). Four chairs, two beginner tows, and two T-bars take you to 22 alpine runs. The resort has night skiing, special events, instruction, and a spectacular view, as well as a 90-meter (300-ft.) half pipe for snowboarders.

Though the area is small, all skill levels are covered, with two beginner trails, three blue trails, and five black-diamond runs, including Coffin and Inferno, which follow the east slopes down from 1,230 meters to 750 meters (4,100 to 2,500 ft.).

Rental packages and a full range of facilities are available. Lift tickets good for all-day skiing are C$29 (US$19) for adults, C$16 (US$11) for seniors, C$22 (US$15) for youths, and C$16 (US$11) for children under 12.

Mount Seymour Provincial Park, 1700 Mt. Seymour Rd., North Vancouver (☎ **604/986-2261;** snow report 604/ 986-3999; www.mountseymour.com), has the area's highest base elevation; it's accessible via four chairs and a tow. Lift tickets on weekdays are C$19 (US$13) all day for adults and youths 13 to 18, C$15 (US$10) for seniors, and C$9 (US$6) for children 6 to 12; on weekends C$26 (US$17) all day for adults, C$15 (US$10) for seniors, C$21 (US$14) for youths 12 to 19, C$12 (US$8) for children 6 to 12. Nighttime skiing is C$19 (US$13) for adults, C$17 (US$11) for seniors, C$17 (US$11) for youths 12 to 19, and C$9 (US$6) for children 6 to 12. In addition to day and night skiing, the facility offers snowboarding, snowshoeing, and tobogganing along its 22 runs. There are 26 kilometers (16 miles) of cross-country trails. The resort specializes in teaching first-timers. Camps for children and teenagers, and adult clinics, are available throughout the winter.

Mount Seymour has one of Western Canada's largest equipment rental shops, which will keep your measurements on file for return visits. Shuttle service is available during ski season from various locations on the North Shore, including the Lonsdale Quay SeaBus. For more information call ☎ **604/ 986-2261.**

Cypress Bowl, 1610 Mt. Seymour Rd. (☎ **604/926-5612;** snow report 604/926-6007; www.cypressbowl.com), has the area's longest vertical drop (525m/1,750 ft.), challenging ski and snowboard runs, and 16 kilometers (10 miles) of track-set cross-country ski trails (including 5km/3 miles set aside for night skiing). Full-day lift tickets are C$35 (US$23) for adults, with reduced rates for youths, seniors, and children. Cross-country full-day passes are C$12 (US$8) for adults, with reduced rates for youths, seniors, and children. Snowshoe trail tickets are available for C$5 (US$3.35). Discounts for half-day, nighttime, and multiday tickets are available. **Cypress Mountain Sports,** 510 and 518 Park Royal S., West Vancouver (☎ **604/878-9229**), offers shuttle service to and from the ski area. Round-trip tickets are C$9 (US$6).

Cypress Mountain Sports stocks a complete selection of downhill, cross-country (including backcountry, skating, racing, and touring), and snowboarding equipment and accessories. The rental and repair department, staffed by avid skiers, offers a broad selection of equipment. Rental and repair prices are quite reasonable. The store also offers guided hikes in summer and snowshoe treks in winter.

SWIMMING & WATER SPORTS　　Vancouver's midsummer saltwater temperature rarely exceeds 65°F (18°C). Some swimmers opt for fresh- and saltwater pools at city beaches (see "Beaches," above). Others take to the water at public aquatic centers.

The **Vancouver Aquatic Centre,** 1050 Beach Ave. at the foot of Thurlow Street (☎ **604/665-3424**), has a heated, 50-meter Olympic pool, saunas, whirlpools, weight rooms, diving tanks, locker rooms, showers, child care, and a tot pool. Adult admission is C$3.85 (US$2.55). The new, coed **YWCA Fitness Centre,** 535 Hornby St. (☎ **604/895-5777**), in the heart of downtown, has a six-lane, 25-meter ozonated (much milder than chlorinated) pool, steam room, whirlpool, conditioning gym, and aerobic studios. A day pass is C$12 (US$8) for adults. UBC's **Aquatic Centre** (☎ **604/822-4521** for the pool schedule, or 604/822-4522), located next door to the Student Union Building, has designated hours when facilities are open for public use. Adult admission is C$3.75 (US$2.50); youths and students, C$2.75 (US$1.85); seniors, C$2 (US$1.35).

TENNIS　　The city maintains 180 outdoor hard courts that have a 1-hour limit and accommodate patrons on a first-come, first-served basis from 8am until dusk. Local courtesy dictates that if people are waiting, you surrender the court on the hour. (Heavy usage times are evenings and weekends.) With the exception of the Beach Avenue courts, which charge a nominal fee, all city courts are free.

Stanley Park has four courts near Lost Lagoon and 17 courts near the Beach Avenue entrance, next to the Fish House Restaurant. **Queen Elizabeth Park**'s 18 courts service the central Vancouver area, and **Kitsilano Beach Park**'s 10 courts service the beach area between Vanier Park and the UBC campus.

You can play at night at the **Langara Campus** of Vancouver Community College, on West 49th Avenue between Main and Cambie Streets. The **UBC Coast Club,** on Thunderbird Boulevard (☎ **604/822-2505**), has 10 outdoor and 4 indoor courts. Indoor courts are C$10 (US$7) per hour, plus C$3 (US$2) per person; outdoor courts are C$3 (US$2) per person.

Bayshore Bicycle and Rollerblade Rentals, 745 Denman St. (☎ **604/688-2453**) rents tennis rackets for C$10 (US$7) per day.

WINDSURFING   Windsurfing is not allowed at the mouth of False Creek near Granville Island, but you can bring a board to Jericho and English Bay Beaches or rent one there. Equipment sales, rentals (including wet suits), and instruction can be found at **Windsure Windsurfing School,** 1300 Discovery St., at Jericho Beach (☎ **604/224-0615**). Rentals start at C$17 (US$11) per hour.

6

Shopping

*B*lessed with a climate that seems semitropical in comparison to the rest of Canada, Vancouverites never really developed a taste for indoor malls. Instead, the typical Vancouverite shops on the street—parking the car or, better yet, leaving it at home—and browsing from one window to the next, always on the lookout for something new. Below are a few suggestions on where to start exploring.

1 The Shopping Scene

ROBSON STREET   It's been said that the corner of Robson and Burrard gets more foot traffic than any other corner in Canada. Urban myth? Who knows. Anyway, it's a busy, colorful parade of humanity, many from Asia (hence the sushi bars and shops with Japanese signs), most with money. Look for high-end fashions, with a focus on clothes for the younger set.

SOUTH GRANVILLE   The 10-block stretch of Granville Street—from Sixth Avenue up to 16th Avenue—is where Vancouver's old-money enclave of Shaughnessy comes to shop. Classic and expensive men's and women's clothiers, and houseware and furniture boutiques predominate. This area is also the heart of Vancouver's gallery row.

WATER STREET   Though a little too heavy on the knick-knack shops (it's the wrought-iron lamp stands that bring them out), Water Street and Gastown are by no means just a tacky tourist enclave. Look for antique and cutting-edge furniture, galleries of First Nations art, and funky basement retro shops.

MAIN STREET   Antiques, and lots of 'em. From about 19th up to 27th, Main Street is chock-a-block with antique shops. Rather than outbid each other, the stores have evolved so that each covers a particular niche, from art deco to country kitchen to fine Second Empire. It's a fun place to browse, and if your eyes start to glaze over at the thought of yet another divan, the area also has cafes, bookshops, and clothing stores.

GRANVILLE ISLAND   A rehabilitated industrial site beneath the Granville Street Bridge, the Public Market is paradoxically one of the best places to pick up salmon and other seafood. It's also a great place to browse for crafts and gifts. Particularly interesting is Kid's Market, a kind of mini-mall for children, complete with Lilliputian entranceway, toy and craft and book stores, and play areas and services for the not-yet-10 demographic.

ASIA WEST   If you've never been to Hong Kong, or are just itching to get back, this new commercial area on Richmond's No. 3 Road between Capstan and Alderbridge is the place to shop. Stores in four new malls—the Yaohan Centre, President Plaza, Aberdeen Centre, and Parker Place—cater to Vancouver's newly arrived Asian community by bringing in goods direct from Asia. If the prices seem a bit high, a simple inquiry is often enough to bring them plummeting down as much as 80%.

PUNJABI MARKET   India imported. The 4 blocks of Main Street on either side of 49th Avenue contain the whole of the subcontinent, shrunk down to a manageable parcel. Look for fragrant spice stalls and sari shops and textile outlets selling luxurious fabrics—at bargain-basement prices.

2 Shopping A to Z

ANTIQUES
Bakers Dozen Antiques. 3520 Main St. ☎ **604/879-3348.**

This charming shop specializes in antique toys, model ships and boats, folk art, and unusual 19th- and early 20th-century furniture.

Mihrab. 2229 Granville St. ☎ **604/879-6105.**

Part museum, part subcontinental yard sale, Mihrab specializes in one-of-a-kind Indian antiques for the house and garden. Think intricately carved teak archways, or tiny jewel-like door pulls, all selected by partners Lou Johnson and Kerry Lane on frequent trips to the subcontinent.

Potter's Gallery. Westin Bayshore Hotel, 1601 W. Georgia St. ☎ **604/685-3919.**

Established in 1924, this store sells Chinese and Japanese art as well as Kurf Sutton's fine porcelain flowers.

Three Centuries Shop. 321 Water St. ☎ **604/685-8808.** www.
threecenturiesshop.com.

French and English decorative arts, especially from the art
deco and art nouveau periods, are featured at this store, three
doors down from the Gastown Steam Clock.

Uno Langmann Limited. 2117 Granville St. ☎ **604/736-8825.**
www.langmann.com.

Catering to upscale shoppers, Uno Langmann specializes in
European and North American paintings, furniture, silver,
and objets d'art from the 18th through early 20th centuries.
Open Wednesday to Saturday from 10am to 5pm.

Vancouver Antique Centre. 422 Richards St. ☎ **604/669-7444.**

Housed in a heritage commercial building, this maze contains
14 separate shops on two levels, specializing in everything
from china, glass, and jewelry, to military objects, sports, toys,
retro, '50s and '60s collectibles, home furnishings, and watches.
There are even more shops in the neighboring buildings.

BOOKS

Blackberry Books. 1663 Duranleau St. ☎ **604/685-4113** or 604/
685-6188.

Books about art, architecture, and fine cuisine are the specialties of this Granville Island store, which also has a wide variety of more general categories. New titles are displayed with
staff reviews posted beside them.

Chapters. 788 Robson St. ☎ **604/682-4066.**

There was grumbling amongst the literati when this big-box
baddie came to town a couple years back. Since then Chapters
seems to have won folks over with the sheer quality of its
book-buying experience—stores are pleasant and well
planned, with little nooks and comfy benches; coffee is often
available on the ground floor. And though it pains a local
booster like myself to say it, Chapters' book selection is—
gasp—every bit as good as homegrown favorite Duthie's. Also
at 2505 Granville St. (☎ **604/731-7822**).

✪ **Duthie Books.** 2239 W. Fourth Ave., Kitsilano. ☎ **604/732-5344.**

Since 1957, this locally owned chain has been synonymous
with good books in Vancouver. Though its recent financial
troubles and retrenchment have left Duthie's with just one

store, it remains a particularly good place to find local authors, in addition to an excellent inventory of Canadian and international titles. The staff is knowledgeable, and the shop offers custom services such as special, by-mail, and out-of-print ordering.

Granville Book Company. 850 Granville St. ☎ **877/838-BOOK** or 604/687-2213. www.granvillebooks.com.

Located in the heart of Vancouver's entertainment district, this bookstore has a great selection and staff with a true love for books. The generous opening hours (till midnight daily and 1am on Fridays and Saturdays) make this a great spot for browsing after dinner or before a movie.

✪ **International Travel Maps and Books.** 552 Seymour St. ☎ **604/687-3320.** www.itmb.com.

Best selection of travel books, maps, charts, and globes in town. The selection of special-interest British Columbia guides is impressive, with topics ranging from backcountry skiing and minimum-impact hiking to off-road four-wheeling. This is the hiker's best source for detailed topographic charts of the entire province. One of the city's secret bargains is the bin of free outdated provincial maps near the door that often includes maps of the parks around Whistler (outside Vancouver, the province changes slowly enough that they're still accurate).

Kidsbooks. 3083 W. Broadway. ☎ **604/738-5335.**

Largest and most interesting selection of children's literature in the city; also has an amazing collection of puppets, and regular readings. Also at 3040 Edgemont Blvd., North Vancouver (☎ **604/986-6190**).

Little Sister's Book & Art Emporium. 1238 Davie St. ☎ **604/669-1753.**

What makes one book literature and another pornography? Canada Customs officers used to routinely duck this difficult question by simply seizing whole shipments of Little Sister's books. They stopped only after the Supreme Court ruled that—whatever the answer to the question—it wasn't for Customs to decide. To see for yourself, come down and browse this West End bookstore's large selection of lesbian, gay, bisexual, and transgender books, videos, and magazines, as well as its huge adult novelties department.

CHINA, SILVER & CRYSTAL

One local artisan, **Martha Sturdy,** has a shop downtown, across the street from the Hotel Vancouver. There's also a great array of sophisticated international china and crystal in the downtown stores. On Granville Island you can observe potters, silversmiths, and glassblowers as they work their magic.

Gallery of BC Ceramics. 1359 Cartwright St. ☎ **604/669-5645.** www.bcpotters.com.

This Granville Island gallery loft is owned and operated by the Potters Guild of British Columbia. It presents a lively, juried collection of more than 70 sculptural and functional ceramic works. The gallery also carries a full range of books for ceramics enthusiasts. Closed on Mondays.

✪ **Martha Sturdy Originals.** 3039 Granville St. ☎ **604/737-0037.**

Designer Martha Sturdy—once best known for her collectible, usable, handblown glassware trimmed in gold leaf—is now creating a critically acclaimed line of cast-resin housewares, as well as limited-edition couches and chairs. Expensive, but, if you've got the dough, well worth it. Open Monday to Friday from 10am to 6pm, Saturday from 10am to 8pm, and Sunday from noon to 5pm.

CHINESE GOODS

T&T Supermarket. 181 Keefer St. ☎ **604/899-8836.**

Racks and racks of goods you won't find at home (unless your home is China), but the real entertainment is the seafood bins and the produce section, where strange and ungainly comestibles lurk: fire-dragon fruit, lily root, and enoki mushrooms.

Ten Ren Tea & Ginseng Co. 550 Main St. ☎ **604/684-1566.**

Whether you prefer the pungent aroma of Chinese black or the exotic fragrance of chrysanthemum, jasmine, or ginger flower, you must try the numerous varieties of drinking and medicinal teas in this Chinatown shop. It also carries Korean, American, and Siberian ginseng for a lot less than you might pay elsewhere.

Tung Fong Hung Foods Co. 536 Main St. ☎ **604/688-0883.** www.tung-fong-hung.com.

If you've never been to a Chinese herbalist, this is the one to try: jars, bins, and boxes full of such things as dried sea horse,

thinly sliced deer antler, and bird's nest. It's lots of fun to explore and potentially good for what ails ya. Chinese remedies can have side effects, however, so before ingesting anything unfamiliar, it's usually wise to consult the on-site herbalist.

CIGARS & TOBACCO

Just remember, if the cigars are Cuban, you'll have to light up on this side of the border.

✪ **La Casa del Habano.** 980 Robson St. ☎ **604/609-0511.**

Directly across from Planet Hollywood on Robson Street, Casa del Habano has Vancouver's largest walk-in humidor. Cigars range in price from a few dollars to over a hundred. Better customers are occasionally invited to relax in the private smoking room. Members have small lockers/humidors where they can store their purchases along with a bottle of fine cognac or single-malt scotch.

Vancouver Cigar Company. 1093 Hamilton St. ☎ **604/685-0445.** www.vancouvercigar.com.

The selection here is reputed to be the city's most extensive, featuring brands such as Cohiba, Monte Cristo, Macanudo, Hoyo De Monterrey, Romeo y Julieta, Partagas, Ashton, and A. Fuente. The shop also carries a complete line of accessories.

DEPARTMENT STORES

The Bay (Hudson's Bay Company). 674 Granville St. ☎ **604/681-6211.**

From the establishment of its early trading posts during the 1670s to its modern coast-to-coast chain, the Bay has built its reputation on quality goods. You can still buy a Hudson's Bay woolen "point" blanket (the colorful stripes originally represented how many beaver pelts each blanket was worth in trade), but you'll also find Tommy Hilfiger, Polo, DKNY, and more. The store doesn't accept pelts anymore, but it does take all major credit cards.

Hills of Kerrisdale. 2125 W. 41st Ave. ☎ **604/266-9177.**

This neighborhood department store in central Vancouver is a city landmark. Carrying full lines of quality men's, women's, and children's clothes, as well as furnishings and sporting goods, it's a destination for locals because the prices are often lower than those in the downtown core.

DISCOUNT SHOPPING

The strip of West Fourth Avenue between Cypress and Yew Streets has recently emerged as consignment-clothing central. New shops open regularly.

In-Again Clothing. 1962 W. Fourth Ave. ☎ **604/738-2782.**

Good variety of seasonal consignment clothing. The selection keeps up with fashion trends. Don't forget to look at the collection of purses, scarves, and belts.

Second Suit for Men & Women. 2036 W. Fourth Ave. ☎ **604/732-0338.**

This resale- and sample-clothing store has the best in men's and women's fashions, including Hugo Boss, Armani, Donna Karan, Nautica, Calvin Klein, and Alfred Sung. The inventory changes rapidly.

Upstairs on 4th. 2144 W. Fourth Ave. ☎ **604/732-3924.**

This upstairs shop is jam-packed with men's and women's secondhand clothing, some of it quality, all of it cheap, cheap, cheap. It takes a bit of browsing, but if you find something good in here, guaranteed it'll be a steal.

And elsewhere in the city is . . .

Wear Else? Clearance Centre. 78 E. Second Ave. ☎ **604/879-6162.**

Carrying the same items as its retail shops, this outlet store offers savings of 30% to 80% on Tommy Hilfiger, Jones New York, and other designer collections.

FASHIONS
For Children

Isola Bella. 5692 Yew St. ☎ **604/266-8808.**

This store imports an exclusive collection of rather expensive, high-fashion newborn and children's clothing from designers like Babar, Babymini, Milou, Petit Bateau, and Paul Smith.

✪ **Please Mum.** 2951 W. Broadway. ☎ **604/732-4574.**

This Kitsilano store sells attractive Vancouver-made toddlers' and children's cotton clothing.

For Men & Women

Vancouver has the Pacific Northwest's best collection of clothes from Paris, London, Milan, and Rome, in addition to a great assortment of locally made, cutting-edge fashions. International designer outlets include **Chanel Boutique,**

900 W. Hastings St. (☎ **604/682-0522**); **Salvatore Ferragamo,** 918 Robson St. (☎ **604/669-4495**); **Gianni Versace Boutique,** 757 W. Hastings St. (☎ **604/683-1131**); **Versace's Versus,** 1008 W. Georgia St. (☎ **604/688-8938**); **Polo/Ralph Lauren,** the Landing, 375 Water St. (☎ **604/682-7656**); and **Plaza Escada,** Sinclair Centre, 757 W. Hastings St. (☎ **604/688-8558**).

It seems that almost every week a new designer boutique opens in Yaletown, Kitsilano, or Kerrisdale.

✪ **Christine and Company.** 201–657 Marine Dr., West Vancouver. ☎ **604/922-0350.**

More than 20 years ago, Christine Morton started out selling delicate, antique, lacy sleepwear along with a few of her own lingerie creations. She then expanded to silky blouses and heirloom-quality trousseau lingerie. And she's now regarded as the city's hottest bridal-wear designer.

✪ **Dorothy Grant.** Sinclair Centre, 250–757 W. Hastings St. ☎ **604/681-0201.**

Designed to look like a Pacific Northwest longhouse, this shop is where First Nations designer Dorothy Grant exhibits her unique designs as well as her husband's (acclaimed artist Robert Davidson) collection of exquisitely detailed Haida motifs, which she appliqués on coats, leather vests, jackets, caps, and accessories. The clothes are gorgeous and collectible. She also carries contemporary Haida art and jewelry.

Dream 311. W. Cordova. ☎ **604/683-7326.**

Big-name designs can be found anywhere, but this little shop is one of the few places to show early collections—clothing and jewelry—of local designers.

Leone. Sinclair Centre, 757 W. Hastings St. ☎ **604/683-1133.**

Shop where the stars shop. Versace, Donna Karan, Byblos, Armani, and fabulous Italian and French accessories are sold in this very elegant building; valet parking provided.

Lulu Island Designs. Steveston Landing, 119–3800 Bayview St., Richmond. ☎ **604/275-0558.**

Inside this historic cannery, amid artifacts from Steveston's days as a 19th-century Japanese fishing village, you'll find high-quality embroidered and silk-screened shirts.

Roots Canada. 1001 Robson (corner of Burrard). ☎ **604/683-4305.**

For more than 20 years, this chain has featured sturdy, Canadian-made casual clothing. The flagship store on Robson is in the heart of the busiest shopping area of Vancouver. You'll find leather jackets, leather bags, footwear, outerwear, and athletic wear for the whole family. There are many other locations around town, including in the Pacific Centre, 701 W. Georgia St. (☎ **604/683-5465**).

Straiths. Hotel Vancouver, 900 W. Georgia St. ☎ **604/685-3301.**

If Valentino, Ungaro, Bally, and Testoni are your preferences, then visit this well-known shop, which features the best clothing and accessories from the world's leading designers, at designer prices (though if you're visiting from the States, you may discover that many items carry the same price tag, and the currency conversion becomes a 30% discount).

Swimco. 2166 W. Fourth Ave. ☎ **604/732-7946.** www.swimco.com.

Located near Kitsilano Beach, this store caters to swimmers and sunbathers. You will find a large variety of bikinis and bathing suits in the latest prints and colors for men, women, and children. Check out the latest in active beachwear, shorts, and tops.

Venus & Mars. 315 Cambie St. ☎ **604/687-1908.** www.venusandmars.nu.

This Gastown boutique features Vancouver designer Sanné Lambert's work, specializing in one-of-a-kind handmade gowns and velvet robes.

✪ **Zonda Nellis Design Ltd.** 2203 Granville St. ☎ **604/736-5668.**

Rich colors and intricate patterns highlight this Vancouver designer's imaginative handwoven separates, pleated silks, sweaters, vests, and soft knits. Nellis has also introduced a new line of hand-painted silks and sumptuous, sheer hand-painted velvet eveningwear.

Vintage Clothing

Deluxe Junk Co. 310 W. Cordova St. ☎ **604/685-4871.** www.deluxejunk. com.

The name fits—there's tons of junk. Amid the polyester jackets and worn-out dress shirts, however, are some truly great finds. Some real bargains have been known to pop up.

Legends Retro-Fashion. 4366 Main St. ☎ **604/875-0621.**

Specializing in unique retro clothing, Legends is well known among vintage purists for its cache of one-of-a-kind pieces. Most of the clothes, such as evening dresses, shoes, kid gloves, and other accessories, are in immaculate condition.

Tapestry Vintage Clothing. 321 Cambie St., Gastown. ☎ **604/687-1719.**

Consignment shop with an interesting collection of vintage women's clothing.

True Value Vintage Clothing. 710 Robson St. ☎ **604/685-5403.**

This underground shop has a collection of funky fashions from the 1930s through the 1990s, including tons of fake furs, leather jackets, denim, soccer jerseys, vintage bathing suits, formal wear, smoking jackets, sweaters, and accessories.

FIRST NATIONS ART

You'll find First Nations art all over the city. You don't have to purchase a pricey antique to acquire original Coast Salish or Haida work. As the experts at the **Museum of Anthropology** explain, if an item is crafted by any of the indigenous Pacific Northwest artisans, it's a real First Nations piece of art. The culture is ancient yet still very much alive. Pick up a copy of *Publication No. 10: A Guide to Buying Contemporary Northwest Coast Art* by Karen Duffel (available at the Museum of Anthropology), which details how to identify and care for these beautifully carved, worked, and woven pieces.

Even if you're not in the market, go gallery-hopping to see works by Haida artists **Bill Reid** (the province's best-known Native artist) and **Richard Davidson,** and by Kwakwaka'wakw artist and photographer **David Neel.**

Coastal Peoples Fine Arts Gallery. 1024 Mainland St. ☎ **604/685-9298.** www.coastalpeoples.com.

This Yaletown boutique offers an extensive collection of fine First Nations jewelry. The motifs—bear, salmon, whale, raven, and others—are drawn from local myths and translated into 14-karat or 18-karat gold and sterling-silver creations. Inuit sculptures and items made of glass or wood are also worth a look. Custom orders can be filled quickly or shipped worldwide.

⭗ **Images for a Canadian Heritage.** 164 Water St. ☎ **604/685-7046.**

This store and the Inuit Gallery of Vancouver (see below) are government-licensed First Nations art galleries, featuring traditional and contemporary works such as native designs on glass totems and copper plates. With a collection worthy of a museum, this shop deserves a visit whether you're buying or not.

Inuit Gallery of Vancouver. 345 Water St. ☎ **604/688-7323.**

Home to one of Canada's foremost collections of Inuit and First Nations art. The prices are oriented toward serious buyers, but it's worth a visit.

⭐ **Leona Lattimer Gallery.** 1590 W. Second Ave. ☎ **604/732-4556.**

This beautiful gallery presents museum-quality displays of Pacific Northwest First Nations art, including ceremonial masks, totem poles, limited-edition silk-screen prints, argillite sculptures, and expensive gold and silver jewelry. Prices start at a few dollars for an original print, and escalate quickly to the three-digits mark for most items.

Marion Scott Gallery. 481 Howe St. ☎ **604/685-1934.** www. marionscottgallery.com.

For more than 20 years, this gallery has been well regarded for its Inuit (Eskimo) and First Nations art collections.

FIRST NATIONS CRAFTS

Bold, traditional, and innovative geometric designs; intricate carvings; strong primary colors; and rich wood tones are just a few of the elements you'll find in First Nations works. Pacific Northwest tribes, including the Haida, Coast Salish, and Kwakwaka'wakw, create crafts, jewelry, and art that are collected throughout the world.

Authentic Cowichan Indian Knits. 424 W. Third St., North Vancouver. ☎ **604/988-4735.**

Freda Nahanee's cottage-industry shop on the North Vancouver Squamish Band Reserve carries thick Cowichan sweaters, carved-silver Kwakiutl jewelry, Squamish woodcarvings, beaded-leather moccasins, and woven baskets. Call ahead for open hours.

Hill's Indian Crafts. 165 Water St. ☎ **604/685-4249.**

In a re-creation of a trading post interior, this shop sells moccasins, ceremonial masks, Cowichan sweaters, wood sculptures, totem poles (priced up to C$35,000/US$23,450), silk-screen prints, soapstone sculptures, and gold, silver, and argillite jewelry.

⭐ **Khot-La-Cha Salish Handicrafts.** 270 Whonoak St., West Vancouver. ☎ **604/987-3339.**

Hand-tanned moose-hide crafts, wood carvings, Cowichan sweaters, porcupine-quill jewelry, and bone, silver, gold, and turquoise accessories are just a few of the selections at this Coast Salish crafts shop.

Museum of Anthropology. University of British Columbia, 6393 NW Marine Dr. ☎ **604/822-5087.**

Works by contemporary First Nations artisans as well as books about the culture and publications on identifying and caring for Pacific Northwest crafts.

FOOD

You'll find **salmon** everywhere in Vancouver. Many shops package whole, fresh salmon with ice packs for visitors to take home. Shops also carry delectable smoked salmon in travel-safe, vacuum-packed containers. Some offer decorative cedar gift boxes; most offer overnight air transport. Try other salmon treats such as salmon jerky and Indian candy (chunks of marinated smoked salmon), which are available at public markets such as Lonsdale Quay Market and Granville Island Public Market.

And even though salmon is the most popular item to buy in Vancouver, coffee flows like water—as does Belgian chocolate.

Cheena BC Limited. 667 Howe St. ☎ **604/684-5374.**

If fresh seafood is on your souvenir list, place your order in advance from this downtown shop. The staff will stow your catch (or selection) in a sturdy carton surrounded by ice packs and have it ready for pickup on the day of your departure. For something different and delicious, try the salmon jerky.

Chocolate Arts. 2037 W. Fourth Ave. ☎ **604/739-0475.**

The works at this West Fourth Avenue chocolatier are of such exquisite craftsmanship, they're sometimes a wrench to eat, occasionally also a hammer or nail—they make little chocolate toolboxes filled with tiny chocolate tools. Seasonal treats include pumpkin truffles around Halloween or eggnog truffles for Christmas. Look for the all-chocolate diorama in the window—it changes every month or so. Worth picking up for a gift are the native masks of thick dark chocolate.

House of Brussels Chocolates. Factory 208–750 Terminal Ave. ☎ **604/687-1524.**

Ever wonder whence cometh the little chocolate hedgehogs that have burrowed their way into every chocolate shop in town? These hazelnut-filled truffles were invented by none other than Brussels Chocolate, which was, alas, unable to secure a patent. They're still the best all-chocolate rodents for sale in the city, however, and if you make it down to the factory on Terminal Avenue, they're also the cheapest. Retail outlets are on Granville Island and in Cathedral Place.

The Lobsterman. 1807 Mast Tower Rd. ☎ **604/687-4531.** www.lobsterman.com.

Live lobsters, Dungeness crabs, oysters, mussels, clams, geoducks, and scallops are just a few of the varieties of seafood swimming in the saltwater tanks at this Granville Island fish store. The staff steams the food fresh on the spot, free. Salmon and other seafood can also be packed for air travel.

Murchie's Tea & Coffee. 970 Robson St. ☎ **604/669-0783.**

This Vancouver institution has been the city's main tea and coffee purveyor for more than a century. You'll find everything from Jamaican Blue Mountain and Kona coffees to Lapsang Souchong and Kemun teas. The knowledgeable staff will help you decide which flavors and blends fit your taste. There's also a fine selection of bone china and crystal serving ware, as well as coffeemakers and teapots.

South China Seas Trading Company. Granville Island Public Market. ☎ **604/681-5402.**

The South Seas have always been a source of intrigue. This shop re-creates a bit of that wonder, with a remarkable collection of rare spices and hard-to-find sauces. Look for fresh kaffir lime leaves, Thai basil, young ginger, sweet Thai chili sauce, and occasional exotic produce like mangosteens and rambutans. Pick up recipes and ideas from the knowledgeable staff.

FURNITURE
Inform. 97 Water St. ☎ **604/682-3868.**

Contemporary designer furniture, including Ingo Maurer, Eurolang, and the designs of co-owner Neils Bentson. The guy riding his mountain bike around the display floor may well be Brian Adams, who stops by occasionally on the way to his recording studio down the street.

VINTAGE FURNITURE

Metropolitan Home. 450 W. Hastings St. ☎ **604/681-2313.**

Modernism is back—sleek lines and elegant simplicity. This showroom bursts with so much current and vintage 20th-century modernist furniture that it's almost a museum.

Panther Decor. 2924 W. Fourth Ave. ☎ **604/733-5665.**

Crammed with furniture, clothing, and housewares from the 1950s to the 1970s. Prices are very reasonable.

GALLERIES

On the first Thursday of every month, many galleries hold free openings from 5 to 8pm. Check the *Georgia Straight* or *Vancouver Magazine* for listings.

Buschlen Mowatt. 111–1445 W. Georgia St. ☎ **604/682-1234.**

The city's leading "establishment" gallery. Look for paintings, sculptures, and prints from well-known Canadian and international artists.

Dianne Farris Gallery. 1565 W. Seventh Ave. ☎ **604/737-2629.**

Contemporary painting and sculpture, from up-and-coming artists and those who already have arrived.

Monte Clark Gallery. 2339 Granville St. ☎ **604/730-5000.**

This cutting-edge gallery—in the otherwise slightly staid confines of south Granville's gallery row—is one of the best spots to look for that rising superstar without the rising prices.

GIFTS & SOUVENIRS

Buddha Supply Centre. 4158 Main St. ☎ **604/873-8169.**

Want money to burn? At Chinese funerals people burn joss—paper replicas of earthly belongings—to help make the afterlife for the deceased more comfortable. This shop has more than 500 combustible products to choose from, including $1-million notes (drawn on the bank of hell), luxury penthouse condos, and that all-important cell phone.

Cows Vancouver. 1301 Robson St. ☎ **604/682-2622.**

Everybody knows at least one cow memorabilia collector, right? T-shirts, tableware, accessories, children's clothes, and trinkets are just a few of the bovine items sold. The ice-cream parlor serves delicious handmade ice cream in freshly baked waffle cones.

Nikaido Gifts. 150–3580 Moncton St., Steveston. ☎ **604/275-0262.**

Wedding kimonos, antique Hina dolls, *yukata* (cotton dressing gowns), plates, dishes, origami, imported teas, and many other lovely Asian items fill this Steveston gift store.

The Ocean Floor. 1522 Duranleau St. ☎ **604/681-5014.**

If you want to bring home a few gifts from the sea, then select from this Granville Island shop's collection of seashells, ship models, lamps, chimes, coral, shell jewelry, stained glass, and marine brass.

JEWELRY

With influences ranging from European and Asian to First Nations, local jewelers offer a wide selection of baubles and bangles in all price ranges.

Forge & Form. 1334 Cartwright St. ☎ **604/684-6298.**

Master Granville Island metal designers Dietje Hagedoorn and Jürgen Schönheit specialize in customized gold and silver jewelry. Renowned for their gold and silver bow ties, they also create unique pieces like "tension set" rings, which hold a stone in place without a setting. Their studio is located just past the False Creek Community Centre.

Henry Birk & Sons Ltd. 698 W. Hastings St. ☎ **604/669-3333.**

Established in 1879, Birk's has a long tradition of designing and crafting beautiful jewelry and watches.

✪ **Karl Stittgen + Goldsmiths.** 2203 Granville St. ☎ **604/737-0029.**

Stittgen's gold pins, pendants, rings, and other accessories demonstrate his eye for clean, crisp design and fine craftsmanship. Each work is a miniature architectural wonder.

The Raven and the Bear. 1528 Duranleau St. ☎ **604/669-3990.**

If you've never seen West Coast native jewelry, it's worth making a trip. Deeply inscribed with stylized creatures from Northwest mythology, these rings, bangles, and earrings are unforgettable. (See also "First Nations Crafts," above.)

MALLS & SHOPPING CENTERS

So maybe it does rain a little in Vancouver in the winter. Locals have two techniques. Some don Gore-Tex outerwear, head out, and embrace the damp. Others go inside. Fortunately, there are numerous indoor shopping centers, some of which stretch for blocks underground. There are even a few downtown shopping centers in renovated landmark buildings that are worth strolling through solely for their architecture.

The Landing. 375 Water St. ☎ **604/687-1144.**

This 1905 Gastown heritage warehouse was renovated into an upscale complex of shops and offices. Inside are designer boutiques such as Polo/Ralph Lauren and Fleet Street, as well as a few good restaurants.

Pacific Centre Mall. 700 W. Georgia St. ☎ **604/688-7236.**

This 3-block complex contains 200 shops and services, including Godiva, Benetton, Crabtree & Evelyn, and Eddie Bauer.

Park Royal Shopping Centre. 2002 Park Royal S., West Vancouver. ☎ **604/925-9576.**

Park Royal consists of two malls that face each other on Marine Drive, just west of the Lions Gate Bridge. The GAP, Coast Mountain Sports, Cypress Mountain Sports, Future Shop, Marks & Spencer, Disney, Eaton's, the Bay, Eddie Bauer, and a public market are just a few of the 250 stores in the center. Next door are also cinemas, bowling lanes, a golf driving range, community and special events, and a food court.

Sinclair Centre. 757 W. Hastings St. ☎ **604/659-1009.** www.sinclaircentre.com.

The Sinclair Centre incorporates four Vancouver landmarks: the Post Office (1910), Winch Building (1911), Customs Examining Warehouse (1913), and Federal Building (1937). Now restored, they house elite shops like Armani, Leone, and Dorothy Grant, as well as smaller boutiques, art galleries, and a food court.

Vancouver Centre. 650 W. Georgia St. ☎ **604/688-5658.**

The Bay, restaurants, a food fair, and more than 115 specialty stores connect underground to the adjoining Pacific Centre Mall (see above).

MARKETS

There are **green markets** scattered throughout the city. You don't have to go grocery shopping to have fun at these enclosed atriums and multilevel spaces; you just need to enjoy sampling food, looking at crafts, tasting British Columbian wines, or simply watching people. There's also a huge **flea market** in an old warehouse by the railway tracks, with as great a mix of stuff as you could possibly imagine.

Chinatown Night Market. 200 Keefer St. and 200 E. Pender St. Phone the Vancouver Tourism Info Centre at ☎ **604/683-2000.**

Across Asia, prime shopping time comes only after the sun has gone down and the temperature has dropped to something bearable. Friday and Saturday nights from May through September, merchants in Chinatown bring the tradition to Canada by closing two separate blocks to traffic and covering them with booths and tables and food stalls offering all manner of things, useful and otherwise. Come down, grab a juicy satay skewer, sip the juice from a freshly cracked coconut, and see what's up.

✪ **Granville Island Public Market.** 1669 Johnston St. ☎ **604/666-5784.** www.granvilleisland.com.

This 50,000-square-foot public market features produce, meats, fish, wines, cheeses, arts and crafts, and lots of fast-food counters offering a little of everything. Open daily from 9am to 6pm. From mid-June through September, the Farmers' Truck Market operates Thursday from 9am to 6pm.

Lonsdale Quay Market. 123 Carrie Cates Court, North Vancouver. ☎ **604/985-6261.** www.lonsdalequay.com.

Located at the SeaBus terminal, this public market is filled with produce, meats, fish, specialty fashions, gift shops, food counters, coffee bars, a hotel, and Kids' Alley (a section dedicated to children's shops and a play area). The upper floor houses a variety of fashion stores, bookstores, and gift shops. Open Saturday to Thursday from 9:30am to 6:30pm, and Friday from 9:30am to 9pm.

New Westminster Quay Public Market. 810 Quayside, New Westminster. ☎ **604/520-3881.**

A smaller version of Granville Island, it is located 25 minutes away by SkyTrain from downtown Vancouver. The market has a variety of gift shops, specialty stores, a food court, a delicatessen, and produce stands. Once you're finished browsing the market, make sure to have a gander at the neighboring Fraser River. A walkway extends along the river and allows great views of the waterfront, the busy boat traffic, and the occasional seal or sea lion.

Robson Public Market. 1610 Robson St. ☎ **604/682-2733.**

Located a few blocks from Stanley Park, this neighborhood market is housed in a modern glass atrium. You'll find produce sellers, two bakeries, a salmon shop, and one of the city's best butcher shops, R. B. Meats, which, in addition to fine steaks, lamb, and poultry, sells meat pies, South African–style dried meats, and other delicacies. The upstairs food court has French, Italian, Greek, Chinese, and Japanese restaurants. Open daily from 9am to 9pm.

Vancouver Flea Market. 703 Terminal Ave. ☎ **604/685-0666.**

Near the train/bus terminal, Vancouver's largest flea market boasts more than 350 stalls. Admittedly, most are stocked with cheap T-shirts, linens, used tools and such, but it's still possible to discover some real finds. Go early or the savvy shoppers will have already cleaned out the real gems. Admission is C60¢ (US40¢) for adults, free for children under 12. Open Saturday, Sunday, and holidays from 9am to 5pm.

MUSIC

Crosstown Music. 518 W. Pender St. ☎ **604/683-8774.**

This small shop is filled with used rock, jazz, and blues CDs, tapes, and albums.

Sam the Record Man. 568 Seymour St. ☎ **604/684-3722.**

Four floors of tapes, CDs, and videos cover a full range of sounds. Many albums here aren't available in the States.

Virgin Megastore. 788 Burrard St. at Robson St. ☎ **604/669-2289.**

With over 150,000 titles housed in a three-story, 42,000-square-foot space, it's Canada's largest music and entertainment store.

Zulu Records. 1972 W. Fourth Ave. ☎ **604/738-3232.**

Located in Kitsilano, Zulu Records specializes in alternative music, local and import, new and used. You will also find a good selection of vinyl and magazines. Staff is happy to make recommendations and bring you up to speed on what's hot in the local music scene.

SHOES

A walking city has to have some great shoe outlets. Vancouver has an abundance of ornate cowboy boots, sturdy Doc Martens, funky clogs, weatherproof hiking shoes and boots, and fine Swiss and Italian footwear.

The Australian Boot Company. 1968 W. Fourth Ave. ☎ **604/738-2668.** www.australianboot.com.

These shoes may look a bit like Doc Martens, but the Australian shoemaker Blundstone has been making them that way for most of the last century. The Australian Boot Company, 1½ blocks west of Burrard Street, carries a wide selection of Blundstone's and R. M. Williams's finest and most rugged footwear.

David Gordon. 822 Granville St. ☎ **604/685-3784.**

This is Vancouver's oldest Western boot, hat, and accessories store. But it's far from stodgy. Boots include an extensive selection of Tony Lama, Boulet, Durango, HH Brown, and Dan Post. You'll also find Vans, Doc Martens, and a lineup of other funky footwear that attracts skateboarders and club kids.

John Fluevog Boots & Shoes Ltd. 837 Granville St. ☎ **604/688-2828.**

This native Vancouverite has a growing international cult following of designers and models clamoring for his under-C$200 (US$134) creations. You'll find outrageous platforms and clogs, Angelic Sole work boots, and a few bizarre experiments for the daring footwear fetishist.

SPECIALTY

Lush. 1118 Denman St. ☎ **604/608-1810.**

Although it has the look of an old-fashioned deli store with big wheels of cheese, slabs of sweets, chocolate bars, dips, and sauces, take a bite and you'd be washing your mouth with soap—literally. All these beautiful, mouthwatering displays are indeed soaps, shampoos, skin treatments, massage oils, and bath bombs. Made from all natural ingredients, these deceptively real looking treats are the perfect pampering gift. Everything is sold by the gram. Various other Lush stores can be found around town, including 100–1025 Robson St. (☎ **604/ 687-5874**). Just follow your nose.

The Market Kitchen Store. 2–1666 Johnston (Net Loft, Granville Island). ☎ **604/681-7399.**

Everything you'd like to have on your kitchen counters or in your kitchen drawers—gourmet kitchen accessories, baking utensils, and gadgets. Anyone need a citrus zester?

Railway World. 150 Water St. ☎ **604/681-4811.**

Lovers of model trains, cars, and planes will be in seventh heaven in this small, jam-packed shop. There are some great Canadian model trains in N, HO, and O gauges, as well as collectors' books and magazines.

Spy-Central. 1463 Robson St. ☎ **604/642-0324.**

A haven for spies, paranoids, and the just plain snoopy, Spy-Central offers cell-phone scanners, miniature cameras, night-vision gear, and a good selection of useful books with titles such as *How to Get Anything on Anyone.* Clumsy shoppers take note: If you break it, they know your credit card number.

Three Dog Bakery. 2186 W. Fourth Ave. ☎ **604/737-3647.**

Beagle Bagels, Scottie Biscotti, or Gracie's Rollovers. Canines will have a hard time deciding on a favorite treat from this gone-to-the-dogs bakery. The store also has leashes, collars, greeting cards, and other dog paraphernalia.

SPORTING GOODS

Boardhead Central.

Not a shop, but a phenomenon. In the past few years, the corner of Fourth Avenue and Burrard Street has become the spot for high-quality snow/skate/surf board gear, and the spot to see top-level boarders and their groupies hanging out. **Pacific Boarder** is at 1793 W. Fourth Ave. (☎ **604/734-7245**). **Thriller** is at 1710 W. Fourth Ave. (☎ **604/736-5651**). **West Beach,** at 1766 W. Fourth Ave. (☎ **604/731-6449**), sometimes hosts pro-skate demos on the half-pipe at the back of the store.

Mountain Equipment Co-op. 130 W. Broadway. ☎ **604/872-7858.** www.mec.ca.

A true West Coast institution and an outdoors lover's dream come true, this block-long store houses the best selection of top-quality outdoor gear: rain gear, clothing, hiking shoes, climbing gear, backpacks, sleeping bags, tents, and more. Memorize the MEC label, you're sure to see it later—at the beach, the bar, the concert hall.

TOYS

The Games People. 157 Water St. ☎ **604/685-5825.**

The Games People carries a huge selection of board games, strategy games, role-playing games, puzzles, models, toys, hobby materials, and other amusements. It's difficult to walk past this store, whether you're an adult or a kid.

Kid's Market. 1496 Cartwright St. (on Granville Island). ☎ **604/689-8447.** www.kids-market.net.

Probably the only mall in North America dedicated to kids, the Kid's Market on Granville Island features a Lilliputian entranceway, toy and craft and book stores, play areas, and services for the younger set, including even a "fun hairdresser."

Kites on Clouds. The Courtyard, 131 Water St. ☎ **604/669-5677.**

This little Gastown shop has every type of kite. Prices range from C$10 to C$20 (US$7 to US$13) for nylon or Mylar dragon kites to just under C$200 (US$134) for more elaborate ghost clippers and nylon hang-glider kites.

WINE

British Columbia's **wines** are worth buying by the case, especially rich, honey-thick ice wines such as Jackson-Triggs gold-medal–winning 1994 Johannesburg Riesling Ice wine, and bold reds, such as the Quail's Gate 1994 Limited Release Pinot Noir. Five years of restructuring, reblending, and careful tending by French and German master vintners have won the province's vineyards world recognition.

When buying B.C. wine, look for the VQA (Vintner Quality Alliance) seal on the label; it's a guarantee that all grapes used are grown in British Columbia and meet European standards for growing and processing.

Summerhill, Cedar Creek, Mission Hill, and **Okanagan Vineyards** are just a few of the more than 50 local estates producing hearty cabernet sauvignons, honey-rich ice wines, and oaky merlots. These wines can be found at any government-owned **LCB** liquor store, such as the one at 1716 Robson St.

(☎ **604/660-4576;** or call 604/660-9463 for the nearest location), and at some privately owned wine stores.

Marquis Wine Cellars. 1034 Davie St. ☎ **604/684-0445** or 604/685-2246. www.marquis-wines.com.

The owner and staff of this West End wine shop are dedicated to educating their patrons about wines. They conduct evening wine tastings, featuring selections from their special purchases. They also publish monthly newsletters. In addition to carrying a full range of British Columbian wines, the shop also has a large international selection.

The Okanagan Estate Wine Cellar. The Bay, 674 Granville St. ☎ **604/681-6211.**

This department store annex, located in the Vancouver Centre mall concourse's Market Square, offers a great selection of British Columbian wines by the bottle and the case.

7

Vancouver After Dark

*V*ancouver is a fly-by-the-seat-of-the-pants kind of town. There's so much to see and do—and the outdoors always beckons—that Vancouverites wait till the day or the hour before a show to plunk their cash down on the barrel. It drives promoters crazy. Not that they stop promoting. Indeed, for a city its size—or twice its size—Vancouver is blessed with entertainment options, from cutting-edge theater companies to a well-respected opera and symphony to folk and jazz festivals that draw people from up and down the coast. And then there are the bars and pubs and clubs and cafes—lots of them—for every taste, budget, and fetish; you just have to get out there and see. Just keep in mind that most dance clubs and even bars downtown charge a cover and have a line on Fridays and Saturdays. There often doesn't seem to be a correlation between the number of people entering and the number of people exiting; you are at the mercy of the bouncers. Some techniques to beat the line: Arrive unfashionably early (before 9pm), make friends with the bouncers or anyone who can get your name on the VIP list, be outrageously beautiful, or drive up in fancy wheels.

For an overview of Vancouver's nightlife, pick up a copy of the weekly tabloid the *Georgia Straight.* It gives up-to-date music and entertainment schedules as well as information about what's going on in the city and surrounding areas. Or get a copy of *Xtra! West,* the free gay and lesbian biweekly tabloid available in shops and restaurants throughout the West End. The Thursday edition of the *Vancouver Sun* contains the weekly entertainment section *Queue.* You can find the publications at bookstores, venues, and curbside boxes.

The monthly *Vancouver Magazine* is filled with listings and strong views about what's really hot in the city. On the Internet, you can check out Vancouver club listings, band profiles, and restaurant reviews at **www.vanmag.com**.

The **Vancouver Cultural Alliance Arts Hotline,** 100–938 Howe St. (☎ **604/684-2787** or 604/681-3535; www.allianceforarts.com), is a great information source for all performing arts, music, theater, literary events, art films, and dance, including where and how to get tickets. The office is open Monday to Friday from 9am to 5pm.

Ticketmaster (Vancouver Ticket Centre), 1304 Hornby St. (☎ **604/280-3311;** www.ticketmaster.ca), has 40 outlets in the greater Vancouver area, and the same monopoly on venues as in most Canadian cities, along with the same steep service charges. With a credit card, tickets can be purchased over the phone and picked up at the venue.

Three major Vancouver theaters regularly host touring performances. The **Orpheum Theatre,** 801 Granville St. (☎ **604/665-3050;** www.city.vancouver.bc.ca), is the refurbished home of the Vancouver Symphony Orchestra. It's an elegant 1927 theater that originally hosted the Chicago-based Orpheum vaudeville circuit. The theater's ornate interior is filled with crystal chandeliers, gilded arches, domes, and an original Wurlitzer organ. The theater also hosts pop, rock, and variety shows.

The **Queen Elizabeth Complex,** 600 Hamilton St., between Georgia and Dunsmuir Streets (☎ **604/665-3050;** www.city.vancouver.bc.ca), consists of the Queen Elizabeth Theatre and the Vancouver Playhouse. It hosts major national and touring musical and theater productions. It's also home to the Vancouver Opera and Ballet British Columbia. The 670-seat Vancouver Playhouse presents chamber-music performances and recitals.

Located in a converted turn-of-the-20th-century church, the **Vancouver East Cultural Centre** (the "Cultch" to locals), 1895 Venables St. (☎ **604/254-9578;** www.vecc.bc.ca), coordinates an impressive program that includes avant-garde theater productions, performances by international musical groups, festivals and cultural events, children's programs, and art exhibitions. Advance ticket sales are through Ticketmaster. See above for phone number.

On the campus of UBC, the **Chan Centre for the Performing Arts,** 6265 Crescent Rd. (☎ **604/822-2697**), showcases the work of the UBC music and acting students, and also hosts a winter concert series. Designed by local architectural luminary Bing Thom, the Chan Centre's crystal-clear acoustics are the best in town.

Generally, bars and clubs are open until 2am every day except Sunday, when they close at midnight.

1 The Performing Arts

THEATER

Theater isn't only an indoor pastime here. There is an annual summertime Shakespeare series, **Bard on the Beach,** in Vanier Park (☎ **604/737-0625**). You can also bring a picnic dinner to Stanley Park and watch **Theatre Under the Stars** (see below), which features popular musicals and light comedies. For more original fare, don't miss ✪ **The Fringe— Vancouver's Theatre Festival** (☎ 604/257-0350; www. vancouverfringe.com). Centered on Granville Island, the Fringe Festival features more than 500 innovative and original shows each September, all costing under C$12 (US$8).

✪ **Arts Club Theatre Company.** Granville Island Stage at the Arts Club Theatre, 1585 Johnston St., and The Stanley Theatre, 2750 Granville St. ☎ **604/ 687-1644.** www.artsclub.com. Tickets C$13–C$45 (US$9–US$30). Senior, student, and group discounts available. Box office 9am–7pm.

The 425-seat Granville Island Mainstage presents major dramas, comedies, and musicals, with post-performance entertainment in the Backstage Lounge. The Arts Club Revue Stage is an intimate, cabaret-style showcase for small productions, improvisation nights, and musical revues such as *The Cripple of Inishmaan* and *The Threepenny Opera.* The old art deco Stanley has recently undergone a glorious renovation and now plays host to longer running plays and musicals, such as *A Closer Walk with Patsy Cline.*

Firehall Arts Centre. 280 E. Cordova St. ☎ **604/689-0926.** www. firehall.org. Tickets C$8–C$18 (US$5–US$12). Senior and student discounts available. Box office Mon–Fri 9:30am–5pm, and 1 hr. before show time.

Housed in Vancouver's Firehouse No. 1, the Centre has for 20 years been home to the cutting-edge Firehall Theatre Company. Expect original, experimental, and challenging plays, such as last year's hit *Filthy Rich* by George F. Walker and Kudelka's *Janus/Janis.* The companies also present dance events, arts festivals, and concerts.

Frederic Wood Theatre. Gate 4, University of British Columbia. ☎ **604/ 822-2678.** Tickets C$15 (US$10) adults, C$9 (US$5) students. No performances in the summer. Box office Mon–Fri 10:30am–3pm. All shows start at 7:30pm.

Forget that "student production" thing you've got in your head. Students at UBC are actors in training, and their productions are extremely high-caliber. For the price, they're a steal. They present classic dramatic works to Broadway musicals to new plays by Canadian playwrights.

Theatre Under the Stars. Malkin Bowl, Stanley Park. ☎ **604/687-0174.** www.tuts.bc.ca. Tickets C$23 (US$15) adults, C$16 (US$11) seniors and children. Box office Mon–Sat 10am–5pm and 7–8pm (show time).

From mid-July to mid-August, old-time favorite musicals like *Annie Get Your Gun, West Side Story, South Pacific* or *Grease* are performed outdoors by a mixed cast of amateur and professional actors. Bring a blanket (it gets cold once the sun sets) and a picnic dinner for a relaxing evening of summer entertainment.

Vancouver Little Theatre. Heritage Hall, 3102 Main St. (enter from the back alley). ☎ **604/876-4165.** Tickets usually C$7–C$12 (US$4.70–US$8). Senior and student discounts available. Box office opens 30 min. before show time.

Works by new Canadian playwrights and an international array of controversial dramatists are presented here by professional, local, and traveling companies.

Vancouver Playhouse. 600 Hamilton, between Georgia and Hamilton sts. in the Queen Elizabeth complex. ☎ **604/665-3050.** Tickets usually C$8–C$16 (US$5–US$11). Senior and student discounts available. Box office opens 30 min. before show time.

Well into its third decade, the company at the Vancouver Playhouse presents a program of six plays each season, usually a mix of the internationally known, nationally recognized, and locally promising.

OPERA
Vancouver Opera. 500–845 Cambie St. ☎ **604/683-0222.** www. vanopera.bc.ca. Tickets usually C$36–C$96 (US$24–US$64). Box office Mon–Fri 9am–4pm.

In a kind of willful flirtation with death, the Vancouver Opera Company alternates between obscure or new (and Canadian!) works and older, more popular perennials, often sung by international stars such as Placido Domingo and Bryn Terfel. The formula seems to work, for the company is over 35 years old and still packing 'em in. The season runs from October through June, with performances normally in the Queen Elizabeth Theatre. English supertitles projected above the stage help audiences follow the dialogue of the lavish productions.

CLASSICAL MUSIC

Fans of chamber music, baroque fugues, Russian romantic symphonies, and popular show tunes will find world-class concert performances in Vancouver.

University of British Columbia School of Music. Recital Hall, Gate 4, 6361 Memorial Rd. ☎ **604/822-5574.** www.music.ubc.ca. E-mail: concerts@ interchange.ubc.ca. Tickets purchased at the door, C$4–C$24 (US$2.70– US$16) adults, C$4–C$14 (US$2.70–US$9) seniors and students. Many concerts are free. The Wed noon hour series costs C$4 (US$2.70).

From September through November, and during January and March, UBC presents eight faculty and guest-artist concerts. They feature piano, piano and violin, opera, or quartets, plus occasional performances by acts like the Count Basie Orchestra. If the concert is in the Chan Centre, go. There are few halls in the world with such beautiful acoustics.

○ **Vancouver Bach Choir.** 805–235 Keith Rd., West Vancouver. ☎ **604/ 921-8012.** Tickets C$15–C$30 (US$10–US$20), depending on the performance. Tickets available through Ticketmaster.

Vancouver's international, award-winning amateur choir, a 150-voice ensemble, presents five major concerts a year at the Orpheum Theatre. Specializing in symphonic choral music, the Choir's sing-along performance of Handel's *Messiah* during the Christmas season is a favorite.

Vancouver Cantata Singers. 5115 Keith Rd., West Vancouver. ☎ **604/ 921-8588.** www.cantata.org. Tickets C$20 (US$13) adults, C$16 (US$11) seniors and students. Tickets through Ticketmaster or at the door.

This semiprofessional 40-person choir specializes in early music. The company performs works by Bach, Brahms, Monteverdi, Stravinsky, and Handel, as well as Eastern European choral music. The season normally includes three programs: in October, December, and March at various locations.

Vancouver Chamber Choir. 1254 W. Seventh Ave. ☎ **604/738-6822.** www.vancouverchamberchoir.com. E-mail: info@vancouverchamberchoir.com. Tickets C$15–C$35 (US$10–US$23) adults, C$13–C$25 (US$9–US$17) seniors and students. Tickets through Ticketmaster.

Western Canada's only professional choral ensemble presents an annual concert series at the Orpheum Theatre, the Chan Centre, and Ryerson United Church. Under conductor John Washburn, the choir has gained an international reputation.

Vancouver New Music. 207 W. Hastings St. ☎ **604/606-6440.** www.newmusic.org. Tickets C$20–C$35 (US$13–US$23) adults, C$16 (US$11) students.

This company presents seven annual concerts, featuring the works of contemporary and avant-garde composers as well as mixed-media performances that combine dance and film. Performances take place at the Vancouver East Cultural Centre between September and June. The society also hosts a biannual new-music festival, but the next one, alas, is not until June 2002.

Vancouver Symphony. 601 Smithe St. ☎ **604/876-3434** for ticket information. www.vancouversymphony.ca. Tickets C$22–C$60 (US$15–US$40) adults. Senior and student discounts available. Box office Mon–Fri 1–5pm and 6pm to show time day of performance.

At its home in the Orpheum Theatre during the fall, winter, and spring, Vancouver's extremely active orchestra presents the "Masterworks" series of great classical works; "Casual Classics," featuring light classics from a single era or composer and a casually dressed orchestra; "Tea & Trumpets," highlighting modern classics and ethnic works, hosted by the CBC's Otto Lowy; "Symphony Pops," featuring selections of popular and show tunes; and "Kid's Koncerts," a series geared toward school-age children. The traveling summer concert series takes the orchestra from White Rock and Cloverdale on the U.S. border to the tops of Whistler and Blackcomb Mountains.

DANCE

For fans of modern and original dance, the time to be here is early July, when the **Dancing on the Edge Festival** (☎ **604/689-0691**) presents 60 to 80 envelope-pushing original pieces over a 10-day period. For more information about other festivals and dance companies around the city, call the **Dance Centre** at ☎ **604/606-6400.**

Ballet British Columbia. 1101 W. Broadway. ☎ **604/732-5003.** www.balletbc.com. Tickets C$18–C$52 (US$12–US$35) adults. Senior and student discounts available.

Just over 16 years old, this company strives to present innovative works, such as those by choreographers John Cranko and William Forsythe, along with more traditional fare, including productions by visiting companies such as American Ballet

Theatre, the Royal Winnipeg Ballet, and the Moscow Classical Ballet. Performances are usually at the Queen Elizabeth Theatre, 600 Hamilton St.

2 Laughter & Music

COMEDY CLUBS

Vancouver TheatreSports League. Arts Club Stage, Granville Island. ☎ 604/738-7013. www.vtsl.com. Shows Wed–Thurs 7:30pm, Fri–Sat 8, 10, and 11:45pm. Weekends C$15 (US$10) adults, C$11 (US$7) seniors and students; weeknights C$7 (US$4.70).

Part comedy, part theater, and partly a take-no-prisoner's test of an actor's ability to think on his or her feet, TheatreSports involves actors taking suggestions from the audience and spinning them into short skits or full plays, often with hilarious results. Since moving to the Arts Club Stage, Vancouver's TheatreSports leaguers have had to reign in their normally raunchy instincts for the more family-friendly audience— except, that is, for Friday and Saturday at 11:45pm, when the Red-Hot Improv show takes the audience into the R-rated realm.

Yuk Yuk's Komedy Kabaret. Plaza of Nations, 750 Pacific Blvd. ☎ 604/687-5233. Cover C$5–C$10 (US$3.35–US$7). Shows Tues–Thurs 9pm, Fri–Sat 9 and 11pm.

A constantly changing lineup of leading Canadian and American stand-up comics play at Yuk Yuk's. Amateurs take the stage for Wednesday night open mike. In the 200-seat theater, it's hard to get a bad seat.

STRICTLY LIVE

Besides the listings below, every June the **du Maurier International Jazz Festival** (☎ 604/872-5200) takes over many venues and outdoor locations around town. The festival includes a number of free concerts. The **Vancouver Folk Festival** (☎ 604/602-9798) takes place outdoors in July on the beach at Jericho Park. The **Coastal Jazz and Blues Society,** 316 W. Sixth Ave. (☎ 604/872-5200), has information on current and upcoming events throughout the year.

The Commodore Ballroom. 868 Granville St. ☎ 604/739-7469. www.commodoreballroom.com. Tickets C$5–C$50 (US$3.35–US$34).

Every town should have one, but sadly very few do: a huge old-time dance hall, complete with suspended hard-wood dance floor that bounces gently up and down beneath your nimble or less-than-nimble toes. And though the room and floor date back to the jazz age, the lineup nowadays includes many of the best modern bands coming through town. Sightlines are excellent. Indeed, the Commodore's one of the best places I know to catch a midsized band—and thanks to a recent renovation, the room looks better than ever.

The Roxy. 932 Granville St. ☎ **604/684-7699.** www.roxyvan.com. Cover C$5–C$8 (US$3.35–US$5).

Live bands play every day of the week in this casual club, which also features show-off bartenders with Tom Cruise *Cocktail*-style moves. The house bands Joe's Garage and Dr.Strangelove keep the Roxy packed, and on weekends lines are long. Theme parties (often with vacation giveaways), Extreme Karaoke, Canadian content, '80s only, and other events add to the entertainment.

The Starfish Room. 1055 Homer St., near Helmcken St. ☎ **604/682-4171.** Cover C$3–C$30 (US$2–US$20), depending on the act.

The Room itself is a big echoing chamber with less-than-optimum sightlines, yet Starfish promoters consistently bring in some of the best talent on tour. Lineups include international recording stars as well as local artists, playing everything from jazz and blues to Celtic to lounge, funk, and, in rare fits of nostalgia, even punk. Jon Spencer Blues Explosion, the Paperboys, Kevin Kane, and Jeff Buckley are just a few of the acts that have played here recently. Tables can be a bit of a squeeze, especially when local groups like the Colorifics take the stage.

The WISE Club. 1882 Adanac St. ☎ **604/254-5858.** Cover depends on show; C$15 (US$10) for most bands.

Folk, folk, and more folk. In the far-off reaches of East Vancouver (okay, Commercial Drive area), the WISE Hall was unplugged long before MTV ever thought of reaching for the power cord. Bands are local and international, and the room's a lot of fun—like a church basement or community center—with alcohol.

Yale Hotel. 1300 Granville St. ☎ **604/681-9253.** www.theyale.com. Cover Thurs–Sat C$3–C$15 (US$2–US$10).

This century-old tavern on the far south end of Granville is Vancouver's one and only home of the blues. Visiting heavyweights have included Koko Taylor, Stevie Ray Vaughan,

Junior Wells, and Jeff Healey. The pictures in the entryway are a who's who of the blues. When outside talent's not available, the Yale makes do with what's homegrown, including Long John Baldry and local bluesman Jim Byrne. Shows are Monday to Saturday at 9:30pm. On Saturday and Sunday, there's an open-stage blues jam from 3 to 7pm.

ALMOST LIVE

Over the past few years, DJs have slowly replaced bands on the local music scene. Bars that exclusively book live music are nearly nonexistent; many places feature DJs only, and a few offer a mix.

Babalu. 654 Nelson St. (at Granville). ☎ **604/605-4343.** Cover C$3–C$7 (US$2–US$4.70).

Located about halfway down the Granville Street strip, this hopping little club offers R&B, swing, salsa, Latino, and jazz to a late 20s and 30s crowd. Midweek belongs to the house band, The Smoking Section, while on other nights there are visiting acts or DJs. A tiny dance floor means constant jostling, but no one in this good-natured crowd ever seems to mind. Open Thursday to Sunday.

Chameleon Urban Lounge. 801 W. Georgia St. (entrance on Howe St.). ☎ **604/669-0806.** www.chameleonlounge.com. Cover Mon–Thurs C$5 (US$3.35), Fri–Sat C$7 (US$4.70).

Under the landmark Hotel Georgia, the Chameleon feels like a scene out of a Fellini movie. Set in a high-ceilinged, plush basement lounge, it features live jazz, funk, and salsa most evenings, offers a full martini menu, and attracts a very urban crowd. No Doubt, Weezer, Jason Priestly, Christopher Walken, and many more celebs have dropped in for an evening.

Hot Jazz Society. 2120 Main St. ☎ **604/873-4131.** Cover C$10–C$12 (US$7–US$8) only for special acts, otherwise no cover.

Playing everything from Dixieland to swing, Latin to progressive, this club caters to dedicated fans of both jazz and dance. The dance floor is packed no matter who is playing. On Tuesday nights the Wow Big Band plays swing tunes, and on Thursday nights dance lessons are included in the price of admission. Call for more details.

✪ **The Purple Onion.** 15 Water St. ☎ **604/602-9442.** www.purpleonion. com. Cover C$5–C$8 (US$3.35–US$5).

Some clubs do DJ to survive, some have bands; the Onion serves up both, all for the same cover. The Club room is dance floor pure and simple. At the moment, an '80s dance party is alternating nights with house. Down the hall and round a left turn is the Lounge, where the house band squeals out funky danceable jazz for a slightly older crowd three nights a week. There's karaoke on oh-so-dead Sunday. During the Jazz Festival, this place hops.

The Sugar Refinery. 1115 Granville St. ☎ **604/683-2004.** No cover.

This tiny hole up a darkened stairway on the unfashionable end of Granville Street is immensely popular. Try as I might, I don't get it. The room is cramped and narrow, the sightlines horrible. Bands are still able to find a spot and perform. When there's a DJ, the decidedly lo-fi sound system has all the resonance of your little brother working the family turntable. But people are voting with their feet, and I'm outnumbered.

3 Bars, Pubs & Other Watering Holes

Visitors to Vancouver need to know that when it comes to liquor regulations, our city is a bizarre and Byzantine place. For historical and political reasons too difficult to get into, bars and pubs are still seen by officialdom as a Bad Thing, so new pub licenses are impossible to come by. What are available are restaurant licenses and, as Vancouverites love a drink as much as anyone, there are many restaurants that look suspiciously like pubs. The trick is that patrons in a restaurant can drink only if they eat or—here's the Kafkaesque kicker—have the intention of eating. So, if a waitress in a place that looks for all the world like a pub asks if you'll be eating, take the appetizer menu, smile, and say "Yes." As long as the menu's on the table, odds are the establishment's liquor license is safe. Occasionally, after a few pints you'll be asked to buy some fries or wings or even a large chocolate chip cookie in order to satisfy the letter of the law. Take it in stride, or take off for a new pub (er, restaurant); just please, don't take offense—remember, it's our bureaucrats, not us.

RESTAURANTS MASQUERADING AS BARS

The Alibi Room. 157 Alexander St. ☎ **604/623-3383.** www.alibiroom.com.

Higher-end trendy restaurant/bar brought to you at least in part by *X-Files* star Gillian Anderson, the Alibi Room offers upstairs diners modern cuisine and a chance to flip through shelves full of old film scripts. Monthly script readings provide a venue for ever hopeful wanna-be screenwriters. Downstairs there's a DJ. Located on the eastern edge of Gastown.

✪ **The Atlantic Trap and Gill.** 612 Davie St. ☎ **604/806-6393.**

Regulars in this sea shanty of a pub know the words to every song sung by the Irish and East Coast bands that appear onstage most every night. Guinness and Keith's are the brews of choice, and don't worry too much about ordering food. As the song goes: *"I'se the bye that orders the pint, I'se the bye that drinks her, keep your menus up in sight, and the government's none the wiser."* Or something like that.

Cellar Jazz Cafe. 3611 W. Broadway. ☎ **604/738-1959.**

Jazz has a loose definition on the West Coast. In this dark downstairs Kitsilano boîte, the often-as-not live sounds stretch to include funk, fusion, jazz, and occasionally even hip-hop. Local jazz aficionados swear by this place and almost begged us not to list their favorite hangout for fear of crowds.

DV8. 515 Davie St. ☎ **604/682-4388.** www.dv8lounge.com.

Even skate rats and snowboarders have to alight sometime, and this little Davie Street eatery is where the tribe comes to quaff pints and swap a brand of shoptalk incomprehensible to anyone born before Reagan took office. Bask in their youth. Enjoy the beer. DJs and live music weekly. Also check out the gallery space for monthly changing exhibits of innovative artwork.

✪ **The Jupiter Cafe.** 1216 Bute St. ☎ **604/609-6665.** www.jupitercafe. com.

Located just off busy Davie Street in the West End, the Jupiter Cafe combines a postapocalyptic industrial look with lounge chic. Black ceilings, exposed pipes, and roof struts mix surprisingly well with chandeliers, velvet curtains, and plush chairs. More importantly, the Jupiter is open late (till 4am some nights). True, it can be a challenge to flag down your waiter, but that gives you more time to scope out the crowd: gay and straight, funky and preppy, casual and dressed to kill. A huge outdoor patio provides a pleasant refuge from the street, but on colder nights, it's the exclusive domain of die-hard smokers. The menu—burgers, pastas, and pizzas—is largely decorative.

Monsoon Restaurant. 2526 Main St. ☎ **604/879-4001.**

What this slim little bistro in the otherwise sleepy section of Main and Broadway does really well is beer and fusion-induced tapas, accompanied by a buzzing atmosphere generated by interesting and sometimes beautiful people.

✪ **Naked.** 432 Richards St. ☎ **604/609-2700.**

Naked is located up a marble staircase on the top floor of a former bank building downtown. The room is something out of Arabian Nights; rich warm light from candles and lanterns diffuses through billowing swaths of fabric hanging round low divans, couches, and foot-high tables. It's the perfect place to meet friends for cocktails—early or late—and share some food, served up by the kitchen of the downstairs Ballantynes Restaurant. Among the menu offerings are shiitake mushroom–and–bean sprout salad rolls and smoked-salmon sushi. DJs spin acid and/or jazz and other down-tempo grooves, without drowning out all conversation. Open Thursday to Sunday.

Urban Well. 1516 Yew St. ☎ **604/737-7770.**

The tanned and taut from nearby Kits Beach drop into the Well as the sun goes down, and often don't emerge until the next day. Monday and Tuesday there's comedy, with DJs the rest of the week. Regulars line up on the patio counter to people-watch, while inside there's a tiny dance floor for demonstrating once again that you can get down in beach sandals.

✪ **The Whip Gallery Restaurant.** 209 E. Sixth Ave. ☎ **604/874-4687.**

The Whip's the one place in the city where the wall art and the clientele match. The folks sipping and munching look like they could—and probably did—produce the art hanging on the walls. Young and angry isn't the look here. Whip customers have some success under their belts and are mellowing into their 40s and 50s. Food is above average, which is good, 'cause they occasionally do insist you order something. Jazz combos sometimes set up in the corner.

ACTUAL BARS

The Arts Club Backstage Lounge. 1585 Johnston St., Granville Island. ☎ **604/687-1354.**

The Arts Club Lounge has a fabulous location under the bridge by the water on the edge of False Creek. Crowd is a mix of tourists and art school students from neighboring Emily Carr College. Friday and Saturday, there's a live band in the evenings. Most other times, if the sun's out, the waterfront patio is packed.

✪ **The Brickhouse Bar.** 730 Main St. ☎ **604/689-8645.**

Anthropologists and urban planners often speak of Gentrifiers— that tribe of mostly younger humanity who move into a down-at-the-heels neighborhood and by their presence and earning ability transform "gritty" into "funky," and then as the even-more-upscale yuppies arrive, into just plain freaking expensive. Main Street is still in the funky stage, and an evening at the Brickhouse is your chance to watch the tribe at play. The warm and bustling bar has pool tables and comfy couches from which to watch artists and dot-commers and their upscale cousins vie for table time, bar space, and reproductive success. And if that palls, you can watch the fish in the wall-length tropical tanks. The tapas menu from the upstairs bistro is superb.

Fred's Uptown Tavern. 1006 Granville St. ☎ **604/605-4350.** www.fredstavern.com.

As the *Georgia Straight* recently noted, the best sign that Vancouver's bar scene is under-served is this: Fred's, a pleasant little downstairs tavern with neither band nor DJ nor dance floor, charges a cover (usually about C$5/US$3.35). What's more, there's a line to get in. So what's the attraction? A TV for every sightline, a cadre of buxom serving staff supplying an endless stream of pints, and a crowd of early 20-somethings so intent on each other that it really doesn't matter where they meet.

✪ **The Irish Heather.** 217 Carrall St. ☎ **604/688-9779.**

A bright and pleasant Irish pub in the dark heart of Gastown, the Heather boasts numerous nooks and crannies, some of the best beer in town, and a menu that does a lot with the traditional Emerald Isle spud. The clientele is from all over the map, including arty types from the local gallery scene, urban pioneers from the new Gastown condos, and kids from Kitsilano looking for some safe but authentic grunge.

✪ **The Lennox Pub.** 800 Granville St. ☎ **604/408-0881.**

Part of the renewal of Granville Street, this new pub fills a big void in the neighborhood; it's a comfortable spot for a drink without having to deal with lines or ordering food. The beer list is extensive, containing such hard-to-find favorites as Belgian Kriek, Hoegaarden, and Leffe. There is a great selection of single-malt scotches. The pub has a turn-of-the-20th-century feel with lots of brass, wood paneling, and a long bar. The menu covers all the pub-food basics.

A SPORTS BAR

The Shark Club Bar and Grill. 180 W. Georgia St. ☎ **604/687-4275.** C$5 (US$3.35) cover on the weekend after 9pm.

The city's premier sports bar, where men are men and dress the part—except on Halloween, when a squad of erstwhile jocks shows up dressed in white hot pants and fringed halter tops like Dallas Cowboys cheerleaders. Anyway, the Shark Club—in the Sandman Inn—features lots of wood and brass, TVs everywhere, and on weekend evenings, lots of young and beautiful women who don't look terribly interested in sports. Despite this—or because of it—weekend patrons often score.

BARS WITH VIEWS

If you're in Vancouver, odds are you're here for the views. Everybody else is. The entire population could go make more money living in a dull flat place like Toronto, but we stay 'cause we're addicted to the scenery. As long as that's your raison d'être, you may as well do it in style at one of the places below.

Cardero's Marine Pub. 1583 Coal Harbour Quay. ☎ **604/669-7666.**

On the water at the foot of Cardero Street, this Coal Harbour pub and restaurant offers an unmatched view of Stanley Park, the harbor, and the North Shore. Overhead heaters take away the chill when nights grow longer.

✪ **Cloud Nine.** 1400 Robson St. (42nd floor of the Empire Landmark Hotel). ☎ **604/662-8328.** Cover C$5 (US$3.35) Thurs–Sat.

View junkies will think they've died and gone to heaven. As this sleek hotel-top lounge rotates 6° a minute, your vantage point circles from volcanic Mount Baker to the Fraser estuary to English Bay around Stanley Park to the towers of downtown, the harbor, and East Vancouver. And who knew paradise served such good martinis?

The Creek Restaurant and Brewery. 1253 Johnson St.   ☎ **604/685-7070.**

Located in the Granville Island Hotel, this watering hole offers an unmatched view of False Creek and great brews to boot. The food's also pretty good. Atmosphere is laid-back hip. Inhabitants are mostly 30-somethings who've discovered there's no office fire so serious it can't be quenched with another round.

The Flying Beaver Bar. 4760 Inglis Rd. ☎ **604/273-0278.**

A unique West Coast tradition: Beaver and Cessna pilots pull up to the floating docks and step ashore to down a few in the floatplane pub. Located beneath the flyway of Vancouver International, the Beaver offers nonflyers great views of incoming jets, along with mountains, bush planes, river craft, and truly fine beer.

The Sylvia Lounge. 1154 Gilford St. ☎ **604/681-9321.** www.sylviahotel. com.

One of the city's oldest hotels and the West End's first "high-rise," the Sylvia—overlooking English Bay Beach—features a ground floor lounge beloved mostly for its view, location, and history. For a time in the 1950s, the Sylvia was the hippest cocktail bar in town. Fifty years later, it's a quiet, low-key room with reasonably priced drinks and a view out over the water. A great place to duck into either before or after a stroll along English Bay.

LOUNGES

Bacchus Lounge. 845 Hornby St. (in the Wedgewood Hotel). ☎ **604/608-5319.** www.wedgewoodhotel.com.

Step into Bacchus and bask in the low light cast by fireplace and tealights, its Turneresque wall paintings, and the irony-free evocation of piano bars of yore. Lounge has (or had) staged a hip, self-aware second coming, but for Bacchus it's still and forever the days of Ike and Mamie's first White House term. The piano man in the corner pounds out Neil Diamond, and the crowd of boomers and their children hum along.

Georgia Street Bar and Grill. 801 W. Georgia St. ☎ **604/602-0994.**

The Dr. Jekyll and Mr. Hyde of the downtown lounges, the GSB&G on weeknights has the quiet piano-plinking feel of a hotel bar (in, fact, it's attached to the Hotel Georgia). On weekends—or anytime during the summer Jazz Festival—a band squeezes into one corner, refugees from the downstairs

Chameleon Lounge squeeze into another, and the suits, jeans, khakis, and Kangol caps shake it up on the tiny dance floor.

Gerard Lounge. 845 Burrard St. ☎ **604/682-5511.**

Upscale taken to the edge of hyperbole, the Gerard faithfully re-creates the atmosphere of an English club, including not just the rustic oil paintings and dead animals on the walls, but also the lesser sons of the local (Hollywood) nobility having a bit of a rip with the native girls. The Gerard is also known for its exotic cocktails and Tuesday Chocoholic's Buffet.

✪ **Gotham Cocktail Bar.** 615 Seymour St. ☎ **604/605-8282.**

A clear case of the law of unintended consequences: The lounge adjoining this new steak house was designed for a male clientele—thick leather benches and a room-long mural of sensuous women in Jazz Age clothes. Men certainly did show up—well-off suits in their 30s and 40s particularly—but they were soon a tiny minority midst the great gaggles of women, all seemingly sharing Ally McBeal's age, romantic aspirations, and hem length.

4 Dance Clubs

Au Bar. 674 Seymour St. ☎ **604/648-2227.** Cover C$5–C$7 (US$3.35–US$4.70).

An address is unnecessary for Au Bar; the long Seymour Street corral of those not-quite-beautiful-enough for expedited entry immediately gives it away. Inside, this newest of downtown bars is packed with beautiful people milling from bar to dance floor to bar (there are two) and back again. Observing them is like watching a nature documentary on the Discovery Channel: Doelike women prance and jiggle while predatory men roam in packs, flexing pecs and biceps. To maintain some form of natural order, black-clad bouncers scan the room like game wardens, searching the horizon for trouble in paradise.

The Legion. 2205 Commercial Dr. Cover $6 (US$4). For up-to-date info on Vancouver's swing scene, call the **Swing Hotline** at ☎ **604/377-1394.**

Swing's not dead, but the boom has definitely come and gone. Some of the more talented hep cats can still be found cuttin' a rug on Tuesday, Friday, and Saturday on the 3,400-square-foot dance floor upstairs in the Legion auditorium. Not sure about your moves? Dance lessons are included with the cover and are at 7:30pm on Tuesday nights for the Lindy Hop and 8:30pm on Friday and Saturday nights for East Coast Swing. The evening is all ages, so alcohol's out, but you can go downstairs and sign yourself into the Legion pub where the draught is very cheap.

✪   **Luv-a-fair.** 1275 Seymour St. ☎ **604/685-3288.** Cover C$2–C$6 (US$1.35–US$4).

Where the pale-skinned go to sweat: '80s early in the week, then Brit pop, alt-rock, house, and industrial mayhem as they head toward the weekend. Girls dance on the catwalk, guys— a cuter, less attitude-filled bunch than elsewhere, says my female companion—shake their stuff on the floorboards. Behind the chain-link fence in the upstairs mezzanine are the pool table and Foosball.

The Palladium Club. 1036 Richards St. ☎ **604/687-6794.** Cover varies, up to C$10 (US$7).

Dancing is the order of the evening at this industrial space with a dance floor the size of Texas and a ceiling soaring up so high you can hardly make out the duct work. Monday, young 20-somethings dive into the '80s. Tuesday, Wednesday, and Saturday, it's house. Sunday night, the Goths come out to play. For the boogie-less, there's pool.

The Rage. 750 Pacific Blvd. (Plaza of Nations). ☎ **604/685-5585.** Cover Fri C$5 (US$3.35), Sat C$7 (US$4.70).

Tune in to radio station Z95 on the weekends after 8pm and you'll hear exactly what's going on in this airplane hangar of a dance club: Five bars and speaker stacks loud enough to liquefy your brain make this the weekend house party to beat.

Richards on Richards. 1036 Richards St. ☎ **604/687-6794.** www.richardsonrichards.com. Cover Fri–Sat C$8 (US$5) for the club, concerts C$10–C$30 (US$7–US$20).

Dicks on Dicks has been packing 'em in longer than you'd care to know. What's the attraction? For years, the club was a notorious pickup spot. Things have mellowed a touch since then, but as the line of limos out front on busy nights attests, Dicks is still hot. Inside there are two floors, four bars, a laser light system, and lots of DJ'ed dance tunes. Occasional live acts have included the likes of Junior Wells, James Brown, and, just recently, 2 Live Crew and Jack Soul.

Sonar. 66 Water St. ☎ **604/683-6695.** www.sonar.bc.ca. Cover varies, C$5–C$10 (US$3.35–US$7) and up to C$20 (US$13) for special events.

Loud bass. Flashing lights. The endlessly thrumming rhythms of house. It's a combination that really works best with the aid of psychogenic substances with four-letter initials. Of course, the Sonar crowd of ravers-on-holiday already know that.

Stone Temple Cabaret. 1082 Granville St. ☎ **604/488-1333.** Cover C$5–C$20 (US$3.35–US$13).

Don't let the name fool ya, this is disco, pure and simple. A moderate-size dance floor in the front room features lights, smoke, booming bass, and a collegiate crowd swigging from beer bottles as they get down. The back room has plush banquettes and a balconied upstairs with pool tables. Open Tuesday to Sunday.

✪ **Voda Nightclub.** 783 Homer St. (in the Westin Grand Hotel). ☎ **604/684-3003.** Cover C$5 (US$3.35).

Voda has quickly made a name for itself, attracting folks young, old, and in-between, with the only real common denominator being cash. Intriguing interior boasts a mix of waterfalls, rocks, and raw concrete—like a beautiful piece of 1950s modernism. The small dance floor basks in the warm light from the hundreds of candles everywhere. Tuesday is Salsa night, with the 15-piece salsa band performing Latin tunes. Thursdays are disco, with a mix of DJs and bands filling out the rest of the week.

Wett Bar. 1320 Richards St. ☎ **604/662-7707.** www.wettbar.com. Cover C$3–C$7 (US$2–US$4.70).

The '80s live on here, from the Artist once again known as Prince to spleen-shattering bass levels to squads of steroid-injected bouncers, complete with earphones, attitude, and, in the case of the Chief Beef, a full Kevlar vest and handcuffs. What's he guarding against? Judging by the clientele, willow-thin girls bopping timidly round their purses, desperately trying not to look uncool. Open Tuesday to Saturday.

5 Gay & Lesbian Bars

The near complete lack of persecution in laid-back Vancouver has had a curious effect on the city's gay scene—it's so attitude-free it's often hard to tell apart from the straight dance world, male go-go dancers and naked men in showers notwithstanding. Many clubs feature theme nights and dance parties, drag shows are ever-popular, and every year in early August, as Gay Pride nears, the scene goes into overdrive. The **Gay Lesbian Transgendered Bisexual Community Centre,** 2–1170 Bute St. (☎ **604/684-5307**), has information on the current hot spots, but it's probably easier just to pick up a free copy of *Xtra West!,* available in most downtown cafes.

The Dufferin Pub. 900 Seymour St. ☎ **604/683-4251.** www.dufferinhotel. com.

Buff at the Duff is a city institution; other drag shows might be raunchier, but none have quite the style. Shows are Monday to Thursday. Friday and Sunday the go-go boys strut their stuff (and yes they do take it all off). The rest of the time—and before, during, and after many of the shows—the DJs keep you grooving.

Heritage House Hotel. 455 Abbott St. ☎ **604/685-7777.** Cover C$4–C$10 (US$2.70–US$7) some nights.

This aging beauty of a downtown hotel plays host to three separate gay bars. Downstairs, the lesbian **Lotus Cabaret** has a big bar, little alcoves for sitting, an adequate dance floor, and an upbeat atmosphere. The crowd is mixed, except for Friday when it's women only. **Charlie's Lounge** on the main floor is casual and elegant. Saturday night's "Charlie's Angels" is women only, sorry guys! The most endearing of the three is **Chuck's Pub.** More than slightly seedy, with comfortable wicker chairs and the cheapest draught in town, Chuck's is home on Friday evenings to Guys in Disguise, an amateur drag-queen revue. None of the acts is especially talented, but the patrons and performers all seem to know each other, and everyone sings along.

Homers. 1249 Howe St. ☎ **604/689-2444.**

Billed as a "neighborhood club," this casual pub has a relaxed atmosphere. There's no heavy cruising, but there are billiards tables, a great pub menu, inexpensive food and drinks, and the occasional surprised cruise ship passenger.

Lava Lounge. 1176 Granville St. ☎ **604/605-1154.** Cover C$2–C$10 (US$1.35–US$7).

Great things were expected when Howard Johnson's bought this sleazy hotel and closed the in-house club for renovations. It reopened with a different name, but the same decor, all the way down to the floor plants. That aside, and whatever your orientation, it's well worth coming here just to see the Lush. Thursday nights is the Electrolush Lounge night, when the show tunes on the turntable are matched to the clips from Busby Berkeley musicals flickering on the walls. The crowd is gay but not flamboyantly so. Indeed, the clientele could be confused with that of a jock bar were it not for the tall and striking drag queens swishing about and good-looking men dancing together. On non-Lush nights acts vary from live to DJ and from house to reggae to retro. Tables surround and overlook the dance floor.

Numbers Cabaret. 1098 Davie St. ☎ **604/685-4077.** Cover Fri–Sat C$3 (US$2).

A multilevel dance club and bar, Numbers has been around for 20 years and hasn't changed a bit. Extroverts hog the dance floor while admirers look on from the bar above. On the second floor, carpets, wood paneling, pool tables, darts, and a lower volume of music give it a neighborhood pub feel.

✪ **The Odyssey.** 1251 Howe St. ☎ **604/689-5256.** Cover Mon, Thurs, and Sun C$3 (US$2), Fri–Sat C$5 (US$3.35), Tues C$1 (US65¢), Wed no cover.

If this is what lay over the rainbow, I don't think anyone ever told Dorothy. Odyssey is the hottest and hippest gay/mixed dance bar in town (alley entrance is for men, women go in the front door). The medium-sized dance space is packed. Up above, a mirrored catwalk is reserved for those who can keep the beat. Shows vary depending on the night. Monday it's Sissy Boy, Saturday it's Fallen Angel go-go dancers, Sunday it's the Feather Boa drag show. And on Thursday, it's Shower Power—yes, that is a pair of naked men in the shower above the dance floor. No, you're not in Kansas anymore.

The Royal Hotel. 1025 Granville St. ☎ **604/685-5335.**

This recently renovated gay bar has constantly changing theme nights. At the moment, Monday night is Divas Inc, a popular drag show. On Tuesday, the Empress of Vancouver hosts gay bingo. Thursday night's Libido's Lounge features Latin funk. Friday nights, the Royal is packed with professionals and other nine-to-fivers kicking off the weekend.

Index